LONDON

City of
the Romans

LONDON

City of the Romans

RALPH MERRIFIELD

University of California
Berkeley and Los Angeles

© Ralph Merrifield 1983
First published 1983 by
University of California Press
Berkeley and Los Angeles

Typeset and Printed in Great Britain.

Library of Congress Cataloging in Publication Data

Merrifield, Ralph.
    London, city of the Romans.

    1. London (England)—Antiquities, Roman.   2. London
(England)—History—To 1500.   3. England—Antiquities,
Roman.   4. Romans—England—London.   I. Title.
DA677.1.M46   1983   936.3′1203   82–40412
ISBN 0–520–04922–5

Contents

Preface

This book is a synthesis of many people's studies of the origin and early history of London, of which I have endeavoured to make a coherent story. Our knowledge of this subject has been vastly increased in recent years by archaeologists who have rescued and interpreted the buried material evidence. Over the last ten years, in particular, an immense effort has been directed to this purpose, particularly in the City by the Department of Urban Archaeology of the Museum of London, and in north Southwark by the Southwark and Lambeth Archaeological Excavation Committee. As a result, we now have very much more evidence than in 1965, when I first attempted a synthesis of this subject (*The Roman City of London*).

The main approach then was archaeological and topographical, since much of the data had been collected by random observation on building-sites, and gave little indication of any sequence of events. Scientific excavation in advance of builders' work has since been carried out on a very much larger scale than was then possible, so that we now have evidence of a chronological sequence from many sites, some very large, and can hardly avoid trying to interpret it in historical terms.

Unfortunately, the archaeological sequence cannot usually be slotted into the chronology of history with any precision, owing to the difficulty of close archaeological dating. In order to reconstruct what was happening in London at a given period, therefore, we can only put together all datable finds of that period with the indications of what appears to have happened then on a variety of sites, and try to make sense of it against the background of history as we understand it. We construct a hypothesis, which may not be the only one that could be based on the same evidence, particularly if the dates of the site-phases could be shifted by ten years or more, as is usually possible. Often one hypothesis seems to stand out as much more likely than any other, but this is a purely subjective judgement. Should we therefore decline to relate archaeology to history until we have much more data, as some archaeological purists would demand? I do not think so, for hypotheses help to identify areas where more information is required, and make it more likely that the required data will be sought. They will do no harm unless they come to be regarded as established truths, and are no longer checked against new evidence when it is obtainable.

I have tried to take into account all data known to me, though some evidence of importance, particularly from very recent excavation, may well have been overlooked because I did not realise its significance at the time of writing. Cost of production has also made it necessary to omit a study of the extraordinarily rich evidence for the religious life of Roman London, which would have required copious illustration. Only material of this kind directly relevant to the history of the city itself has therefore been included.

Acknowledgements for generous help and co-operation must be made to the Department of Urban Archaeology of the Museum of London, whose Chief Archaeologist, Brian Hobley, first encouraged me to undertake this task. I am particularly indebted to Peter Marsden, who has made notable contributions in this field, and has constantly made his knowledge available to me. Chris Green, John Maloney, Gustav Milne and Steve Roskams provided valuable information and useful ideas in discussion, and Trevor Hurst took great trouble to supply me with admirable photographs. A major contribution to this book was made by Chris Unwin, who as cartographer and artist produced all the maps and original line-drawings, and re-drew the site-plans. I am also much indebted to the Southwark and Lambeth Archaeological Excavation Committee, whose Director, Harvey Sheldon, and staff gave me much information and generously supplied excellent photographs, fully documented by Laura Schaaf. Geoff Parnell gave me important information concerning his excavations in the Tower of London, and provided a photograph, as also did Tony Johnson for the Shadwell excavation and H. Sheldon for the Highgate kilns. Mark Hassall kindly advised on various historical matters, and Dr J. P. C. Kent discussed the problem of the late silver ingots and permitted me to quote his views. Hugh Chapman, John Clark, Jenny Hall, Jean Macdonald and Geoff Marsh of the Museum of London read the text and made helpful suggestions, while Jean Macdonald also kindly plotted the Iron Age distribution map. I am particularly grateful to Harvey Sheldon for a close examination of the text, resulting in the removal of a number of misconceptions, obscurities and infelicities, with the moderation of over-bold statements and prejudiced views. The extent to which such faults remain is in no way his responsibility, however, but should be attributed to the perverseness of the author.

Finally, I am much indebted to my wife, who typed the much-corrected manuscript and produced the index.

The Plates

Maps, Plans and Diagrams

I

London before the Roman Conquest

There is a persistent legend of a pre-Roman London, for which Geoffrey of Monmouth must be held largely responsible. According to his *History of the Kings of Britain*, written in Latin and finished about 1136, Brutus, a leader of the Trojans and great-grandson of Aeneas, came to Britain and founded a city on the Thames which he called Troia Nova, later corrupted to Trinovantum. Lud, brother of Cassivellaunus, subsequently built walls around it, and called it Caerlud, or Lud's City. Geoffrey's sources are unknown and his whole 'History' is a farrago of bits of real history as recorded by early chroniclers and romanticised fiction, with the latter predominating. Some details may be based on tradition, others on an attempted explanation of known facts or names, and civic pride then as now readily gave birth to myths. Inevitably the legend of London put together by Geoffrey of Monmouth or his unknown predecessor had a long life, and has left to this day in many Londoners a wish to believe in a pre-Roman origin for their city. The discovery by City archaeologists recently of a few sherds of pottery of the Early Bronze Age on a site in Newgate Street at once produced enthusiastic headlines about prehistoric London. Let us therefore consider what historical and archaeological facts, if any, underlie this persistent legend that London existed before the Roman conquest.

The pre-eminence of the London area has always been ensured by its geographical advantages—natural in origin but improved by human skills. It stands on a tidal river which has always given easy access to ships—until the development of giant tankers and bulk carriers since World War 2 made its estuary a more convenient unloading place. The river has always provided a convenient means of entry into the heart of the rich lowland zone of Britain; and the Thames valley itself, with its copious water-supply, well-drained gravels, fertile silts and brick-carths, and abundant timber for building and fuel, has attracted settlers since the time of the first Neolithic farmers. The importance of the Thames as the gateway into Britain and the natural means of communication for a prosperous population has always been much enhanced by the convenient fact that it lies immediately opposite an even more important water-way on the other side of the North Sea. The river Rhine gives access to the very heart of Europe, and provides a route for the transport of goods, men and ideas. Together the two water-ways gave the London region a certain cosmopolitan character long before London itself was born.

Bronze Age London

European contacts are most evident in the later part of the Bronze Age—a period of innovation and technical advance, in which new inventions and improvements of foreign origin appeared in the Thames valley earlier than in any other part of the country. A good example of this is the bronze sword with leaf-shaped blade, effective for slashing because its greater weight was in the lower part of the blade. It rapidly ousted the older so-called 'rapier'—a much elongated dagger of the British Middle Bronze Age which could be used for stabbing only. The earliest examples of the new sword known in Britain, dating from the late eleventh century BC, are imported weapons of a type that originated in the Upper Rhine valley and Switzerland, and these are almost confined to the Thames valley between Brentford and Barking.[1] They were copied with small changes of design by British smiths, and the concentration of those copies in the London region strongly suggests that they were made there. A similar pattern of distribution is found with other imported weapons and their copies throughout the Late Bronze Age, and some of these Thames type copies have been found widely distributed on the Continent, strongly suggesting an export trade from the Thames valley.[2]

Specialists in Bronze Age metalwork have long believed that there was manufacture of bronze goods as well as trade in them in the London region, but until recently their arguments have been based only on the typology and distribution of tools, weapons and other artifacts that have been found in great quantities in the river bed. No riverside occupation site of the people who lost or deposited this wealth of bronze material in the river was known, until a series of rescue excavations took place in Egham, on the western fringe of suburban London, between 1972 and 1978. At the southern end of Runnymede Bridge a substantial wharf was found with pile-driven timbers, and 80m south of it were occupation deposits of the same period, with post-holes and spreads of daub suggesting the presence of huts. There were many metal fragments in these deposits, including two imported bronze objects, a vase-headed pin and a notched razor that were probably made in north or central Europe. The presence of amber beads also indicated continental trade. More important, however, were fragments of casting debris, strongly suggesting that bronze-working took place on the site. These included a miscast razor still partly encased in its clay mould. The assemblage has been archaeologically dated to the eighth or ninth century BC, a date confirmed by radio-carbon samples.[3]

Earlier trial trenches about 300m further south had produced material that was roughly contemporary with this, or a little later, notably a hoard of bronze scrap, including fragments of swords, knives and spearheads, with more complete but damaged socketed axes, gouge and spearhead. It was evidently deposited by a bronze-smith, probably in the eighth or ninth century BC. Elsewhere on the same site was found a stone mould for casting socketed axes of South Welsh type, a class also represented in the hoard. There is little doubt that it was brought from Wales by a migrant smith, who apparently found it worth while to establish his workshop in this manufacturing centre by the Thames.[4]

The attraction of this area, remote from sources of copper ore and tin, for the manufacturing of bronze goods was evidently due mainly to its convenience for trading, not only in the finished products but also in the scrap material—broken and obsolete tools and weapons—that was now increasingly used by the bronze-smiths. Also, the use of lead in the alloy to facilitate casting—a characteristic technique of the late Bronze Age—now made it necessary to assemble three separate ingredients, so that the proximity of the source of one of these (e.g. copper in Wales) had become less important to the manufacturer than the general convenience of transport provided by the Thames.

We seem therefore to have a sizeable settlement at Egham on the south bank of the river, extending at least 400m inland, and perhaps enclosed by a ditch. It might well be as large as a medium-sized hill-fort, though like the hill-forts it was probably not occupied continuously throughout its area. It seems to have flourished as a trading and manufacturing centre for a few centuries only towards the end of the Bronze Age, and to have had neither predecessor nor successor in that place, though evidence for Middle Neolithic occupation about 2000 years earlier was found there.

It is most unlikely that Egham was an isolated phenomenon in the lower Thames valley. The greatest concentrations of Bronze Age tools, weapons and ornaments have been dredged from the river further downstream, and it would be surprising if there were no comparable settlements, engaged in the same sort of activities, between Brentford and Battersea, where these have been found in great quantities. Many of these finds are earlier than the Egham settlement, belonging to the Middle Bronze Age and the beginning of the Late Bronze Age; many are contemporary; and many others are later, belonging to the closing phase of the Bronze Age, when influences from the Hallstatt civilization of Central Europe were reaching the Thames valley in the seventh century BC—a phase apparently unrepresented at Egham, which may already have been abandoned. It has also been demonstrated that there are concentrations of later Bronze Age *land* finds in some of these areas, notably at Syon Reach, and even in the City itself, where the latest phase of the Bronze Age is well represented.[5]

The picture that seems to have emerged is of a lower Thames valley already engaged in many of the activities that later made London rich—importing from the Continent, trading with other parts of Britain, manufacturing and exporting to the Continent and even Ireland. It was in fact making full use of its great water highway. But, as far as we know, these activities had no single centre—certainly not a centre that remained unchanged for centuries. Flood deposits covered the Late Bronze Age riverside area at Egham, and changes in the river course or rises in the water level may well have forced the abandonment of many of them.

Some people have thought that this may explain the great losses of bronze equipment in the Thames, but it is unlikely that the flooding of occupation sites can account for more than a tiny proportion of them. Disasters of this kind resulting in permanent abandonment seldom occur without warning; and if they did, it would usually be possible to salvage at least the larger objects of value, such as swords. Losses by accident are more likely to occur at regular crossing-places, by the wrecking of ferries or misfortunes at difficult fords. It is at these points also that tribal skirmishes are likely to occur, and any of these circumstances may have resulted in the loss of weapons and equipment. Even so, the great quantities of such material dredged from the lower Thames, particularly in west London, taken in conjunction with similar finds in rivers and pools elsewhere, is difficult to account for except by the hypothesis that much of it was deliberately deposited as votive offerings, either to appease a local river deity or as part of a funerary ritual—possibly for both purposes. Colin Burgess has in fact postulated a new water-oriented cult that replaced the old sky and earth-oriented religion in the Middle Bronze Age, and has suggested that this may have been due in part to climatic deterioration. On this hypothesis, new religious centres on the Thames and in the Fens replaced the old sacred sites of the Wessex uplands soon after 1400 BC.[6] If so, one or more of these is likely to have been located somewhere in what is now west London.

Religious centres, trading centres and regular crossing-places all require land-routes of some kind into the interior, and the wharf at Egham would not have been worth constructing if there had not been tracks leading from it that no doubt communicated ultimately with the North Downs Ridgeway, the great prehistoric route from Kent to Wessex. No Bronze Age centre could become permanently predominant, however, because its landward tracks had no marked superiority over those of its rivals. The intensive Thames-side activity of this period did not therefore create a London, but rather a succession of 'little Londons' that could be abandoned without much regret if local riverside conditions deteriorated.

The London area in the Iron Age

The introduction of the general use of iron in the sixth century BC did not at first disrupt the long-established trading pattern that linked the Thames valley with Europe, and the local smiths adopted the new metal while continuing to use their skill in bronze-working. This was now applied to more ornamental purposes, however, and on the evidence of their distribution iron daggers with decorative sheaths, partly made of bronze, were made in the lower Thames valley from about 550 50 300 BC (I).[7] Brooches also testify to continued contact with the

I   Iron daggers and bronze sheaths, probably of local manufacture, from the Thames at Hammersmith, early Iron Age, fourth century BC. *Museum of London*

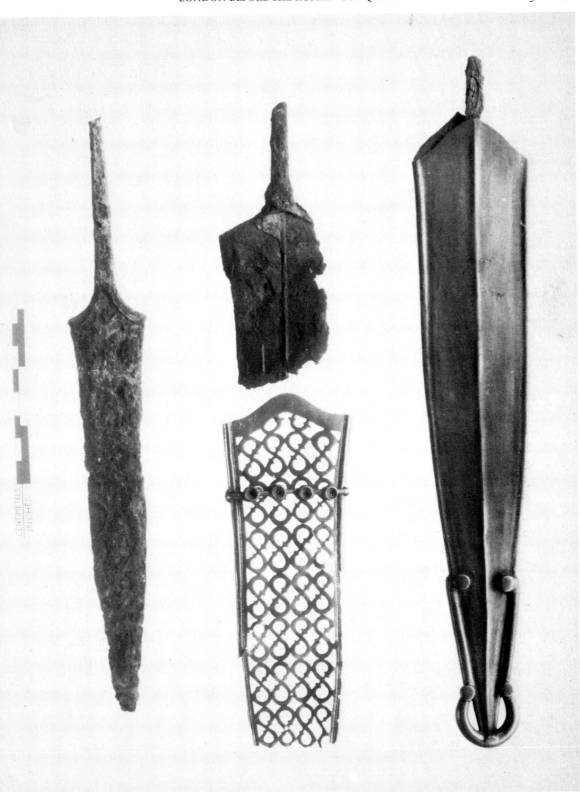

continent of Europe during this period. It seems likely, however, that the volume of long-distance trading declined, probably because iron, the essential new metal, was to be found almost everywhere, unlike bronze, an alloy for which the ingrdients had to be sought in distant places, and which was therefore worth saving for scrap and trading widely.

From about 300 to 100 BC, there seem to have been very few continental imports, and such developments as occurred, for example in iron swords, were mostly insular and were relatively uninfluenced by foreign fashions. This decline in overseas trade must have had a devastating effect on the communities of the lower Thames valley, and it is perhaps not suprising that evidence for their very existence during this period is sparse. A few swords from the river in west London may date from the second century BC, but may equally well be somewhate later.[8] It has also recently been suggested that the huts and temple excavated by Professor Grimes at Heathrow (2) may not be earlier than the second or third century BC, although the bulk of the pottery and other finds from this site is now considered to be Late Bronze Age of about 700BC.[9] A somewhat similar but unenclosed group of circular huts at Little Waltham, Essex, also associated with a possible shrine of some kind, is dated between the mid-third and late second century BC. It is of course unlikely that occupation ceased in the London area, however much trade

2 Reconstruction of later prehistoric settlement on site of Heathrow airport, by Alan Sorrell. *Museum of London*

3 Bronze parade helmet from the Thames near Waterloo Bridge, later first century BC. *British Museum*

and prosperity dwindled, and subsequent developments suggest that there was some continuity of the Thames cult and perhaps also of the craft of local smiths.

With the Belgic incursions and settlements in south-eastern Britain, for which we have Caesar's authority, close intercourse with the Continent was restored, as is well demonstrated by the introduction of coins of Gaulish type that were later copied in Britain. Between about 100 BC and the Roman conquest of AD 43 a number of spectacular bronze objects, decorated in a style and technique that is distinct from contemporary continental work, found their way into the long-

favoured stretch of the Thames between Brentford and Waterloo Bridge. They include the well-known horned helmet (**3**), shield bosses, the horn-cap of a chariot, horse-bits, a sword-scabbard and, perhaps latest of all, the magnificent parade-shield from Battersea (**4**). It is the equipment of a warrior aristocracy, some of it for show rather than practical use, and its deposition in the Thames seems to continue the already ancient tradition of offering valuables to the river. Whether it represents also the continuation and final flowering of the craftsmanship of local smiths is perhaps more doubtful. Certainly there was a striking concentration of fine British-made bronzes of this period in the Thames at west London, but a long-established practice of making votive offerings at a place sanctified by tradition might be sufficient to explain them. It is perhaps no coincidence that the principal land-find of the first century BC–first century AD in the area is a group of small bronze boars and other animals found with a miniature wheel on Hounslow Heath.[10] This was evidently a cult deposit, and we are reminded that an enigma of local archaeology at an earlier period is the square temple-like structure associated with the Late Bronze Age settlement at Heathrow. For this period it is at present unique, and if it is in fact later than the main occupation of the site, it is still likely to be considerably earlier than the Romano-Celtic temples that resemble it, and of which it seems to be a rare precursor.[11]

It is also significant that the name of the river Brent, the tributary of the Thames that partly encircles west London, according to Ekwall means 'high or holy river'.[12] Religious traditions attached to specific places are long-lived, as we know from more recent history, and a concentration of valuable offerings in one particular part of the river Thames may indicate merely that an earlier place of pilgrimage in the neighbourhood was still remembered. They do not necessarily suggest the proximity of a centre of wealth and power.

A possible pre-Roman *oppidum* in west London

John Kent, however, has pointed out that the numismatic evidence does seem to indicate the existence of such a centre for a limited period in the earlier part of the first century BC, somewhere a few miles to the west of the historic centre of London.[13] There is a remarkable concentration of the curious imported gold coins called Gallo-Belgic B around this area (**5,1**, fig 1). The basic type is similar to other Gallo-Belgic coins and their British derivatives—a much devolved male head on the obverse and a horse on the reverse—but is characterised by the almost complete obliteration of the head on the obverse die. It seems likely to have been the product of a break-away group of a tribe that asserted its independence by mutilating the traditional coinage in this way. These curious coins seem to have come from the south-western corner of Gallia Belgica, the territory of the Caleti around Dieppe, so there is no obvious geographical reason why the London area

4 Bronze parade shield with glass inlay ornaments, from the Thames at Battersea, early first century AD. Length 2ft 6½in (77.5cm). *British Museum*

5   (1) Gallo-Belgic B gold stater from Mitcham Common.
(2) Potin coins from Shepperton.
Probably first half of first century BC. *Museum of London*

should be their centre of distribution in Britain. They are predominately land finds, and cannot be accounted for in the same way as the valuables from the river. Most were presumably accidental losses or personal possessions hidden and abandoned. A gold starter of this kind represented considerable wealth, and would presumably not have been used in casual trade, but rather for such purposes as tribute, reward for major services, bride-price, and similar payments of social importance in the life of an individual.

The other coinage that Kent would associate with the hypothetical political and trading centre on the Thames is of quite a different category. These are the numerous small British-made coins of base metal with a large tin content, usually called potin or speculum (5,2). They were intrinsically or little value, and evidently served as the small change of commerce. As such they were distributed widely and had a long life, in some cases extending to the Roman conquest itself. Most, however, survived in hoards, which have a particular concentration in the London area between Sunbury and St James's Park, though some are scattered more widely in Kent and there is an outlier in Norfolk (fig 1). This might suggest that they were deposited by refugees fleeing from the London area when some disaster overtook the supposed Thames-side *oppidum*.

It may be noted also that one type of iron currency bar, the so-called plough-shaped variety, has a distribution approximately centred on the London area.[14] Caesar describes the money of the Britons as coins of gold and bronze (evidently the tin alloy coins that look like bronze) and iron ingots of fixed weights. Although their weight is rather variable, it was presumably this type of iron currency bar that he encountered, since the others have a more westerly distribution. The possibility remains, however, that these were made simply as votive plough-shares. It may be significant that most were found in the Thames itself, and that there is an outlier from the great votive deposit at Llyn Cerrig in Anglesey. Like the decorated bronzes from the Thames, they may therefore indicate merely the continuation of the river cult.

Taking all this evidence together, however, a fair case can be made for the revival or re-establishment of some kind of centre of trade and political influence on or very near the Thames in the western part of Greater London, at a date not far removed from 100 BC. Whether its location in the general area of the probable

Gallo Belgic B gold stater
Gallo Belgic B gold quarter stater
Potin coin Class I
currency bar, plough shaped
round symbol = hoard

Fig. 1   Distribution map of Gallo-Belgic B gold coins, potin coins Class I and plough-shaped currency bars, showing concentration of coins in Brentford/Kew area. *J. Macdonald and C. Unwin*

Bronze Age centres was due to geographical advantages such as easy crossing places and good routes into the interior, or merely to a surviving religious tradition is uncertain. If the hypothetical *oppidum* really existed—and no trace of it, or of any particular concentration of occupation has yet been detected by archaeologists working in the area—its position may have been determined by a combination of these circumstances.

In any case it cannot have lasted very long, for it is inconceivable that it would not have been mentioned in Julius Caesar's account of the events of 55–54 BC[15] if it had still existed at that date; as we shall see, he must have passed very near its site. Kent's view is that it was a settlement of the Trinovantes that came to an end around 60 BC, as a result of the expansion of the power of Cassivellaunus. He suggests that it was this hostile encroachment on the Trinovantian western territory that led to the dispersal of refugees and the concealment of the coin-hoards. The alternative possibility, that the hoards were deposited as a result of Caesar's own arrival, cannot of course be reconciled with the hypothesis that they were the coinage of a Thames-side settlement that must already have ceased to exist. It is a curious coincidence, and Kent wryly dismisses it as such, that Geoffrey of Monmouth should have used the name 'Trinovantum' for his mythical pre-Roman London.

The Thames as a frontier

In pre-Roman times, as later in the Saxon Heptarchy, the Thames formed a natural political frontier, and during tribal warfare could perform a useful function as a defensive barrier. When this role was predominant, its more positive use as a water highway and trade route must always have been diminished. This was evidently the situation in the middle of the first century BC, when it would have been difficult for a Thames-side emporium to have survived and carried out its proper functions, even under the protection of a chieftain as powerful as Cassivellaunus. We know from Julius Caesar's account that although he obviously controlled a considerable part of the north bank of the lower Thames—probably at least the whole of that part west of the Lea—he found it necessary to have his tribal headquarters inland, where it was protected by forests and marshes as well as by strong man-made defences.

Caesar is explicit that Cassivellaunus' territory was separated from the maritime tribes by the Thames, and that the Roman army entered it when it crossed the river. He also tells us that Cassivellaunus had previously been continuously at war with the other tribes, and that only fear of the Romans had forced them into a temporary and uneasy alliance with him. Almost certainly outside this alliance were his principal recent opponents, the Trinovantes of Essex, whom Caesar described as about the strongest tribe of south-eastern Britain. Cassivellaunus had killed their king and forced his son Mandubracius to flee for his life. He had crossed to the Continent and put himself under Caesar's protection, thereby providing one of the pretexts for invasion. The principal one, however, was that the Britons had been assisting the Gauls in their resistance to the Romans.

Caesar tells us that the coastal parts of Britain were inhabited by immigrants from Belgic Gaul—i.e. from the part of northern Gaul that included modern Belgium but extended as far south as the lower Seine—and that these people came as raiders but settled to till the soil. He also says that most of them were still called by the names of the continental tribes from which they came. Unfortunately he does not specify these tribes, but one of them is likely to have been the Atrebates, a tribe of Belgic Gaul to the north of the Somme. Colonists of this tribe were probably already established south of the Thames to the west of the Cantiaci of Kent. It was because he already had contacts in Britain that Caesar sent Commius, a prince of the Atrebates whom he had made king, as a sort of ambassador to the Britons before the invasion of 55 BC. Unfortunately Commius was captured before he could reach his friends, but was released and returned to Caesar soon after the successful landing by the Romans. Later, in 52 BC, he was to turn against Caesar and become a leader of the Gallic resistance. A Roman attempt to murder him by treachery made him their implacable enemy, and he escaped to Britain, where he founded a powerful dynasty ruling the British Atrebates.

A less clearly defined political relationship between Britain and Gaul at an earlier date was the rule of Divitiacus, king of the Suessiones, between the Oise and the Marne, around the modern Soissons. He seems to have been recognized as high king not only by other continental Belgic tribes, but also, according to Caesar, in Britain as well.[16] The people of Kent were described by Caesar as the most civilised inhabitants of Britain, with a way of life very similar to that of the Gauls, and it was in Kent that the most fully Belgicised British culture developed at a somewhat later date. This is characterised by the rich cremation burials and fine pedestal jars of the Aylesford and Swarling cemeteries. North of the Thames, similar pottery and burials occur in Hertfordshire, in territory that was certainly controlled by Cassivellaunus at the time of Caesar's invasion. He was therefore long regarded as a Belgic chieftain and leader of a Belgicised tribe, the Catuvellauni. Both ideas have now been challenged. The Belgic burials in Hertfordshire almost certainly belong to the period after Caesar's invasion, when it is by no means certain that this territory would have been retained by Cassivellaunus or his descendants; it may well have reverted to the Trinovantes, who helped Caesar. This tribe is likely to have been predominantly non-Belgic, but seems in somewhat later times to have had a Belgic ruling-class, which may already have been establishing itself.[17]

Cassivellaunus, the outstanding personality in Britain at this time, is in fact a mystery about whom scholars are likely to remain divided. Harding regards him not as a Belgic chieftain but as the descendant of much earlier warrior-immigrants from the Marne region of northern France.[18] His skill in the use of war-chariots, which the Romans found so disconcerting, was an accomplishment long lost in Gaul and suggests that he was heir to a military tradition established in Britain at an earlier date. It could in fact account both for his successes against the Belgic or

Belgicised chieftains of south-eastern Britain and for their willingness to accept him as war-leader in time of emergency.

The Catuvellauni, known to us only from later writers, are also becoming increasingly nebulous, and their association with Cassivellaunus is based only on the similarity of name, and the presence in this area several generations later of the dynasty of Tasciovanus, considered to be rulers of the Catuvellauni and probably descendants of Cassivellaunus. Kent, however, thinks that these may have been kings of the Trinovantes throughout, rather than Catuvellaunian conquerors who imposed their rule; and puts forward the hypothesis, on numismatic grounds, that Cassivellaunus moved westward after his defeat by Caesar, and perhaps founded a royal house of the Durotriges in Wessex.[19]

In this mesh of conflicting theory, it is clear only that Cassivellaunus ruled on the north bank of the Thames; that he was on bad terms with his neighbours to the east, the Trinovantes, and had probably recently encroached on their territory; and that he was feared and distrusted, though respected, by the tribes to the south of the river, who probably considered themselves more civilised because of their closer links with Gaul. It was not a recipe for success in Britain's initial encounter with the Romans.

Julius Caesar's invasions

Caesar's first attempt in 55 BC, however, was abortive, not as a result of any British victory, but through Roman inexperience of the rough seas and strong winds of the Channel, which prevented the cavalry from landing and thereby hamstrung Caesar's attacking force. More serious than this was the damage inflicted on his ships by the storm; the warships, which had been beached, were waterlogged, and the transports, which were at anchor, were badly damaged and lost irreplaceable equipment. The Britons, who had sued for peace after the first successful landing, were given new heart, and had the best of an attack on a legion that was foraging for corn; it was rescued with difficulty by Caesar with the other legion. This encouraged the Britons to collect a large force and attack the Roman camp, but they were defeated and put to flight. Again they sued for peace, and Caesar, thankfully one imagines, limped back to Gaul with his damaged ships before winter made the passage more difficult.

The following year he returned with a much larger force—no less than five legions and 2000 cavalry in an armada of 800 ships. This was much more than a punitive expedition and reconnaissance in force; there can be little doubt that Caesar intended conquest, and that his prime motive was personal ambition. This time the Romans landed without opposition and made their camp. The main force pressed on into the interior and first encountered the enemy at a river in Kent, probably the Stour. The Romans drove off the British chariots and cavalry, and successfully stormed a stronghold in the woods, probably the hill-fort of Bigbury near Canterbury. The following day, however, dispatch riders brought news of yet another disaster to the Roman ships as a result of a sudden gale, and the army hastily returned to its base camp. Here they found that nearly all the ships had been damaged, and about 40 had been totally destroyed. This caused ten days' delay, for Caesar had at last learnt his lesson, and ordered that all the ships should be beached and enclosed with a fortification. He was then able to resume the campaign, and led the main army back to the place they had previously reached. They now found that Cassivellaunus, whom the Britons had appointed to supreme command by common assent, had assembled much larger forces. He had considerable success at first by guerilla tactics and skilful use of chariots and cavalry fighting in open order. Two legions and the cavalry, however, successfully repelled a massed British attack while they were foraging, and completely routed the enemy. Following this defeat Cassivellaunus' unenthusiastic allies dispersed, and it was now apparent that the only real resistance to overcome was that of Cassivellaunus and his own tribe, who retreated to their territory across the Thames.

As always, Caesar's actions were prompt and decisive. He at once led his army to the Thames, which he must have reached in the neighbourhood of London. Here he found a difficult ford which had been strongly defended with sharp stakes fixed in the river-bank and also concealed in the river-bed itself. It seems likely that these defences had been prepared earlier for inter-tribal warfare, and if so they were no doubt duplicated at other regular crossing-places of a river that had become a hostile frontier. Caesar, however, believed that this was the only place where the Thames could be crossed, and so gives us our one clue to its location. Approaching from the east, he evidently crossed at the very first ford he reached, and as this was the nearest to the river-mouth it is not surprising that it was difficult. If he had pushed further up the river, he would certainly have found other fords which would have been easier crossing-places, although these would probably have been even more strongly defended. It would, however, have been quite out of character for him to have done so. He had always achieved success by rapid, decisive moves regardless of difficulties, relying on the efficiency and courage of his army to overcome them. This was, however, evidently a regular crossing-place well above the tidal limits of the river. Now the greatest concentration of river-finds of the pre-Roman Iron Age—and for that matter of the Bronze Age also—lies to the west of the City, beginning at Waterloo Bridge and continuing to Brentford and beyond, with the stretch of river between Wandsworth and Hammersmith particularly rich in Iron Age finds.

As we have seen, there is good reason to believe that many of these weapons and ornaments were deposited as votive offerings, and the river cult is most likely to have been centred on regular crossing-places. There is an interesting parallel from Ashanti, where the spirit of the river Tano was worshipped as a god in recent times; here a primitive shrine or altar, sometimes only a large stone from the river, was set up at each ford and offerings were thrown into the river there.[20] There is a strong suspicion, therefore, that there was at least one ford downstream of Brentford, probably in the Hammersmith–Wandsworth area, and a ford in regular use is likely to have been an easier crossing-place than the one described by Caesar.

Claims have often been made for places further up the river as the site of Caesar's crossing, particularly Brentford and Coway Stakes near Walton, where stakes have been found in the river-bed. The latter need not be seriously considered, since the stakes ran across the river and were clearly not defensive, but perhaps the remains of fishing weirs. Brentford has always had its supporters, however, since Montague Sharpe recorded the discovery there of rows of oak stakes in lines parallel with the bank between Brentford and Isleworth.[21] Some of them are said to have been sharpened and pointing outwards at an angle of 45°. These could, however, have been the tie-beams of a wooden embankment or quayside, and of course their period is unknown. Some support for a possible pre-Roman date is provided by the discovery of a similar sharpened stake re-used in a Romano-British structure on the foreshore at Syon Reach in 1928, and another found nearby in a Roman level during an investigation in 1966–7. Roy Canham suggested that both were derived from an earlier feature.[22]

Nevertheless, even if this structure of piles and stakes does prove to be of the right date and to be defensive—and further investigation is clearly needed whenever opportunity arises—it will not provide conclusive evidence that this was the place where Caesar crossed in 54 BC. Cassivellaunus would presumably have prepared similar defences at all likely crossing-places and, as I have suggested, had probably already done so against his British enemies. It seems quite incredible that Caesar should have come as far as this, passing other probable fords on his way, and yet remained convinced that he was crossing at the only possible place.

It is much more likely that he arrived at the Thames by the most direct route through north Kent and crossed at Westminster, where we have reason to believe there was a regular crossing of some kind 90 years later. At this point any ford upstream in the west London area would have been screened from view by the curve of the river. There is reason to suppose that there was a short period of somewhat higher river-level in the later pre-Roman Iron Age than in the early Roman period,[23] and this may account for the depth of water in Caesar's time at a place that seems to have been a regular ford a little later.

Caesar describes how the infantry attacked at the same time as the cavalry, although they had only their heads above water, and that the large British force drawn up on the opposite bank behind its defences was overpowered by the speed of their attack and fled from the river. The apparent ease of the victory as soon as the difficulty of the crossing had been overcome suggests that Cassivellaunus' army was divided, with some parts of it guarding other potential crossing-places upstream. At this point, however, he seems to have given up all hope of victory in a pitched battle, and disbanded most of his troops, keeping only about four thousand charioteers to harass the Romans by guerrilla tactics in the densely wooded country, where the Britons alone knew the lanes and pathways by which they could attack and retreat.

While the Romans were finding their way into the interior, envoys from the Trinovantes arrived, offering to surrender and obey Caesar's orders. They also asked for protection against Cassivellaunus and that Mandubracius should return to them to rule as king. In return, Caesar demanded hostages and grain for his troops; both were supplied forthwith—another indication that the Roman line of march was not far from Trinovantian territory, though there is no reason to suppose it was actually within it. Several other tribes now followed the example of the Trinovantes, sending envoys and offering surrender. Caesar names these tribes—the Cenimagni, Segontiaci, Ancalites, Bibroci and Cassi—but we know nothing more about them, nor where they were located. Harding has conjectured that the Cenimagni might be the tribe to the north of the Trinovantes later known as the Iceni, and that their name could be related to that of the Gaulish tribe of Cenomani, whose territory was in western Gaul well to the south of Gallia Belgica.[24] Unless their ruler had been taking an active part in the campaign, however, it seems unlikely that a plenipotentiary of the Iceni could have been on the spot so quickly. It is probable that at least one of these tribes was local, for it was from their envoys that Caesar learnt he was not far from the hidden stronghold of Cassivellaunus, which was protected by forests and marshes. Since their very names seem to have disappeared a century later, it may be suspected that several were minor tribes of the south-east who had been subjugated, those to the north of the river by the Trinovantes and Cassivellaunus; those to the south by the Belgic kingdoms that were to become the Cantiaci and Atrebates, and may already have been called by those names. Kent at least contained more than one tribe at this time, since no fewer than four kings of that region are named. We may even suspect that, in spite of its Gallic 'civilisation', south-eastern Britain still contained aboriginal elements that retained their tribal identity. Caesar's description of the sharing of women between related men suggests the existence of a social organization that would have been as unfamiliar to the Gauls as to the Romans.[25]

Caesar led his army to the place that had been indicated—a densely wooded spot fortified with rampart and ditch, where great numbers of men and cattle had been congregated. The Romans attacked from two sides, and as usual when they were able to engage at close quarters, the force of their onslaught routed the Britons, who fled after a short resistance. We do not know where this stronghold was, though it is likely to have been within twenty or thirty miles of London. Wheathampstead, on a gravel plateau above the river Lea in Hertfordshire, has been favoured by many archaeologists since excavations there by Mortimer Wheeler in 1932.[26] This was a settlement protected by massive earthworks, enclosing on at least three sides an area of 90–100 acres (36–40 ha). Such occupation as has been found in a very limited excavation is of the latter part of the first century BC,[27] after the time of Caesar, but there seems no reason why such a strongly defended site should not have been re-occupied, whatever the fate of the followers of Cassivellaunus.

In the meantime, Cassivellaunus, who was still able to exercise some authority south of the Thames, had ordered the four kings in Kent to attack the Roman naval camp there. This failed, and a successful sortie by the Romans inflicted heavy losses on the Kentish tribes. By this time Cassivellaunus had had enough, and sent envoys to obtain terms of surrender, using the ubiquitous Commius as an intermediary. Caesar also needed to extricate himself before the onset of winter, so granted terms under which hostages were to be surrendered and an annual tribute paid; also Cassivellaunus was strictly forbidden to molest Mandubracius and the Trinovantes. As soon as he had received the hostages, Caesar packed his troops into the available ships and returned to Gaul, probably hoping to return to complete the conquest the following year. For the rest of his life, however, he was fully occupied elsewhere, and no Roman troops were to set foot in Britain for nearly 90 years.

It is very clear from Caesar's account,[28] not only that no Thames-side settlement that could be regarded as a precursor of London then existed, but that the long-exploited advantages of the Thames as a water-highway and entrance to Britain were not compatible with its use as a defended frontier in inter-tribal warfare. They could only be restored when both sides of the river were at peace and preferably under control of a single power. Moreover, they would not be fully exploited until trade between Britain and the Continent regained the importance it seems to have had at certain times in the later Bronze Age.

Britain between the invasions

Developments that might have led to the establishment, or re-establishment, of an emporium on the Thames did in fact take place in the 97 years that elapsed between the departure of Caesar and the invasion of Claudius in AD 43. The process of absorption of minor tribes into greater kingdoms, which seems to have been at an early stage in Caesar's time—certainly south of the Thames—continued, so that the south bank became the northern limit of the two kingdoms of the Cantiaci and Atrebates only, while the north side of the river was shared between two peoples, the Trinovantes and the Catuvellauni, who are difficult to distinguish from one another politically or culturally. The Cantiaci do not appear to have been a completely unified kingdom, but the Atrebates further west were ruled by the powerful dynasty founded by Commius, whose princes were proud to call themselves 'sons of Commius', perhaps even in the second generation. North of the Thames, an even more powerful dynasty had been founded by Tasciovanus, a Catuvellaunian by the conventional view, although Dr Kent suggests that he may have been a Trinovantian.[29] In view of the mobility of these rulers, who on occasion seem to have been able to take over a new kingdom when driven out of the old, it may be wiser to consider the conflicts of this period as dynastic rather than tribal struggles, in which case the tribal label perhaps doesn't matter very much. What little we know of these rulers is based almost entirely on their coins, which are fortunately now inscribed with abbreviations of their names, sometimes with an indication of their parentage, and occasionally with an abbreviation of the name of the place where they were minted.[30] The chief mint of Tasciovanus was at Verulamium, where the pre-Roman settlement, which lay to the south-west of the later Roman city, commenced about 15 BC, probably as a successor to the Wheathampstead *oppidum*. For a brief period he also issued coins at Camulodunum, and his coins are widely distributed in Essex. If the spread of coins is an indication of political influence, as is usually assumed, Tasciovanus seems to have exercised some measure of control over a fair part of eastern Britain north of the Thames and south of the Fens, and also in north Kent. It seems that a powerful kingdom consisting of a confederation of tribes north of the Thames was established, and an extension of its power south of the river had been achieved over the peoples of north Kent. The rule of Tasciovanus was contested by a rival named Athedomarus, however, whose coins are found extending over much of the same area north of the Thames. A successor or conqueror of Athedomarus was Dubnovellaunus, a Kentish king who also ruled in Essex.

In this confusing struggle for power, Cunobelinus, the son of Tasciovanus, finally emerged as the victor, and from the distribution of his coins recovered control over all the territory north and south of the Thames that was ever ruled by his father. He made Camulodunum his capital, and it was here that his coins were minted.

Until the reign of Cunobelinus, the southern bank of the Thames to the west of the Kentish tribes had remained the northern boundary of the Atrebatic kingdom established by Commius, which extended to the south coast in Hampshire and west Sussex. This dynasty, however, was weakened by internal dissension, and Cunobelinus gained control of the Thames in this western area also, where soon after AD 20 his brother Epaticcus was established as ruler in the northern tribal centre of the Atrebates at Calleva (Silchester). The kingdom of Verica, the son of Commius who had successfully ousted his elder brothers, seems now to have been reduced to south-east Hampshire and west Sussex. One of these brothers, Eppillus, had established himself as ruler of Kent until he also was driven out by Cunobelinus, who now practically controlled the whole of the Thames basin, and was powerful enough to have established a Thames-side trading centre if he had wished to do so. Although trade with the Continent had increased and Cunobelinus was happy to import wine, fine pottery and other luxuries, he found Camulodunum perfectly adequate as a port, and his loosely knit 'empire' of tribes under related and subordinate rulers required as yet no unified administration, for which a more central capital might have been convenient.

After the departure of Caesar, the Romans, while not interfering directly with Britain, continued to watch over its affairs, and through trade and cultural contacts extended their influence over the Belgic rulers of the south-east. Rome, in fact, became the natural refuge for chieftains who were driven out by the dynastic warfare or by the fraternal rivalry that made these Belgic kingdoms inherently unstable. Tincommius, son of Commius, probably ousted by his brother Eppillus, fled to Augustus as also did Dubnovellaunus of Kent and Essex, presumably when expelled by Cunobelinus.[31] Adminius, a son of Cunobelinus who was banished by his father, sought refuge with Caligula, an event which gave rise to the grotesque posturing of that emperor on the Channel coast. No emperor needed to look far for a pretext for invasion, and when Claudius in AD 43 required

both a military triumph and employment for surplus legions, this was provided by the aged Verica, who had finally been driven from the dwindling kingdom of the Atrebates by Cunobelinus. The great Belgic king himself had sensibly maintained friendly relations with the Romans while pursuing his career of conquest, but his recent death had not only divided his kingdom, but left it in the hands of his two sons, Caratacus and Togodumnus, who were openly anti-Roman.

There is no suggestion from historical or archaeological evidence that there was any settlement of importance in the London area throughout this period of dynastic struggles, when the principal trading places were at the tribal centres of Camulodunum, Verulamium, Calleva, and the unnamed capital of the southern Atrebates, later known as the Regni, in the neighbourhood of Selsey and Chichester. Former claims that there was a trading settlement on the Thames just before the Roman conquest can now be discounted.[32] They were based on a number of pieces of the fine Italian (Arretine) pottery, of the kind imported by Cunobelinus and his contemporaries, said to have been found in the City of London and Southwark. These have not survived the close scrutiny of modern scholarship. One has been re-identified as later Gaulish ware; the others are highly suspect as genuine London finds, because they are complete (very unusual in London except in pottery from burials) or from a collection that contains other improbable foreign material said to have been found in London.[33]

The other evidence that has sometimes been cited is the name 'Londinium' itself, which must be derived from a native word. Its derivation from a personal name 'Londinos', supposedly from a Celtic adjective 'londo-', meaning 'fierce', 'merry' or 'active', has been rejected by modern scholars, although they have nothing to put in its place.[34] Margaret Gelling has suggested that some of the obscure place-names of Roman Britain, among which she includes Londinium, may belong to a linguistic stratum older than the use of Celtic speech in Britain.[35] In view of the intensive Bronze Age activity in this area, it would certainly not be surprisingly if a pre-Celtic place-name had survived. There is no reason whatever to suppose that it was applied to any settlement of importance at the time of the Roman conquest, however. It may have lingered merely as the name of a farm— or even a natural feature, if we are dealing with an unknown language.

We need not suppose that the London area was uninhabited at this time; indeed there are one or two inhumation burials from central London that antedate the earliest evidence for Roman activity on their respective sites, but may not be much earlier. One of these was found in the 1976 excavations in the Tower of London, and another was more recently excavated in Southwark, beneath the early Roman road to the bridge (6). Southwark excavations have also produced a considerable part of a decorated pot of non-Belgic type, attributed to the period first century BC—first century AD, found in the lower fill of a water-channel, the

6   Pre-Roman male burial found in Borough High Street, Southwark, beneath Roman road leading to the bridge. *SLAEC*

upper fill of which contained pre-Flavian pottery, at 201–211 Borough High Street. The channel seems to have been a natural water-course that was filled when the Roman road to London Bridge was constructed.[36] There were evidently people in the neighbourhood, probably living on higher ground to the south, but there is as yet nothing to suggest occupation on a larger scale than that of isolated homesteads.

If there had been a Thames-side *oppidum* little more than a century earlier, however, memory of it would certainly have been preserved among the local people and passed on to their Romano-British descendants. Is it possible that vague traditions had survived to the time of Geoffrey of Monmouth? It is certain that the romantic legend of 'New Troy' was created in the early twelfth century to gratify the pride of a self-confident city then struggling to win self-government and establish itself as a commune. Its starting point, however, must have been the tribal name, and just possibly a memory of the second half of the Latinised name of an earlier tribal capital, '——— *Trinovantum*'—'——— of the Trinovantes'. John Clark, however, has pointed out that the *civitas Trinovantum* mentioned by Caesar was erroneously interpreted by the historian Orosius in the fifth century as meaning the 'city' instead of the 'tribe' of the Trinovantes, and it is likely that the whole edifice of 'New Troy' was erected on this simple error, compounded by later writers who assumed that 'Trinovantum' was the city's name.[37]

2

The Claudian Conquest
and the
Beginning of Londinium

The prerequisite conditions for the development of London were created by the Roman conquest of AD 43, which imposed a single firm control over both sides of the river Thames. It was a control that was to be rapidly extended not only over the Thames but over the entire lowland zone of Britain with all its riches. Moreover the conquest brought in its train a vast improvement in landward communications. The new roads that were laid out as an essential instrument of conquest and exploitation made possible speedy travel by marching armies and wheeled traffic at all seasons. The barrier of the Thames had to be finally and permanently breached if they were to be effective. The requirement was obviously a bridge—no problem for Roman military engineers in a country where timber was abundant. It required a considerable investment of labour, however, and it is unlikely that more than one bridge over the lower Thames was envisaged. Later generations managed well with a single bridge between the estuary and Kingston, and only the phenomenal growth of London's own population in the last three centuries made it necessary to build others. The Roman roads, however, had to come to the bridge, so that for the first time a single centre of land communications was established on the river. Water traffic, which in the past had created transient settlements of importance on the river banks, continued to be essential, especially for the transport of bulky or heavy material, and under an imperial power eager for commercial exploitation the Thames became again the principal gateway of Britain. Although ships could certainly pass through it, presumably under a drawbridge, as we know from wrecks upstream, the bridge naturally became the terminus for most of this traffic. From the beginning, then, the bridgehead was an unrivalled centre of communication by land and water, and the development of a major city there was inevitable. The sequence of events that gave birth to London is clear and incontrovertible, but the precise date of the building of the first London Bridge and the circumstances of the founding of Londinium are much more doubtful.

The invading Roman army of AD 43 under its general Aulus Plautius initially took the route through Kent that had been followed by Julius Caesar nearly a century earlier, as was inevitable if the short sea crossing from Gaul was used. More fortunate or better informed than Caesar, however, Aulus Plautius landed, not on an open beach, but in the natural harbour of Richborough, where the double ditch defending his beachhead can still be seen. His landing at this point seems to have taken the Britons by surprise, and was unopposed. Their leadership was shared by the two sons of Cunobelinus, Caratacus and Togodumnus, who decided to make the river Medway rather than the Thames their main line of defence. Here they fought a major battle that was to decide the whole campaign. It continued into the second day, but in spite of the Britons' courage and determination the professionalism and discipline of the Roman army, accompanied by equal courage, inevitably prevailed and the Britons were ultimately routed. This was the decisive battle of the campaign, and thereafter only local resistance was encountered. Aulus Plautius then advanced to the Thames, which he successfully crossed in two places. Unfortunately we have no first-hand account, as we have with Caesar, of these and subsequent events. According to Dio[1], who wrote nearly 200 years later, but probably had access to earlier accounts that are now lost, the first crossing was in hot pursuit of fugitives 'at a point near where the river flows into the sea and at high tide forms a pool'. Here there was a concealed ford which the Britons knew, but the pursuing Gaulish auxiliaries were forced to swim. Other troops crossed by a bridge a little further upstream, so that the Britons were attacked from more than one direction and suffered heavy losses. They fled, probably into Essex, and the pursuing Romans found themselves bogged down in impenetrable swamps, where they lost many men.

All this must have happened fairly near the site of London, which was probably later selected because of its proximity to the tidal limit of the Thames at that time. Unfortunately there seems no way in our present state of knowledge to establish precisely where this was. The reference to the pool formed at high tide might suggest a point further downstream where the river begins to widen out into the estuary, and where it is just possible that there was a low-water ford in the first century AD. Yet the Romans who crossed by the bridge were soon able to concert their attack with the Gauls who swam across at the hidden ford, so that the two crossings probably really were only a little way apart, as Dio says. It is unlikely that the bridge was downstream of London Bridge, where no bridge but the late nineteenth-century Tower Bridge has ever been built in recorded history, and where even the great Victorian engineers preferred the enormous and difficult task of tunnelling. Both crossings therefore were presumably somewhere within what is now called Inner London.

It is probable that the Roman sword with ornamental sheath of the first century AD, found in the Thames at Fulham (**7**), was lost by an officer of the invasion force, so that part of the army at least may well have crossed by the long-established fords in the west London area.

But what was the bridge? It seems unlikely that the political unification of the

7 Roman officer's sword, with bronze sheath-frame decorated with Romulus and Remus suckled by wolf, first half of first century AD, from the Thames at Fulham. *British Museum*

two sides of the river under the growing empire of Cunobelin had proceeded to a point where a bridge had become necessary, even if the Britons had been capable of building it. It is even more unlikely that a wooden bridge, which could easily be burnt, would have been permitted to remain to assist the Roman army in its crossing. It is much more likely that this was a floating bridge hastily constructed by Roman engineers to overcome an obstacle of which they had been fully aware since Caesar's invasion. If they had brought the necessary equipment with them, a temporary bridge of this kind could probably have been assembled very quickly, though the second crossing could hardly have followed the first as rapidly as Dio's narrative might suggest.

At this point, with the Thames successfully crossed and the main opposition in south-eastern Britain overcome, a curious halt was called to the campaign, and on the pretext that the invaders had suffered heavy casualties an appeal for reinforcements was sent to the Emperor Claudius at Rome. There is no doubt that this was by prior arrangement, and that it had always been intended that Claudius, who needed a military success to consolidate his political position, should personally take up the leadership of the campaign at the point where Julius Caesar himself had abandoned it. The timetable, however, had been thrown out by Plautius' early success, which brought him across the Thames much more quickly than had been expected. Claudius was still in Rome when he received the message, and he hastily embarked at Ostia with his Praetorian Guards and the corps of elephants that was intended to overawe the Britons. From there he sailed to Marseilles, and then partly by river and partly by overland marches passed through Gaul and crossed the Channel. The journey to the Thames under the most favourable circumstances cannot have taken less than six weeks.

I have in the past argued that it was during this period of inactivity that Aulus Plautius built the first London Bridge—as a more permanent piled structure by which the Emperor and even his elephants could cross the river with fitting dignity. He could easily have done so, for Julius Caesar built a pile bridge across the Rhine, a wider river, in ten days from the first collection of timber.[2] Plautius' principal problem at this time must have been to keep his men occupied, so he may well have built a bridge, but if so, it now seems unlikely to have been in the Southwark–City area, and therefore could not be described as the first London Bridge.

It seems certain that Plautius was in control of both sides of the Thames in the strategically important London area before the arrival of Claudius, for Dio's statement that the Emperor fought a battle to cross the river can be discounted. Suetonius and the inscription from Claudius's triumphal arch in Rome both inform us categorically that he suffered no losses during his brief stay in Britain, and casualties would have been inevitable in a contested river-crossing.[3] There is little doubt that everything possible was done to prepare for the triumphal entry of this most unwarlike of emperors into Camulodunum, short of the actual capture of the *oppidum*. There was therefore a large Roman army in the London area, even allowing for the probable detachment of Vespian and *Legio II Augusta* to commence the conquest of the west. Where was it based? It is a reasonable assumption that it was at London and that Londinium, like so many lesser towns

8   Roman legionary helmet, mid-first century AD, from the Thames at London. *British Museum*

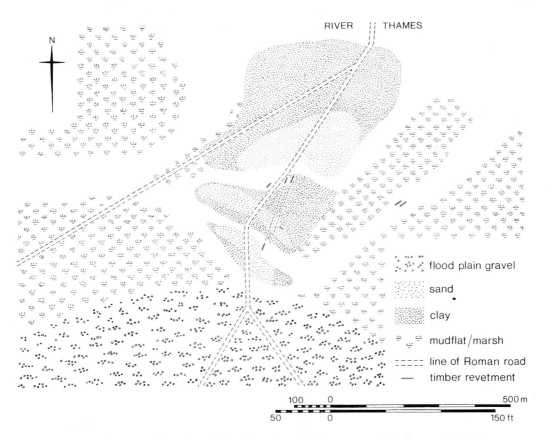

RIVER ‖ THAMES

N

flood plain gravel

sand

clay

mudflat/marsh

line of Roman road

timber revetment

100　0　　　　　　　　　　500 m

50　　　0　　　　　　　　　150 ft

Fig. 2　Natural topography of north Southwark, with Roman roads leading to the bridge.
C. Unwin after S.L.A.E.C.

of Roman Britain, began its existence as a fort controlling a strategic river-crossing at the time of conquest. It is, however, an assumption that archaeologists have as yet failed to confirm. Such new evidence as we have, although inconclusive, points to a later date for the construction of the approach roads to London Bridge and the first Roman occupation of Southwark. By implication it points therefore to a later date for the construction of the first London Bridge and the beginning of Londinium.

A small professional team has been working in Southwark since 1970, and gradually a clearer picture has emerged of the ancient topography of north Southwark, archaeologically of great importance as the southern bridgehead of London Bridge from Roman times to the present day. As such it should reflect the history of the northern bridgehead which is the site of the City itself. The earliest archaeological levels in Southwark, however, are more accessible than they are in the City, where the overburden of later deposits is thicker, later destruction by massive foundations and double cellars has been more extensive, and the greater value of land has until recently inhibited investigation.

A significant new discovery is that north Southwark is not nearly such an obvious place for a river-crossing as it appeared to be a few years ago. We knew then that Borough High Street overlay a natural sandy area that was a few feet higher than the original ground level to the east and west, and imagined this to be a sand-spit giving easy access to the river from the higher ground to the south—the sort of natural feature that a military engineer looking for a convenient place to build a bridge could hardly overlook. Thanks to a painstaking study of the natural contours and surfaces of north Southwark by Alan Graham, however, based on builders' test-bores as well as excavations, we now know that the higher area of sandy gravel was merely an 'eyot' (island), separated from the higher gravels to the south by three water-courses, probably minor channels of the Thames, each of which would have to be bridged. Between these channels were two other islands consisting of small sand-banks and areas of silt forming mud-flats—not the easiest terrain for road-building and settlement (fig 2).[4]

As might be expected, the earliest structures in Southwark were the roads—apart from a channel revetment that may have been a support for a temporary bridge at 201–211 Borough High Street and a drainage ditch at 106–114 Borough High Street, both of which were probably an essential part of the preparation of the ground for road construction.

One road is clearly a diversion to the north-east, towards the bridgehead, of Watling Street, the great highway through north Kent from the invasion port of Richborough. It changes from its north-westerly course just south of St George's Church, and runs first north and then north-north-east. Its line has now been plotted with fair precision from the east side of Borough High Street just north of St George's Church, across to the west side of the modern road, where it curves to its final course towards the bridge, underlying Borough High Street, where it was observed in a GPO trench opposite Nos 93–99.

The other road was first found by Dr Graham Dawson in 1969 in Montague Close, immediately north of Southwark Cathedral. It has since been shown to run from that point in a north-easterly direction, and would have met the first road just east of the present London Bridge. Their junction, approximately midway between the mediaeval and modern bridges, does not give the precise position of the Roman bridgehead, which has been lost by erosion and lay some distance to the north of the present river-bank. Whichever was the primary road—and it is by no means certain that this was the Watling Street extension—probably continued on its course for a little way before swinging to the north on the bridge approach, which was almost certainly at right angles to the river-bank. The junction does however confirm evidence from the north bank suggesting that the Roman bridge was on or very near the site of Old London Bridge. There is little doubt that a Roman north-south roadway underlies Fish Street Hill, and that this was the central axis of Londinium, as would be expected if it led from the bridge to the city centre.[5] An excavation in 1981 on the east side of Fish Street Hill

9 Measuring NE corner of wooden structure (A), possibly a support for the Roman bridge, Fish Street Hill, 1981 (view to W). A first-century waterfront (B) of later construction abuts it on the right and terminates beside it. See also 22, p 92. *Museum of London*

showed that the first-century waterfront was interrupted at that point, and immediately to the south was the north-eastern corner of an earlier rectangular timber structure that may well have been a support for the Roman bridge itself (**9**).

The destination of the Montague Close road to the south-west is also significant. Unless there was a change of direction it must have reached the Thames at or near the hypothetical ancient crossing from Lambeth to Westminster, which now seems considerably more probable. It was postulated by Margary and others to account for the alignments of Watling Street, north and south of the river, which disregard London Bridge and the City, and would if projected meet at this point.[6] This road or rather these roads, since there is as yet no archaeological evidence to confirm the continuation of Watling Street North to the south of Marble Arch, should represent a primary route from the Channel port of Richborough to Verulamium, the most important tribal centre in south-east Britain after Camulodunum. As a trackway the route may well have existed before the Roman conquest, and is likely to have been of some importance when rulers at Verulamium, such as Tasciovanus, had political and trading interests in Kent. The construction of a major highway leading to the site of the new bridge from the general direction of Stangate, the old ferry site north of Lambeth Palace, strongly suggests not only that there was a river-crossing at this point in early Roman times, but that there was Roman activity somewhere in west London when London Bridge was built and before Londinium was founded. It would not be surprising if the original purpose of the road was to bring labour and material for the construction of the bridge to its southern end.

The roads were of the rammed gravel construction that is usual in the London area, and the material from which they were made is likely to be of very local origin. Alongside the more westerly road were quarry pits that were later partially filled with clay. This road was about 6m wide in its earliest phase, but was later widened to about 10m, and eight superimposed surfaces were found, indicating that it continued to be of importance, and strongly suggesting that the Westminster crossing remained in use after the building of London Bridge (**10**).[7]

The more easterly road that linked the new bridge with Watling Street and Stane Street was about 8m wide in its early phases and may have been wider later. Five surfaces were observed in its surviving thickness of 0.7m. Where it passed over the marshy ground of a silted channel at 210–211 Borough High Street it was laid on three layers of oak logs, reduced to only layer as it reached firmer ground to the north. Still further north, at 106–114 Borough High Street, where the ground was again unstable, it was constructed on a timber raft and was contained, at least on its eastern side, within a line of vertical stakes which may originally have held horizontal planks set on edge.[8] It is likely that the underlying timbers

10 Gravel metalling of Roman road in Montague Close, Southwark, leading from the bridge probably to a crossing at Westminster. Several resurfacings are visible and the thickness of the gravel deposits is at least 1.5m (view to E). *SLAEC*

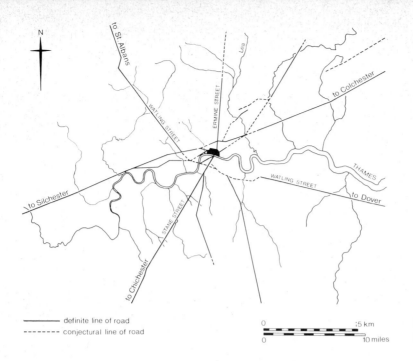

definite line of road
- - - - - conjectural line of road

0   ;5 km
0   10 miles

Fig. 3 Roman roads in the London area

were laid in order to provide a secure foundation or as a working platform, immediately before the construction of the gravel road, although it is just possible that they formed part of an earlier temporary causeway (**11**).

None of the primary road structures are themselves securely dated, though the odd pre-Flavian sherd from construction levels and early Flavian pottery from the make-up of later resurfacing suggests that they were in existence before AD 70, as would be expected. There is, however, a great deal of dating evidence for the earliest activity alongside the roads, from the pottery and coins found in the earliest silt of the adjacent drainage ditches and in the fills of the quarry pits from which the road gravel was obtained. Some Roman pottery, particularly the fine imported wares from Gaul, can now be closely dated, and modern specialists can often give a confident dating within about ten years to a reasonable assemblage of pottery fragments. In Southwark they report a consistent absence of the earliest Claudian pottery, and a general dating of about AD 50–60 for the first debris that accumulated beside the roads.

Much the same story is told by a statistical study of all the coins recorded from Southwark, carried out by M. J. Hammerson.[9] Copper coins (*asses*) of Claudius are abundant, but the great majority are the British copies that seem to have been produced as a token coinage well into the reign of Nero, becoming increasingly cruder and smaller in size. They may well have been issued by the army to remedy the acute shortage of small change at this period. At Southwark the proportion of these irregular copies among the Claudian coins is very high— 92%, approximately the same as that of Exeter (93%), where the legionary base is now considered to have been founded after AD 50, and Lea Mills (90%), where a

11 Timber foundation of main N–S Roman road in Southwark, leading to the bridge; site of 106–114 Borough High Street (view to N). *SLAEC*

supply base was probably established soon after AD 50 by Ostorius Scapula. It is in marked contrast with the proportion found in sites that are known to have been occupied in AD 43, such as Richborough (36%), Hod Hill (33%) and Colchester (58%).

At Colchester also Grade I copies, those nearest to their official prototypes and supposedly the earliest, predominate among the imitations, amounting to 61%, with 21% of Grade II and 8% of Grade III.[10] At Southwark Grade II forms the largest group, and the proportions are Grade I 21%, II 53% and III 26%. The corresponding proportions at Lea Mills are Grade I 6%, II 21% and III 73%. On the assumption that there was a progressive deterioration in the quality of the copies, it is suggested therefore that the beginning of Southwark should fall chronologically between those of Colchester and Lea Mills. It should also be earlier than Usk, believed to have been founded about AD 55, since nearly all the copies found there were very small (20–24mm), whereas at Southwark more than 60% were larger than this. On this basis Hammerson argues that the occupation of Southwark should have begun in the period about AD 50–5.

Since the pottery experts and the numismatist are in accord, the argument from Southwark that the beginning of occupation along the approach roads to London Bridge was not earlier than about AD 50 must be provisionally accepted — provisionally, because past experience has shown that all dating from archaeological evidence alone is subject to revision. Does this also mean that the approach roads to London Bridge, and by implication the bridge and Londinium itself, did not exist before that date? Although it can be argued that the roads initially passed through a militarised zone that was kept clear of occupants and refuse, it is difficult to believe that this state of affairs continued for years rather than months. Clearly the final answer must come from the City, and through no fault of the archaeologists working there it is not yet available. There has been little opportunity in recent years to investigate the earliest archaeological levels in those parts of Londinium where occupation is likely to have begun — at the bridgehead in the neighbourhood of Fish Street Hill; in the central nucleus of the Roman city on both sides of Gracechurch Street, between Cornhill and Lombard Street; and in the intermediate area south of the east-west Roman street that underlies the eastern end of Lombard Street and its junction with Fenchurch Street, and is undoubtedly a primary feature of Londinium. Outside these central areas the first occupation is more likely to have been due to subsequent growth than to the foundation of the Roman city. Somewhere within them we need a site or sites with opportunity for a fully scientific investigation. Above all it is important that there shall be a time for a full investigation of the earliest levels, which are necessarily left until the last, over a reasonable area, and not merely a lucky dip into them in one or two places just before the site is abandoned to the developers. It is a lot to ask on sites of immense capital value where there is strong pressure on archaeologists to finish their work as quickly as possible; moreover, these are sites where the higher and later levels are likely to raise problems of great importance that can only be solved by a horizontal extension of the investigation.

Nevertheless there is no problem of greater historical importance than the origin of London itself, and definitive evidence can only be produced in the heart of the City by the trowel of the archaeologist at work in its deepest levels.

Such information as is at present available is inconclusive. Glimpses of the beginning of Londinium can be obtained from the excavations and observations of Brian Philp, who worked heroically with a few assistants and a band of volunteers through the winter of 1968–9 on a development site immediately east of Gracechurch Street and north of Fenchurch Street.[11] Initial slight occupation seems to have been of brief duration and no structures were found (Period I). This was followed in Period II by the construction of the east–west gravel roadway with its adjacent ditch, and by the dumping of gravel in an open area on the west of the site, and in a more limited area on the east. The more easterly gravel deposit had a straight north-south edge at right angles to the east-west roadway to the south, and was interpreted as a minor north-south street. On either side of it were scattered traces of timber buildings with clay floors. A major replanning followed in Period III, and large new timber-framed buildings were constructed right across the supposed north-south roadway of Period II, while a new east-west roadway or alley crossed the northern part of the site (fig 5). The archaeological dating by coins and pottery of Periods I and II is not precise, and merely places them about the middle of the first century. Period III, however, was brought to an end by the great fire that provides a convenient fixed point in the chronology of London's archaeology—the destruction of Londinium by Boudica in AD 60 (see Chapter 3). Period I is so brief as to be negligible, so that the crucial date for the beginning of Londinium is the commencement of Period II, and the duration of Periods II and III becomes of great importance. On the assumption that Londinium was founded immediately after the conquest, Philp gave Period II an arbitrary date of c 44–50, allowing a full ten years for Period III. As this assumption has been challenged by the evidence from Southwark, it is necessary to consider the case for the duration of both phases. Philp's suggestion is a minimum possible duration of two years for Periods I and II and five years for Period III, though he would prefer a somewhat longer time for both. There is in fact no real evidence for the duration of Period II, for the succession of clay floors observed in a builder's trench in the north-east corner of the site may have extended into Period III; and replanning might have taken place very early if an initial military occupation was replaced by civilian usage as soon as the bridge, main roads and any other major engineering works had been completed. For Period III, however, there is clear evidence of a duration of four or five years at least. The internal wall of one building had been surfaced at four different times with layers of painted plaster, and even if we allow for a somewhat extravagant annual re-decoration, five years must have elapsed between its construction and burning. It is impossible therefore to reduce Philp's minimum duration by very much. Six years would have been the least possible time between the beginning of Period II and the fire of AD 60, and seven or eight would be a more reasonable minimum. This, however, would bring the beginning of Londinium comfortably within the date range of AD 50–5 postulated on the Southwark evidence for the building of London Bridge. A date in the earlier part of this range—say 50–3—would be more acceptable, and more in accord with the numismatic evidence from Southwark presented by Hammerson.

This hypothesis, however, raises a serious problem. We are left with an awkward gap of between seven and ten years after the first arrival of Aulus Plautius at the Thames. What sort of occupation was there in the London area during this not inconsiderable period, and where was it? The principal Roman base in the early years of the conquest was at Camulodunum, which could be supplied directly by sea, but the continuation of Richborough as a base implies also the continued use of the Channel crossing and the overland route through Kent. This way into Britain must always have been preferred for passenger traffic at least—as it has been ever since. But it is dependent on the provision of a Thames crossing, and if this was not at Southwark it must have been further upstream. The existence of at least a ford at Westminster now seems likely, as we have seen, and it is hardly possible to avoid the conclusion that a temporary bridge would have been built either there or at one of the easier crossing-places a little further upstream in west London, where there are firm gravels on both sides of the river. As the conquest proceeded forts are known to have been built to protect minor river-crossings at Chelmsford, Water Newton, Great Casterton and Dorchester-on-Thames; it is quite inconceivable that the most important river-crossing of all should not have received similar protection, probably on a much larger scale. Moreover, travellers to and from the Channel would soon have required accommodation there. The Thames crossing, never a mere incident on the journey, was the obvious point for a halting-place, even before the Roman road system made it the natural centre for redistribution. Some sort of transit camp and a *mansio* for official messengers would have been needed within a year or two at most. Where was all this before Londinium existed?

We know remarkably little about the early military activities of the Romans in the London area, and this is due partly to the difficulty of access to the archaeology of a built-up area, but even more to the neglect of it until very recently, in all parts of London outside the City. Significantly our only real evidence comes from two places on the periphery of the City itself, where it came to light incidentally during investigations into other aspects of the Roman and mediaeval town.

Professor Grimes, excavating the site of the bombed church of St Bride in Fleet Street, found the curved south-east corner of a Roman ditched enclosure beneath the north-west corner of the church. Its angle was about 90°, and the enclosure must have extended across the line of Fleet Street, which is believed to overlie one of the two principal roads to the west out of the Roman city. It is likely therefore to antedate both the road and the city. The large ditch was U-shaped rather than V-shaped like the usual military ditch, and Grimes considered that the angle was too tight for a normal fort.[12] Nevertheless the military interpretation seems more likely than any other, and the position, on relatively high ground dominating the crossing of the Fleet to the site of the Roman city, is one where an early fort might be expected. Since we now have such a long period in which some kind of military occupation may be expected in the neighbourhood the probability is increased. It could be a fort of the invasion period, when it is likely that the army of Aulus Plautius was distributed in strategically placed forts on both sides of the river; it could equally well have been constructed years later while Londinium and its bridge were being built.

The second find, which was on the opposite side of the City, is more definitely military, but gives us only a tantalising glimpse of the early presence of the Roman army. Hugh Chapman, excavating in 1972 on a site at the corner of

12 Military ditch with 'ankle-breaking' gully at bottom, excavated at corner of Aldgate and Duke's Place. *Museum of London*

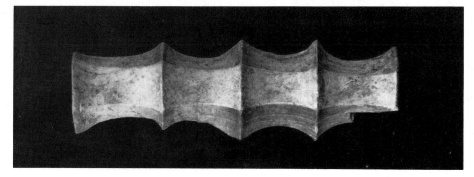

13   Bone handle-grip of Roman legionary sword, found in the fill of early military ditch, Aldgate. Length 3.4 in (8.6 cm). *Museum of London*

Aldgate and Duke's Place, just within the Roman city wall, found that the earliest feature on the site was a typically military V-shaped ditch, with 'ankle-breaking' gully at the bottom (**12**). This ran on a north-easterly alignment diverging from that of the Aldgate–Aldgate High Street roadway, which overlies the line of the Roman highway from the city gate at Aldgate to Camulodunum. There was no sign of silting at the bottom, but a degree of weathering at the sides, suggesting that the ditch was filled not at once but after a fairly short time. The tip-lines indicated filling from the south, evidently by levelling earth ramparts constructed with the brick-earth excavated from the ditch. It must therefore have been the northern edge of a fortified enclosure, the main area of which lay to the south. The fill of the ditch was remarkably clean, containing only five undateable pottery sherds. It did, however, contain one object which indicates the presence of Roman soldiers. This was part of the bone handle-grip of a typical legionary sword (**13**)[13].

We have no means of dating this early military occupation. All that can be said is that following the filling of the ditch and the levelling of the rampart the area was occupied by two—possibly three—timber buildings, which could not be stratigraphically related to one another. They were, however, clearly constructed after the levelling of the ramparts and the filling of the ditch. In both cases they were destroyed by fire, for which there was evidence of a pre-Flavian date, and which it is reasonable to attribute to the holocaust of 60. The most interesting attribute of these buildings is their alignment, which approximately follows that of the earlier ditch, and bears no relationship to the line of the Roman road through Aldgate to Camulodunum, which adjoins the site to the south. This alignment does not appear here before the building of structures occupied in the period about 70–120, and Chapman makes the reasonable suggestion that the main road from Londinium to Camulodunum lay further south until the replanning of London in the latter part of the first century. He further suggests that its position may be marked by the position of the Roman cemetery that is known to have existed in the neighbourhood of Haydon Street and Haydon

Square, and further east in Alie Street.[14] Roman cemeteries normally lay alongside roads outside the city, and the concentration of burials some 200m south of the known line of the main Roman road has always been puzzling. This cemetery continued in use until the late Roman period, but it is understandable that once established it continued to be used. The burials in Alie Street are considerably nearer Aldgate High Street than is the main concentration at Haydon Street. This suggests an alignment converging with that of the later Roman road through Aldgate, as would be necessary for a road leaving Londinium further south and directed towards the crossing-place of the Lea at Old Ford, which was probably a fixed point from the beginning.

If the Aldgate ditch marks the northern side of an early fort, what was its purpose? Again we are left with alternatives separated in date by at least seven years if current views of the beginning of Londinium prove to be correct. It might have been a temporary base where part of the army of Claudius was assembled for the march on Camulodunum in 43. Or it might equally well have been the edge of a smaller fortified camp set up on the Essex side to serve as a base for the military engineers who were laying out Londinium and building the main highways from it after 50. In either case, its function and period of occupation may have corresponded very closely with those of the ditched enclosure that extended northward from the southern side of Fleet Street.

Since we must build on the scanty information we have, it is clearly of the greatest importance to trace the outlines of both of these possible forts, and to study their relationship, if any, to the topography of the Roman city. Fortunately linear features can be traced by locating them in very few small areas, and the bottoms of early ditches at least have a good chance of surviving the intrusions of later foundations and pits. As yet these are our only real clues to early military activity in London.

If the first London Bridge at Southwark was not built until at least seven years after the conquest, and a regular crossing-place had been established further upstream somewhere in central or west London, there must have been a military presence in the years 43–50 to protect it, and the facilities of a staging-post at least must have been provided. Where was this early Roman settlement, and why didn't it develop into Londinium?

The first question cannot yet be answered for lack of information, and it is most unlikely that this could be obtained merely by watching builders' excavations, in which sparse evidence of the kind found at Aldgate—a filled-in ditch with a single military find—would escape notice. A preliminary requirement is a topographical survey for the whole of Inner London as detailed as that carried out by Alan Graham for northern Southwark.[15] This would at least narrow the areas of possibility, and indicate where scientific excavation might be profitable.

The only possible answer to the second question seems to be that there was a deliberate decision by the Roman Governor to establish a new crossing-place of the Thames further downstream. It seems likely that the principal reason was the need for a major port on the lower Thames. It has often been suggested that the

Roman bridge was built at a point just upstream of the tidal limit of the period. We have no certain knowledge where this was, though it was clearly a long way downstream from the present tidal limit at Teddington, and must have been somewhere in central London. It is likely that the Romans would have preferred to build a bridge on part of the river that was unaffected by the rise and fall of the tide, and there were obvious advantages in placing the bridge as near the estuary as possible, thereby shortening the overland journey from the Channel ports to Camulodunum, the first capital. A more important consideration, however, may have been the need to bring the major roads to the highest point in the river that could conveniently be reached by sea-going ships. Marsden has pointed out the value of the incoming tide to sailing-ships proceeding upstream against both the flow of the river and the prevailing westerly winds.[16] There was need therefore to find a place on the Thames where the requirements of the road system for a regular crossing-place and of shipping for deep water and a tidal flow could be reconciled. The subsequent success of London shows that a wise choice was made, and that the efforts required to build a bridge on a more difficult site than those upstream were well worth while.

The origin of Londinium may be closely connected with the beginning of the economic exploitation of Britain. The rich lowland zone of eastern and southern Britain was secure and orderly, behind the long line of the Fosse Way with its network of forts, and military operations had moved further west. It was time for the new province to show some return for all the effort that had been put into it. The man most concerned with this was the procurator, an offical who was lower in rank than the military governor (*legatus*) and subordinate to him, but who nevertheless had a measure of independence because he was responsible directly to the emperor. His duties were essentially financial, but in a new province particularly were wider than this would imply today. He would have been responsible for all aspects of economic development, and is likely to have been concerned with Londinium from the beginning. The decision to build the bridge and its accompanying roads, however, must have been taken at top level, since this great task would have required the engineering skills and resources of the Roman army, over which the procurator had no authority except by delegation from the governor.

3

The First Londinium, its Death and Rebirth

The origins of Londinium

Throughout the many years of speculation based on scanty evidence, a controversy about the origins of Londinium has continued to reverberate and its echoes have not yet completely died away. Was the city of military origin, as so many Romano–British towns of less obvious strategic importance have proved to be; or was its beginning purely commercial, the result of an influx of Roman traders eager to exploit the new province, as Haverfield maintained?[1] In recent years the former view has prevailed,[2] but the new indications of a later origin for the city and the absence of military equipment from stratified early levels in the City, though not in Southwark, have led to a revival of the hypothesis that London was of purely commercial and civilian origin. Nevertheless, Haverfield's view that 'London began, not at the nod of a ruler, but through the shrewdness of merchants, who detected the unique combination of a harbour, a river crossing and a starting point of many inland routes' still seems unacceptable, since the bridge, roads and whatever port facilities there were must have been created by the decision of the military government and the skills of army engineers. It is inconceivable that Ostorius Scapula, in whose governorship these developments seem to have taken place, did not foresee and intend the commercial exploitation of the site that followed.

It is unfortunate that our only historical reference to Londinium at this period should be a brief statement by the most elliptical and laconic of Roman writers.[3] Tacitus tells us that in 60 it was 'a place not indeed distinguished by the title of *colonia*', with the possible implication that its size and importance merited that rank but that it had never been formally bestowed. A *colonia* was a settlement of Roman citizens with full legal rights as such, and might be defined as a 'first-class city', whereas a *municipium*, or 'second-class city', had less prestige and could be a native town whose citizens had more limited rights of franchise. At a lower level were the *civitates*, or tribal capitals, towns of native Britons with local self-government. According to Tacitus, in 60 there was one *colonia* at Camulodunum,

41

where there was a settlement of veteran soldiers, and a *municipium* at Verulamium, a tribal capital which had received special favour. What then was Londinium? Presumably it had no defined status because it had not yet received a charter. Yet, as we shall see, there is clear evidence of planning, orderly development and public works before 60. It seems likely that these were under the direct control of the procurator's branch of the provincial government, which was probably based at Londinium from the beginning.

Tacitus tells us that in spite of its lack of status, Londinium was teeming with merchants and a famous centre of commerce (*copia negotiatorum et commeatuum maxime celebre*). Significantly, for merchants he used the word *negotiatores* rather than the commoner *mercatores*, strongly suggesting that he is not talking about retail traders but people engaged in commercial and financial transactions on a higher level. In the late Republic, the word *negotiatores* seem to have been applied only to Roman citizens settled in the provinces who lent money upon interest. It was later used more generally, but with a primary meaning of wholesale dealer, banker or agent.[4] *Negotiatores* were in fact a type of businessman who would have been quite at home in the modern City of London. In early Londinium their main purposes were presumably to establish import and export businesses on a large scale, and to invest in the new province by making loans towards the cost of Romanisation and exploitation. Both required the co-operation of the procurator, who in turn was dependent on the *negotiatores* for the transformation of the economy of Britain into that of an effective province of the Roman empire.

The earliest planned feature of which we have knowledge is an east-west road roughly parallel with the river, on the higher ground of the gravel terrace east of the Walbrook. It underlies the eastern end of Lombard Street and part of the western portion of Fenchurch Street—the portion running east-west to the west of Rood Lane. This has in fact been a roadway throughout history, and may fairly claim to be one of the two oldest streets in London. In its earliest form it was a surface of gravel metalling 3–5in (7–13cm) thick, with a square-cut drainage ditch about 2ft 6in (0.75m) wide and 1ft 6in (0.45m) deep along its northern edge. It would be in conformity with usual Roman practice if there were a corresponding ditch on the south side, but this lies beneath the modern road and has not been seen. Later the Roman roadway was to be resurfaced at least seven times, building up a thickness of gravel of more than seven feet.

A parallel east-west roadway 420 Roman feet to the south was almost certainly laid out at the same time as part of the initial planning of Londinium. The distance is the equivalent of $3\frac{1}{2}$ *actus*, the unit of measurement to which Roman surveyors normally worked, and this is the only instance of the earliest town-planning of the city that can as yet be identified. The more southerly road ran along the edge of the gravel terrace that had been selected as the site of Londinium, and immediately to the south of it began the steep slope to the river. This road also survives as a modern thoroughfare that still follows the Roman line for a much greater distance than the Lombard Street–Fenchurch Street road, for the Roman road runs under the existing roadway from the western end of Eastcheap along the northern edge of Cannon Street to St Swithin's Lane. Both of these early streets were much narrower than their modern counterparts, with a roadway of gravel metalling little more than $16\frac{1}{2}$ft (5m) wide. The southern road is as yet less securely dated than the northern, but likewise lay directly on the natural brick-earth and is apparently a primary feature (fig. 4).

Our only real knowledge of the earliest phase of London's occupation comes from the small area immediately north of the Lombard Street–Fenchurch Street roadway and east of the modern Gracechurch Street. The evidence from this site, however, is sufficient to show that the north-south streets at the centre of the first Londinium had no such continuity. This is also true of a minor east-west street, little more than an alley between two buildings, 93ft (37.5m) or 95 Roman feet north of the main east-west road (fig 5); it existed for a few years only before the fire of 60. The buildings associated with it had themselves been constructed across the line of an earlier north-south roadway, which must have had a very short life indeed. Rather surprisingly, therefore, the centre of Londinium seems to have been replanned and rebuilt soon after its first permanent occupation. This would be readily explicable if, as Philp suggests,[5] an early military lay-out gave place to a civilian town, but as we have seen a military beginning on Cornhill is not easily reconciled with the later date for London Bridge indicated by the Southwark evidence. If, however, the Aldgate fort belongs to the invasion period rather than the period of construction, as is quite possible (see p39), another site to accommodate the engineers working on the bridge, roads and port installations would have to be sought, and the gravel plateau of Cornhill opposite the bridge-head would be the most likely place to find it. Unfortunately we know no more of this first phase of settled occupation[6] than that it included two wooden structures separated by a north-south gravel roadway leading from the primary east-west road to the south. The one to the west was a building at least 21ft (6.4m) in north-south length, with a clay floor. Its foundations were wooden posts set in a rectangular foundation trench and packed with clay. The one to the east was probably similar, but only three post-holes of its foundation were seen. Nearly 100ft (30m) to the north of it, however, traces of another building with partition walls 4in (10cm) thick, which should belong to this phase, were observed in a builder's trench, and here a series of clay floors indicated occupation for a considerable time, though it is not clear how many of these belonged to the first building. To the west towards Gracechurch Street, in the central part of the site, was a gravelled area which was to continue as an open space in all the subsequent developments of the Roman city.

No proper judgement can be made of the nature of the first occupation of London from this scanty evidence. We have only a general impression of a regular lay-out of timber buildings alternating with gravel metalling to the north of the major east-west road, and the gravelled area immediately east of Gracechurch Street is more extensive than a mere roadway. There is nothing that is inconsistent with a military lay-out, and the setting of foundation posts in trenches can be paralleled in the timber granaries of the early military base at Richborough.[7] A

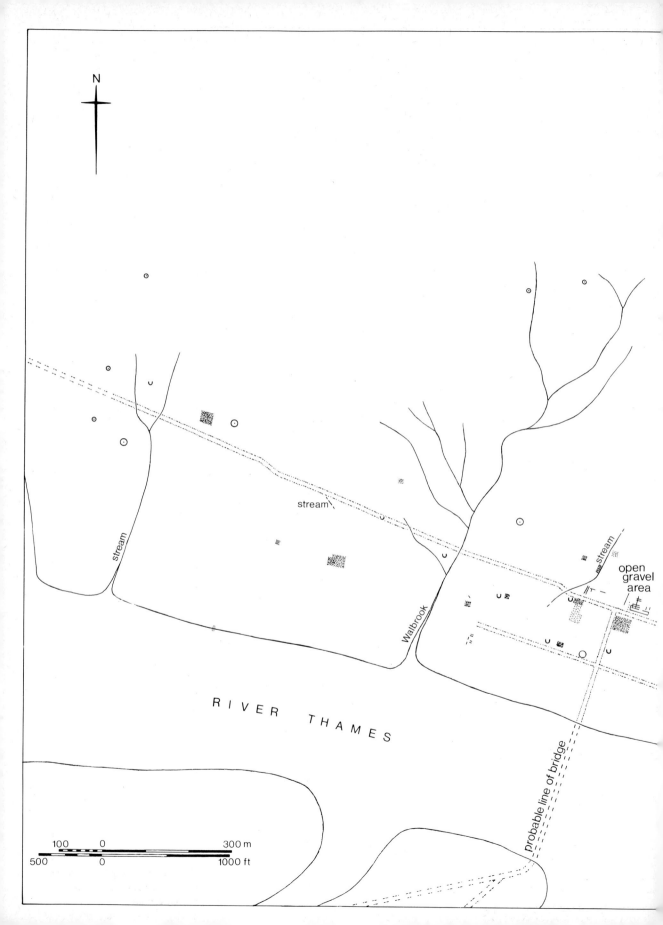

N

stream

stream

stream

Walbrook

open
gravel
area

R I V E R   T H A M E S

Probable line of bridge

100   0   300 m

500   0   1000 ft

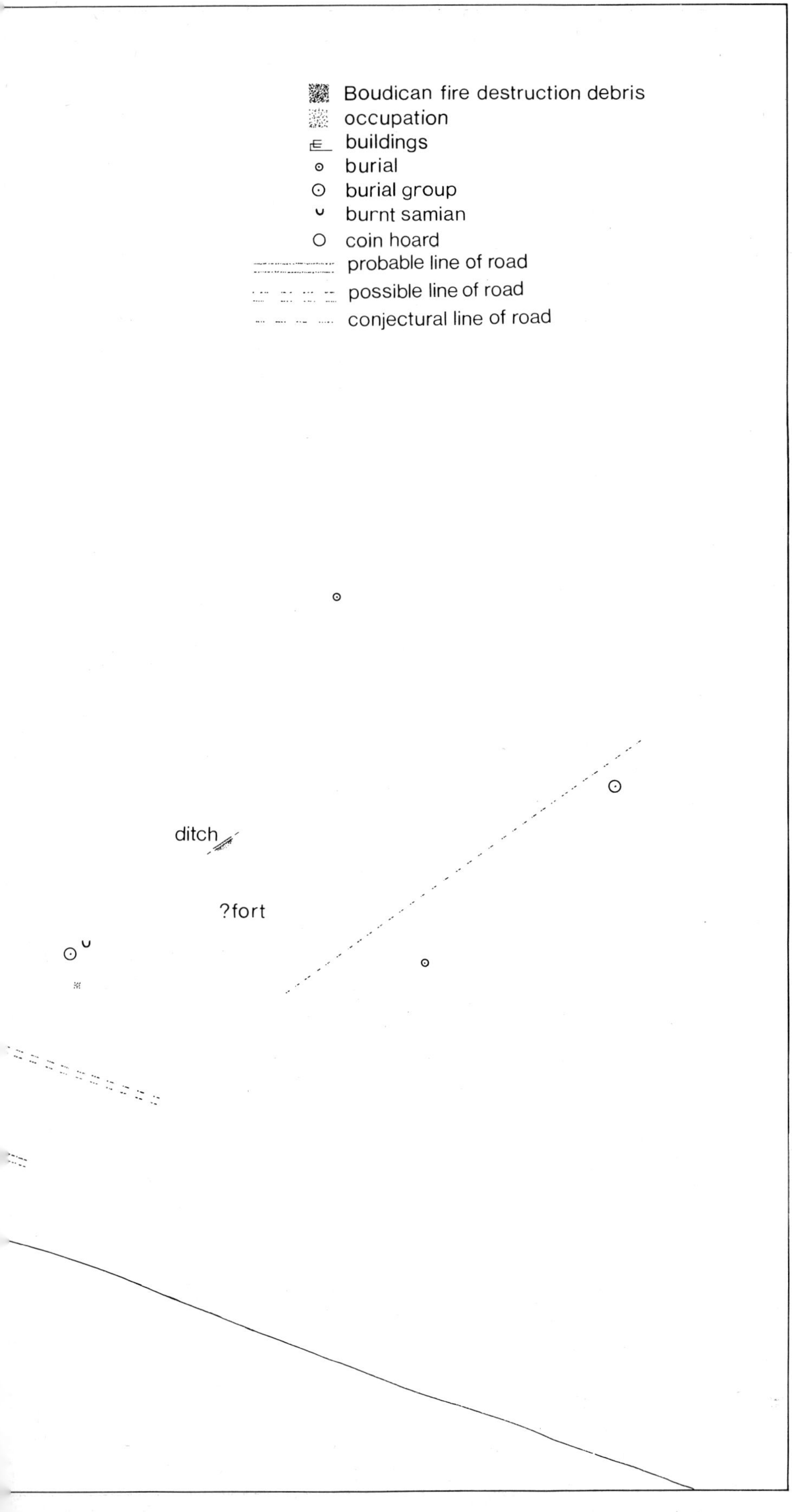

Boudican fire destruction debris
occupation
buildings
burial
burial group
burnt samian
coin hoard
---------- probable line of road
--- -- --- -- possible line of road
-- --- -- ---- conjectural line of road

ditch

?fort

Fig. 4 Map: features of Londinium AD 50–60. *C. Unwin*

similar technique was used in the first two of three timber structures built on a terrace above the river-side at Bush Lane, south of the early east-west road beneath Cannon Street. These were deliberately demolished to make way for the third structure, which seems to have been burnt in 60, and with which the earliest (Neronian) domestic occupation of the site is associated.[8] It seems likely that the first two buildings at Bush Lane, which probably co-existed and may have been storehouses, are contemporary with the first phase on the Gracechurch Street/Fenchurch Street site, and it is noteworthy that there was a change in usage, involving rebuilding, at Bush Lane also before 60. It may also be significant that later in the first century both sites were to be occupied by major public buildings, and may therefore always have been under official ownership and control. Nevertheless a military presence in early Londinium need not imply a primary use as a supply-base—though the army cannot have been indifferent to the establishment of a major port and centre of communications. Imports were in fact already reaching Londinium, as is indicated by amphora sherds found in a corresponding early level on a site immediately to the east, bordering Lime Street[9], though these are evidence only of local consumption and of the provision for people working there of such necessities of Mediterranean civilisation as wine and olive oil. The construction of the Fosse Way, however, as a line of communication that could serve both as the springboard for future operations and a frontier behind which civilian development could begin, gave an obvious strategic importance to the new site, placed as it was at an almost equal distance from the two ends of the line, whereas Camulodunum was distinctly off-centre. The requirements of state gave birth to Londinium, and the army as the executive arm of a military government must inevitably have been involved in its creation, which demanded skills not easily to be found elsewhere. Private enterprise under the civilian control of the procurator's branch of government came later, when the main facilities had been provided.

The centre of early Londinium

It may have been this change in the nature and purpose of the occupation that led to rebuilding in the central area north of the main Lombard Street/Fenchurch Street road, at a date that cannot be later than the beginning of Nero's reign. The latest possible date for the commencement of the new phase seems in fact to be 55. (see p35). The central gravelled area, adjacent to Gracechurch Street and no doubt underlying it, was retained as an open space, and three extensive wooden buildings were constructed to the east of it. Two separate but adjacent buildings lay to the south of a minor east-west road or alley, and the third to the north of it (fig 5). Their foundations were wooden plates, sometimes trough-shaped, set in rectangular trenches and supported, at least intermittently, by pairs of sharpened piles driven into the earth.

On the adjoining site to the east, however, a wall that seems to have been a

Fig. 5 Plan of buildings east of Gracechurch Street, destroyed in AD 60. *C. Unwin after B. Philip*

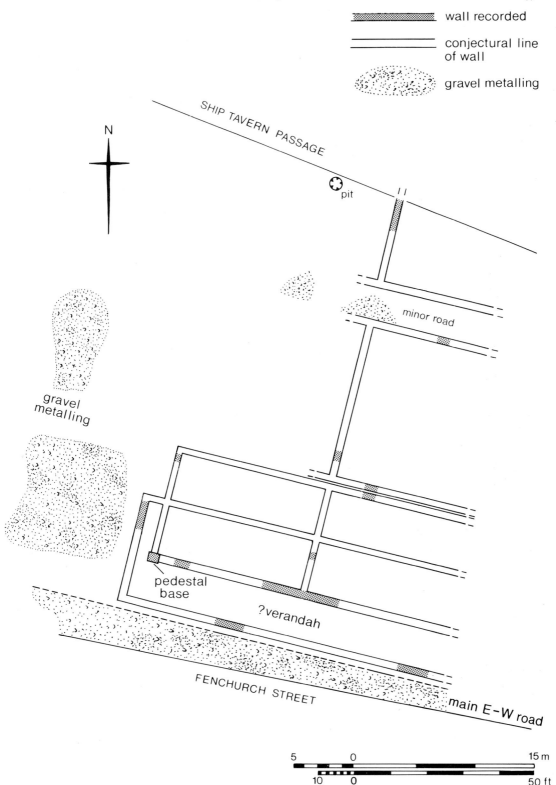

wall recorded

conjectural line
of wall

gravel metalling

N

SHIP TAVERN PASSAGE

pit

minor road

gravel
metalling

pedestal
base

?verandah

FENCHURCH STREET

main E-W road

5   0   15 m

10   0   50 ft

continuation of the main frontage of the southernmost building had substantial foundations of a different character, without piles, consisting of flint nodules set in brownish-white mortar, on which a plank was laid as base-plate. It seems likely that this represents an extension by other builders.

The infilling of the timber-framed walls was of wattle and daub or unfired mud bricks of varying dimensions, bonded with brick-earth so that they tended to become indistinguishable. They were mostly rendered internally with plaster painted white, or occasionally red or green. Floors were invariably of clay (brick-earth), and only in one place on the frontage were roof-tiles found in the fire debris. It must be assumed that the roofs were of thatch, except perhaps on the facade, where the verandah roof may have been tiled or partly tiled. Similarly the complete absence of window-glass fragments strongly suggests that this material was not used.

Nevertheless, the south building had some architectural pretensions, with its verandah or portico about 11ft (3.35m) wide, which extended to the west of the main building, forming a narrower west-facing portico at its western end. In both general plan and constructional details it was remarkable like the contemporary range of shops and work-shops that fronted on Watling Street at Verulamium, and was also burnt in 60.[10] It might be expected that there were more numerous north-south internal cross-walls that could not be observed in partial excavation under difficult circumstances, and that these divided the structure into suites of squarish rooms—a front shop with private quarters behind—as at Verulamium. On this analogy there can be no doubt of its purely civilian function. An interesting feature was a large block of ragstone shaped into rectangular form, which stood on a massive foundation of ragstone rubble concrete with yellow mortar at the south-west corner of the main building within the portico. It presumably supported a pier or column that would have been a striking architectural corner-stone of the structure. This is an important find, since it demonstrates that the ragstone quarries of Kent were already being exploited, and therefore suggests that some ragstone walls in London could be of equally early date.

The timber buildings to the north were of a different character, with semi-basements, and cannot have presented an accessible frontage convenient for shops. The semi-basements might suggest bulk storage, although the re-plastering and repainting of one of them no less than three times within five or six years seem to indicate that it was not merely a storehouse.

All three buildings were planned and constructed by a single agency, as is shown by the fact that the alignment of a north-south internal wall is shared by them all. Moreover the space between the new minor east-west roadway and the main east-west road to the south—a distance of about 98ft (30.1m) or 100 Roman feet—was divided equally between the southern and middle building, for the property boundary indicated by the double wall was almost exactly midway. It seems more likely that the planning and allocation of sites at this early stage of London's development was an act of the provincial government, operating through the procurator's department, rather than any local authority—which in all probability did not yet exist. Development by a private entrepreneur following an initial allocation of land by the state is possible, but in view of subsequent developments in this central area, it seems likely that it was always kept firmly under public control.

As much as possible was squeezed into the space available, no doubt because of the advantages of the central site, for there must have been plenty of room elsewhere. The middle building was placed hard against the southern one with only the two adjacent external walls to indicate that they were not a single structure; while the northern and middle buildings were separated only by the minor east-west roadway, which had no drainage gully, at least on its southern side, and seems to have been merely an alley with gravelled surface extending from wall to wall—a distance of little more than 9ft (2.7m). Moreover the use of piles and substantial foundations for some of the walls suggests that in places there may have been more than one storey.

Unlike the contemporary shops at Verulamium, where internal debris showed that they were in use by tradesmen, including a metal-worker, up to the time of the fire, the buildings on this site provided no evidence of use. The excavators of 1968–9, indeed, were impressed by the lack of internal debris, and were inclined to believe that these premises had been cleared of their contents before their destruction.[11] It was only possible to examine small areas of them, however, and in a later rescue excavation carried out by A. Boddington on the adjoining site to the east, a great quantity of burnt grain was found in a room that must have formed part of the eastern end of Philp's southern building. This was evidently the shop of a corn-chandler, who was obliged to abandon his bulky stock. The burnt grain was up to one metre thick against an internal wall, and was presumably stacked there in sacks before the destruction of 60 scattered it over the floor.

The extent of the open gravelled area to the west is as uncertain as its purpose, but it evidently continued under Gracechurch Street, and this space that seems to have been kept quite clear of buildings is in marked contrast with the closely occupied site of the timber-framed buildings that adjoins it. Peter Marsden has suggested that it may have been an open market-place, as is quite possible.[12] It may, however, have some connection with a mysterious early building on the west side of Gracechurch Street. Two parallel east-west walls with off-set wall to the south are known just north of Lombard Street. These were of ragstone with courses of tiles, and at an early date are likely to have belonged to a building of considerable importance.[13] Unfortunately there is no evidence whether it was built before or after the destruction of 60. All that can be said is that it corresponds in *sequence* with the timber-framed buildings east of Gracechurch Street, since both were succeeded by the same building. Unless, therefore, there was an extra building phase west of Gracechurch Street during the years that the burnt site to the east lay derelict—as is by no means impossible—this structure should be contemporary with the timber-framed buildings destroyed in 60. If it was, it was

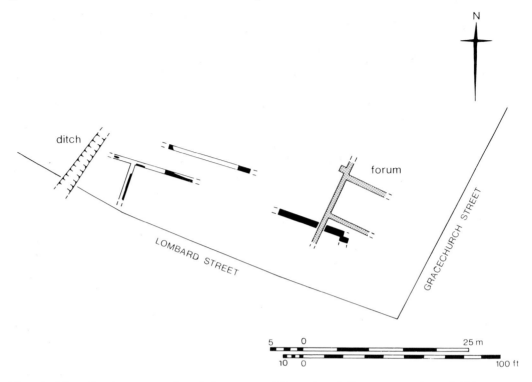

Fig. 6   Plan of early ragstone foundations west of Gracechurch Street, cut and overlaid by west wall of Flavian first forum

probably a public building, and its importance may have demanded an open area around it (fig 6).

An important discovery is that the town already had both a piped water-supply and a fairly sophisticated drainage system. The iron collar of a wooden water-pipe was found on the line of a soil-filled gully that ran along the northern edge of the main road, clearly the remains of a water-main laid in an east-west direction. At the eastern end of the south timber and clay building, where it was extended towards Lime Street, a wooden box drain ran from west to east apparently to remove water from within the building, and it is reasonable to assume that this formed part of a comprehensive drainage system, covering at least the central portion of the town.

Early industrial suburbs

The limits of early Londinium are not immediately obvious, since its vitality was such that there was already building on convenient sites that must have lain well beyond its formal boundary. Many years ago Gerald Dunning attempted to survey the extent of the city before 60 by plotting both burnt sites and unstratified burnt samian pottery of the relevant date.[14] More details can now be filled in, but the overall picture has not greatly changed. Traces of a mid-first-century fire are most concentrated between the southern end of Lime Street and Philpot Lane on the east and the street of Walbrook (on the east side of the Walbrook stream) on the west.

It has often been suggested that the Walbrook would have formed a natural western boundary, but there was undoubtedly early occupation west of the Walbrook, especially in the neighbourhood of the main west road. Early burnt levels tentatively attributed to the holocaust of 60 have been found in King Street and as far west as the GPO site east of King Edward Street. On the east side of the town, as we have seen, there was occupation at Aldgate, only just inside the later city wall that marked the greatest extent of the Roman city. Yet this site, like the GPO site on the west, must have lain beyond the official limits of the pre-Boudican town. These are quite closely defined by the existence of early cemeteries, that under Roman law had to be placed beyond the town boundary. On the east side early cremation urns and cists were found in 1925–6 on the sites of 17–18 Billiter Street and 112–114 Fenchurch Street.[15] A cinerary urn found in Mark Lane to the south and a cremation in a lead canister found in Fenchurch Street in the nineteenth century presumably belong to the same cemetery.[16] The eastern limit of Londinium must then have been not very far east of Mincing Lane and west of Mark Lane and Billiter Street. It seems likely that the regular street grid came to an end just east of this point. Similarly west of the Walbrook the official boundary must lie to the east of the pre-Boudican cemetery in St Martin's le Grand. Here there is some confirmation from the street plan, for there is a curious kink in the alignment of the main Roman road at the bottom of Foster Lane. The displacement of the road at this point either marks a steep slope or indicates that an obstacle was bridged, and there is no evidence of any stream in the neighbourhood. The obstacle may therefore have been an artificial ditch of very early date, marking the western boundary of the pre-Boudican town. Accompanied by an earth rampart it could have formed part of the first defences of Londinium, dating from its very beginning and perhaps already neglected by 60.

If these were the limits of Londinium, how do we account for the outlying occupation at Aldgate and in Newgate Street, beyond the eastern and western cemeteries? We know very little of the former area, where only a small and very narrow site has been excavated. At both ends of it, however, were the remains of shanty buildings of timber and daub that were destroyed by the mid-first century fire.[17] They were not on the alignment of the modern and later Roman road through Aldgate, and there is reason to suppose that the road to Colchester originally lay further to the south. The Aldgate buildings were not therefore part of a roadside ribbon development but in all probability formed part of a larger occupied area that extended further south.

We have a clearer picture from Newgate Street, where the large GPO site was available to archaeologists long enough for an extensive excavation to be carried out. The first building here was a circular hut, contemporary with a ditch that disregarded the alignment of the Roman road through Newgate and presumably antedated it. It is not considered to be pre-Roman, however, and is probably contemporary with small-scale quarrying for brick-earth elsewhere on the site. In the next phase ditches were dug at a right angle to the course of the Roman road, which must then have been in existence. Their purpose was probably to drain the site in preparation for building by carrying away surface water to the inevitable roadside ditch. Two substantial rectangular timber-framed buildings were then constructed, with sill-beams set into the ground at the southern end of the site, near the main road. Further north, away from the road, were traces of several circular huts of wattle and daub. All these buildings were destroyed by a mid-first-century fire, and Steve Roskams, the excavator, has pointed out that the simultaneous burning of several widely separated buildings is unlikely to be accidental, and is therefore almost certainly due to the incendiarism of 60.[18] There was then some delay before rebuilding, and the only sign of activity on the site was the digging of pits with associated gullies, possibly for an industrial purpose. Later buildings here contained work-shops with hearths, some probably used by blacksmiths, and it seems likely that this area was planned as an industrial quarter from the beginning, sensibly placed beyond the cemetery to keep the smoke and fire risk well away from the town. It is quite possible that a parallel development was also taking place on the eastern side of Londinium, as it certainly did later in the first century south of the river in Southwark.

Destruction by Boudica

The glimpses of Londinium between 50 and 60 provided by the archaeological evidence give some indication of the rapid success of the new town, and confirm the impression of teeming activity and commercial eagerness given by the brief words of Tacitus. It was all to end in a disaster from which London was to take years to recover. Prasutagus, client-king of the Iceni of East Anglia, had died, and this had brought to an end the special relationship that the tribe had achieved with its Roman conquerors by early co-operation. Like the Regni of West Sussex and Hampshire it had retained some measure of independence under its own ruler, who was regarded as an ally. Such a relationship was not normally extended beyond the life-time of the favoured individual who was recognised as a client-king, and Prasutagus had been concerned to safeguard the future of his wife Boudica and their two daughters. A man of considerable wealth, derived from the agricultural richness of his tribe, he had endeavoured to do so by making a will leaving half of his property to the emperor and the other half to his family. This brought the minions of the procurator on the scene—probably with instructions to seize the whole estate anyway, for there were precedents for taking the entire personal fortune of a deceased client-king as imperial property. In any case their arrogance and ill-manners led to resistance, which was treated as rebellion. Boudica herself was flogged and her daughters raped. Not surprisingly she vowed vengeance, and the Iceni were joined in their revolt by the Trinovantes to the south, who had seen a Roman *colonia* with its allocation of lands carved out of their tribal territory at Camulodunum; moreover they had witnessed the building there, at British expense, of the great temple of Claudius, which as a symbol of their servitude added insult to injury.

The revolt came at a most inopportune moment for the Romans, since their army was scattered throughout Britain, and the governor, Suetonius Paulinus, with a substantial part of it, was far away in Anglesey engaged in rooting out the Druids from their sanctuary on the island. The colonists of Camulodunum sent to the procurator Decianus Catus for help, but he sent them only 200 ill-equipped men—almost certainly from London. There is the implied criticism that he could have done better, suggesting that troops in excess of this number were at his disposal in London—but Catus no doubt had his own treasure to guard. More promising help was on its way from the north, where the Ninth Legion occupied various forts at the north-eastern end of the Fosse Way. Its commander Petillius Cerialis, however, unfortunately led the legion—or such part of it as he was able to collect at short notice—straight into an ambush somewhere north-west of Camulodunum, from which he escaped with the cavalry alone to take refuge in one of his forts. As a result of its heavy losses the Ninth Legion was no longer an effective force. The colonists of Camulodunum in the meantime had taken refuge within the thick walls of the temple of Claudius, which they held as a citadel, for the colony had no other defences. Their situation was now hopeless, however, and the citadel fell in two days. The first of three great massacres followed; the hated *colonia* was looted and burnt, and the success of the revolt seemed assured.

The procurator, whose ruthlessness and greed had been its immediate cause, quietly slipped on to a ship and escaped to Gaul. Of his possible routes—by ship directly from the port of Londinium by way of the Thames estuary, by road through the friendly territory of Cogidubnus to take ship at Bosham harbour, or by road through Kent to the Channel port of Richborough—he is most likely to have chosen the first, since he had close personal control over shipping at Londinium, whereas the situation in the Channel ports at a time of emergency would have been unpredictable. Moreover, by taking ship directly from Londinium he could escape not only with his life but with all his possessions. If his character can be read correctly from the circumstances of the revolt, this must have been a powerful consideration.

Meanwhile Suetonius Paulinus made all haste for London, pressing on with his cavalry as quickly as possible, and leaving the legionaries to follow at their steady twenty miles a day down the long road from Anglesey. They could hardly have reached Londinium in less than thirteen days, whereas by hard riding Suetonius probably arrived in three or four.[19] If the enemy had been a disciplined army instead of a barbarian rabble, he might well have gone down into history as an even rasher commander than Cerialis. As it was, however, the British rebels wasted a surprisingly long time in looting at Camulodunum and in the Essex countryside, as well as in celebrating their victory, so that Suetonius had time to reach Londinium and take stock of the situation before their arrival. Nevertheless, one wonders whether he knew how bad the situation really was when he decided to make his dramatic dash. It is possible that news of the disaster to the Ninth

Legion had not reached him, and that he expected to find a substantial body of infantry from that legion already in London. He cannot have counted on the arrival in such a short time of the reinforcements for which he had sent from the Second Augusta in the west—and these in fact failed to leave their fortress at Exeter at all, through the excessive caution of the camp prefect who was temporarily in command there. Whatever hopes Suetonius may have had of saving Londinium had to be abandoned when he reached it and learnt the full extent of the disaster. Even then Tacitus tells us that he hesitated, deliberating whether he should stand and fight there—and it is a strong indication of the importance of Londinium in the Romans' plans for the province that he should for one moment have contemplated taking this appalling risk with the force at his disposal, even if some second-grade troops—guards, store-keepers and the like— remained to supplement his cavalry after the two hundred had been despatched by Decianus Catus to Camulodunum. Only one decision was really possible; Londinium had to be sacrificed if the province as a whole was to be saved. In spite of the entreaties of the citizens he determined to withdraw, taking with him those who were willing and able to join his column of march. Its vulnerability on the trek back along Watling Street to Verulamium and beyond to meet the advancing legionaries must have been terrifying, for now no speedy dash for safety was possible.

It is perhaps not surprising that many declined Suetonius' invitation, and these were not only women and the elderly who could not stand the rigours of a forced march. Graham Webster has pointed out that there was an alternative escape route up the Thames into the friendly territory of the Atrebates, whose king, Cogidubnus, had always remained loyal to Rome. Some, no doubt, took refuge at Silchester, the Atrebatic tribal capital, where substantial defences enclosing a large area may well have been constructed at this time.[20] Many others, however, were as reluctant to leave their homes as were later generations of Londoners in times of danger. With the benefit of hindsight this seems incredible folly, but it is one that has been shared in more recent times by many Europeans in both Asia and Africa. The householders of the first Londinium were probably mostly either Roman citizens or well-to-do Gauls and other foreigners who had acquired Roman attitudes, and the Britons with whom they came mostly in contact were likely to have been either a detribalised flotsam engaged in menial activities or the visiting tribal aristocrats with whom they did business. In these circumstances they could hardly be expected to realise either the suppressed hatred of a subject people or the savagery demanded by their gods. We can be quite sure that the procurator's officials made their escape, but the merchants and businessmen who formed the greater part of London's population may have thought that the rebels had no quarrel with them. For whatever reason, although there was ample time to get away, many remained in Londinium to await the hordes of Boudica.

The terrible events that followed their long-delayed arrival demonstrate the complete reversion of the Trinovantes and Iceni to savagery. Inflamed with lust for loot and slaughter they fell on Londinium, where nobody was spared. Death

14 Fragment of South Gaulish samian bowl, burnt black by reduction of iron oxide in the clay, in the Boudican fire of 60. *Museum of London*

by the sword, gibbet or cross was the fate of those who remained in the city, regardless of age or sex. The women in fact, if we are to believe Dio, died even more painfully by obscene torture. The buildings were systematically destroyed by fire—an easy task, since they were mostly timber-framed and thatched—and it is this destruction in 60 (or 61 according to Tacitus and some modern scholars)[21] that gives us the easily recognisable archaeological layer, usually bright red from the oxidised iron in the burnt clay, that marks the death of the first London.

Verulamium was similarly abandoned and met the same fate, and Suetonius made contact with his main force from Anglesey somewhere in the Midlands beyond. It was very small to deal with such a multitude of rebels, consisting of only one complete legion, the XIVth, with a detachment from the XXth. The expected reinforcement from the IInd had not arrived. Fortunately for the Romans, they were able to do battle on ground of their own choosing, within a defile where attack was only possible on a narrow front. The site is not known, but may have been at Mancetter, north-west of Nuneaton and just south of Watling Street, where traces of early defences have been found.[22] In these circumstances, the overwhelming numerical superiority of the Britons gave them no advantage, and a wedge-shaped attack by disciplined soldiers experienced in fighting at close quarters proved irresistible. Whatever Suetonius' defects as a commander-in-chief and governor, he was a brave and effective commander in the field, and won a great victory in which, it is said, 80,000 Britons fell at the price of only about 400 Roman dead, for the Britons' escape was blocked by a ring of wagons occupied by women, whom they had brought with them. Boudica poisoned herself, and the revolt was virtually crushed, although Suetonius continued operations on the pretext that the tribesmen were still disinclined for peace.

His principal motive is likely to have been revenge—understandable enough in the circumstances, for a revolting scene of horror confronted the Roman army when it again entered Verulamium, Londinium and Camulodunum. The Britons had taken no prisoners, and according to Tacitus no fewer than 70,000 people had perished in the three towns and adjacent countryside.[23] This is almost certainly a gross exaggeration, as it is doubtful whether the entire population of this area before the revolt was so large, and many must have escaped by flight. The exaggeration, however, reflects the revulsion felt by Roman soldiers who were by no means squeamish, and had themselves just slaughtered as many. That, however, was in the heat of battle, and an added horror here that probably sent a superstitious shudder through the Roman army was the element of ritual murder to summon the aid of alien gods. It must have seemed that a spirit of evil brooded over the ruins of all three towns, and it may be this more than anything else that delayed their rebuilding and recovery for so long.

Both religious duty and hygiene demanded the disposal of the bodies, and this must have been by mass cremation. No human remains can therefore be attributed with certainty to the massacre. It is possible, however, that some at least of the great number of human skulls found in the stream-bed of the Walbrook were detached from their bodies at this time. They seem to have attracted attention as long ago as the twelfth century, for Geoffrey of Monmouth has a curious story of the mass execution of a legion of Allectus by beheading on the banks of the Walbrook.[24] This tale has no known historical basis and seems to have been invented partly as an explanation of the name of the Walbrook, with an imaginary derivation from the name of the legion's commander, but also in all probability to account for the discovery of skulls, perhaps found in well-digging beside the early mediaeval stream. In more recent times they have been found mostly in the upper waters of the Walbrook on both sides of the city wall (though there are also two found near the main Walbrook crossing at Bucklersbury). The numbers recorded amount to at least 140 from four sites in this area, with a vague reference to 'an immense number' from a fifth. The finders were always impressed by the fact that few if any other human bones were found with them. They were described as being at the bottom of the stream filling on one site, and on gravel at the bottom of sand and silt on another. One skull at least must be earlier than the third century, for it was embedded in the foundations of the city wall, built about 200.[25] It has been suggested that the skulls were rolled by the stream from inhumation burials in the Roman cemetery that was divided by its head-waters in the neighbourhood of Finsbury Circus. The Walbrook, however, was always sluggish, particularly in the period after inhumation burials became common, when it meandered through deposits of silt and is most unlikely to have produced a current strong enough to move a skull. Moreover from the early third century at the latest, when inhumation was only beginning to supplant cremation in Britain, a site that produced 17 skulls was separated from the cemetery by the city wall, through which the streams of the Walbrook passed by barred conduits. Unless, therefore, the skulls are somehow derived from an otherwise unknown pre-Roman inhumation cemetery, and this seems even more unlikely, they really do seem to have come from victims beheaded in the first or second century. The Boudican massacre is the only one attested by history within this period, though executions of criminals by this method might of course have occurred on many occasions. Nevertheless the disposal of the heads in the stream recalls the close connection between Celtic head-hunting practices and the cult of sacred waters, to which Anne Ross has drawn attention.[26] The Walbrook received votive offerings of a less gruesome character many times in the earlier Roman period, but the great massacre of 60–61 seems the only possible occasion when the barbarous rite of head-hunting could be practised on a large scale.[27] It may be significant that the great bronze head of Claudius, probably carried off from Camulodunum at this time, found its way into a river in the territory of the rebel Iceni instead of into the melting pot.

Classicianus, the procurator

Private citizens and foreign traders may have been reluctant to re-establish themselves in Londinium, but Roman officialdom had to return at once in order to rebuild the shattered economy of the province. At its head was the successor of Decianus Catus, who would be primarily responsible for this. The new procurator, Julius Alpinus Classicianus, was a man of very different character, with a greater understanding of the psychology of a subject people. Himself of north Gaulish origin, from a family that had received Roman citizenship several generations earlier and was now of equestrian rank, he appreciated the need for assimilation and Romanisation, and knew that this could not proceed from oppression. Moreover, his father-in-law, a noble of the Treveran tribe, named Indus, had had personal experience of the rebellion of his own tribe forty years earlier, and had himself taken a leading part in the ensuing pacification. It may well have been in memory of this that Classicianus' wife Julia had received her second name (*cognomen*) of Pacata. The Treveri of the Mosel valley had since become fully Romanised and were already one of the most prosperous tribes of Gaul. It was this path that Classicianus hoped the rebel Trinovantes and Iceni would follow. Moreover a similar development in Britain was essential for the accomplishment of his own task. This was made more difficult by the grave danger of famine in south-eastern Britain, for which Tacitus blames the Britons, on the grounds that the Iceni and Trinovantes, who farmed the richest corn-producing area of the province, had failed to sow their fields because of the rebellion. It is possible that the crops were destroyed in the punitive devastation of the rebel territory that followed the defeat of Boudica. Deliberate destruction by the Roman army of food on which it was itself partly dependent seems incredible folly, however, and it is more likely that the loss was the unforeseen result of the massacre and displacement of the farmers who should have tended and harvested it. We know that the army, reinforced from Germany, continued its operations until winter, so the Britons were evidently being harried throughout the harvest season.

Not surprisingly, the new procurator was soon at loggerheads with the governor, his superior officer, who seemed bent on pursuing his vengeance until the spirit of the rebels was totally crushed. Classicianus is accused by Tacitus of encouraging the Britons with the hope that Paulinus would soon be replaced by a new governor with a more conciliatory policy, thereby prolonging their resistance. In this the historian was undoubtedly influenced by his father-in-law Agricola, who had served as a young staff officer in Britain under Paulinus, and always remained loyal to his old commander. It is most unlikely that Classicianus communicated his views to the Britons, though the strained relationship between the governor and procurator must soon have become well-known. Classicianus himself certainly hoped for a new governor with a more conciliatory policy, and did much to expedite this by exercising his right as the holder of an imperial appointment to appeal directly to the emperor. Nero sent a commission of enquiry to Britain, headed by an imperial freedman, Polyclitus—the subject of more sneers from Tacitus. As a result of the commissioner's report, which supported the views of the procurator, Suetonius Paulinus was ordered to cease operations, though retained in office, but shortly afterwards the loss of a few ships provided a pretext for his recall. His successor, Petronius Turpilianus, was evidently briefed to be more merciful, and in his short term of office (one year) succeeded in restoring calm to the troubled province. Two subsequent governors followed the same policy of military inactivity, which was detrimental to the discipline of the troops but made possible steady progress in the Romanisation of the parts of Britain that were already incorporated in the province. This was very much to the taste of the procurator, who was responsible for its economic development.

Classicianus died in office, and one of the most important finds of Roman London was the discovery on two different occasions, separated by more than 80 years, of portions of the massive and imposing monument that was set up above his cremated remains in the eastern cemetery of Londinium. Unfortunately they were not found *in situ*, but like many other Roman sculptures and inscriptions from tombstones in London had been incorporated as building material in a late Roman bastion of the city wall. The first pieces, part of the inscription and a bolster-like ornament from the top, were found in Trinity Place, Tower Hill, in 1852. The inscription, after the normal dedicatory formula DIS MANIBVS ('to the divine shades'), had the name ALPINI CLASSICIANI, preceded by [F]AB. Unfortunately the stone slab containing the beginning of the line was missing, and this was to give rise to a misconception later. Charles Roach Smith in 1859 correctly suggested that the inscription was in all probability from the tombstone of Julius Classicianus, the procurator mentioned by Tacitus, since the name Classicianus is rare. Moreover he was impressed by the quality of the inscription and realised from its size that it came from an imposing monument that was unlikely to be the tombstone of an ordinary citizen.[28] Unfortunately Tacitus does not mention the name Alpinus, and the abbreviation FAB was interpreted by later scholars as the gentile name Fabius. Accordingly they believed it came from the monument of a Fabius Alpinus who had something to do with the fleet (*classis*) and was therefore described or nicknamed by an adjective *classicianus*.[29] They were aware that *Fabia* is also the name of a voting-tribe, and that in inscriptions of this period the tribal name was often incorporated with a Roman citizen's personal name, but discounted this possibility with the argument that there would have been insufficient room on the missing slab for the essential gentile name. It may be suspected also that there was an understandable scholarly reluctance to relate a casual archaeological find to a name from the pages of Tacitus. Fortunately the discovery of another part of the inscription years later in the same place resolved all doubts, and confirmed that Roach Smith's instinct had been right though his actual interpretation had not. In 1935, Frank Cottrill, then serving as archaeological observer in the City of London for the Society of Antiquaries, was called to a site in Trinity Place where a sub-station of the London Passenger Transport Board was being built, and the last remnant of the bastion was exposed. Most of it had been destroyed when the Inner Circle was built in 1882–5, but four courses of its north side remained. Upside down in the bottom course could be seen a second stone slab of the inscription, with the same beautiful lettering. It proved to come from a lower part of the monument, and included the actual title of the procurator, abbreviated PROC. PROVINC. BRIT[ANNIAE] (Procurator of the Province of Britain) and the name of his wife, who had set the monument up in his memory—IVLIA INDI FILIA PACATA I[NDIANA?] VXOR (Julia Pacata Indiana(?), daughter of Indus, his wife). The reconstructed monument is now one of the treasures of the British Museum (**15**). Some might consider it the most important archaeological document of Roman Britain.

Since Classicianus evidently died in Londinium, it may be assumed that his residence, offices and record archive (*tabularium*) were also there, as would also be expected on other grounds. It was the most convenient place because of its easy communications with all other parts of the province, and it must have been the most important port. As we have seen, there is very little doubt that his predecessor was based in Londinium, and the main responsibility for re-establishing the town must have fallen on the procurator's shoulders. Julius Classicianus was undoubtedly a key figure in London's history, though we know practically nothing of his work.

Where for example were his headquarters? Somewhere in the town, between 60 and 70, there must have been a large public building that served as the centre

DIS
MANIBVS
CIVLCFF ... NI CLASSICIAN ...

... NIANNIAE
IVLIA ... CAF ... INDIANA
... F

15 Tombstone of Classicianus, procurator of Britain after 60, reconstructed from fragments found re-used as building material in bastion, Trinity Place. Width c 7½ ft (2.3m). *British Museum*

for the financial and economic administration of the province, and probably also as the procurator's residence. Attention has already been drawn to the early stone building in the centre of the town west of Gracechurch Street. It may have been built before or after Boudica's fire, but it was certainly demolished quite early in Flavian times. It is more than likely, therefore, that it was in existence when Classicianus held office. As yet this is the only pre-Flavian building we know in London with stone walls, and it stands on a central site where a governmental building might be expected. As a stone building it might have survived the fire with only superficial damage, so that it could be reoccupied soon after officialdom returned to London. If, on the other hand, it was built after the fire, there is a marked contrast between this development west of Gracechurch Street and the neglect of the area immediately to the east, which remained derelict for years. Initiative so far in advance of a general recovery might well have been due to the procurator.

In our present state of ignorance no other specific suggestion can be made. An alternative possibility would be a site somewhere on the river-front, since the re-establishment of the port must have been the government's first priority; but as yet we know of no substantial buildings there of such an early date.

4

The Transformation of Londinium,
AD 70–125

The first Forum

The apparent slowness of London's recovery from its destruction in 60 is remarkable, in view of its geographical advantages, but we may be misled by the fact that nearly all our information comes from one central area, which probably reflects the hesitations of official policy rather than lack of vigour in the economic life of Londinium. Commercial life may well have been in full swing on the river-front, and local trading and service industries may already have been springing up elsewhere in the 15 years or more during which Roman officialdom seems to have hesitated about its intentions for London. In this period its status is as obscure as it was before Boudica. Presumably Roman law insisted on some definition for any centre of population, and London was perhaps recognised as a *vicus*—in this case an adjunct not to a fort but to a port and the official establishment of the procurator. Independent Roman citizens in London may well have formed a small self-governing group, *cives Romani consistentes Londinii* ('Roman citizens dwelling in London') as Haverfield suggested,[1] but it is unlikely to have controlled the settlement as a whole, which included wealthy and influential Gaulish and other foreign *negotiatores* who were not Roman citizens, such as Rufus, son of Callisunus, known to us from a fragment of his correspondence (see p98–9). Such *peregrini* (non-citizens) would certainly have expected a share in whatever consitution there was.[2] This must have been a humble one that was subordinated to overriding governmental authority in decisions affecting the development and maintenance of local amenities that were of more than local importance—the bridge, roadways and port facilities. A *vicus* seems the only possible status; Londinium was not yet a city, even of the second rank.

A city charter was evidently not achieved before the Flavian period, and it seems likely that the granting of it is marked by the appearance at last of a major public building on the long-derelict central site north of Fenchurch Street. It also extended west of Gracechurch Street, the line of which it straddled, and involved the demolition of the stone building fronting on Lombard Street which was almost certainly public and may have been the offices of the procurator (p49–50).

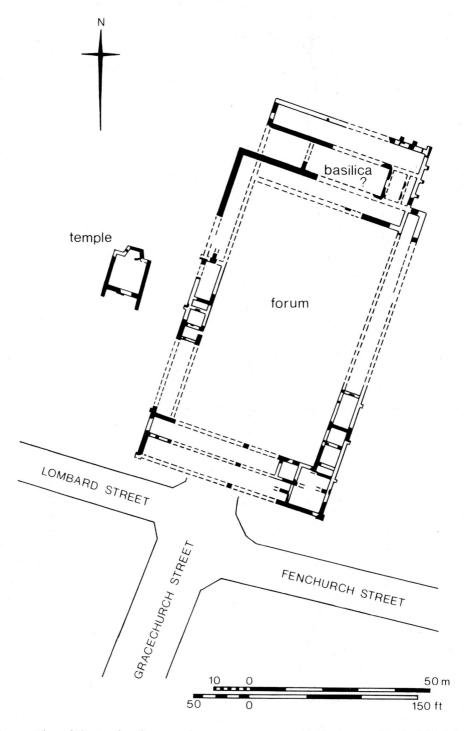

N

temple

basilica
?

forum

LOMBARD STREET

GRACECHURCH STREET

FENCHURCH STREET

10   0   50 m
50   0   150 ft

Fig. 7   Plan of Flavian first forum and contemporary temple. *Reconstructed by P. R. V. Marsden*

The new structure has been recorded piece-meal by five different observers on building-sites, and was investigated more fully by Philp in his rescue excavation east of Gracechurch Street. Peter Marsden has since made a great contribution to City archaeology by carefully replotting and rationalising all these records. From this work there has emerged a convincing if tantalisingly incomplete picture of a forum-like structure with a central courtyard. Single ranges of offices or shops formed the eastern and western sides, while the wider southern range had either a double row of offices or a single row with a wide outer portico—probably the former. The northern side was enclosed by a basilica-like building which extended for only the width of the inner courtyard (fig 7). Cross-walls at its eastern end may indicate the position of a tribunal (raised platform for magistrates). It certainly appears to have the normal central nave and side-aisles of a basilica, though one odd feature is a semi-basement underlying the western end.[3] It seems likely that there was an entrance to the central courtyard in the middle of the southern range, fronting on the main east-west road, although the three walls of this range were observed in a tunnel under Gracechurch Street very near its centre. These were foundations only, however, and may have been over-laid by the entrance. There may also have been an entrance near the middle of the west side, perhaps indicated by a corner wall.

The foundations were of flint and yellow-brown mortar with walls above of ragstone with double or triple courses of bonding tiles. The external walls had brick buttresses which were presumably the bases of engaged columns, so that the building was not lacking in architectural pretentions. Traces of a wall to the west of the western range may indicate that it had an outer colonnade. No external colonnade existed for the eastern range, however, for its external buttresses projected into a narrow north-south roadway. There is also some slight evidence for an east-west roadway immediately to the north, and it has been assumed there would have been a north-south roadway on the west side. Gravel metalling, however, has been observed only immediately west of the west wall of the basilica, and did not extend 36ft (10.9m) or so to the west of it.[4] None has in fact been observed on the line of the supposed north-south road, whose existence must be considered doubtful.

This important public building on the site of the later forum has been variously described as 'the pre-forum building', 'the proto-forum' and 'the first forum', but Peter Marsden's latest reconstruction of it undoubtedly gives it the appearance of a basilica and forum, similar in proportion to many Gaulish fora though smaller than most. It differs from them and resembles British fora in that it did not contain a temple within the forum enclosure for the official worship that was an essential part of civic life. In British fora the shrine seems normally to have been accommodated in the basilica itself. The London building, however, did have a small temple closely associated with it. It lay immediately to the west, either on the opposite side of the hypothetical north-south road or, if the latter did not exist, within the same insula. It was a temple of classical type, facing south, with a cella terminating in an angular apse to the north. There is no doubt that the two buildings were contemporary and were demolished at the same time. The temple had a foundation of flint rubble with yellow-brown mortar, and its walls were built of flanged roofing-tiles, broken and laid in regular courses, with the upturned flanges forming the face of the wall—and roofing-tiles were also incorporated in walls of the structure to the east.[5] The close association of the temple gives some support to the view that this building was in fact a true forum, and that Londinium had received municipal status when it was built.

Its precise dating is therefore of crucial importance, and unfortunately there is room for divergence of opinion on present evidence. Philp dated it to the decade 60–70 on the evidence of eight samian sherds from levels contemporary with the construction—six pre-Flavian and two of date Nero—Vespasian.[6] Cottrill, however, has recorded that one of its walls cut through a pit containing Flavian and earlier pottery, though this material was never published and is now lost.[7] A badly corroded coin of 71, however, survives from this pit, so it is certain that the building was Flavian in date. There is also dating evidence for the narrow north-south road on the east side of the building. This overlay a deposit of rubbish containing no fewer than 57 samian sherds, 25 of them actually beneath the gravel metalling. They include 14 Flavian sherds, one of which, found beneath the road itself, is attributed to the period 75–90.[8] On this evidence Philp dated the road 85–90, suggesting it was built at about the same time as a bake-house with six brick ovens on its east side. This overlay the rubbish deposits and incorporated pre-Flavian and Flavian samian sherds, one not earlier than 75, and two coins of 71. Marsden has argued that the flanking street would have been constructed at the same time as the forum, and that the latter could not therefore have been built before 80–85. Philp pointed out, however, that the rubbish deposits nowhere underlie the forum but gradually accumulated immediately to the east of it, apparently over a considerable number of years, and this suggests that building had been constructed before the accumulation and limited its extension to the west. Unfortunately a break in the stratigraphy makes it impossible to prove.

Certainly in the context of this site a date of construction later than the early Flavian period raises problems, since, in view of subsequent developments, a date in the 80s would give it a remarkably short life. In the wider context of our knowledge of the fora of Roman Britain it would raise even greater difficulties. In the latter part of 79, in the second year of the governorship of Agricola, as we know from an inscription, the great basilica of Verulamium was completed, and it may be assumed that the accompanying forum, if not complete, had been laid out and was at least in process of construction. This immediately follows the winter in which, as Tacitus tells us, Agricola gave encouragement and official assistance in the building of temples, fora and mansions in British towns. The work can hardly have been completed in a few months, however, and it seems likely that it had begun several years earlier under his predecessor, Frontinus, probably not later than 75. It was an impressive building, with a basilica 385ft (117m) by 120ft (36.5m), and a forum piazza about 310ft (94m) by 205ft (62m) internally. Beside this our London structure makes a very poor showing, with its basilica 148ft

(45m) by 75ft (22.75m) and piazza courtyard 220ft (67.25m) by 130ft (40m). If Londinium had been given a new status it must have been that of *municipium*—the same rank as Verulamium. Is it conceivable that Londinium, approaching the zenith of its prosperity in the 80s, would have been permitted to set such a bad example as a *municipium*, at a time when it was official policy to encourage the lower-ranking civitas to invest in impressive public buildings as a mark of Romanisation? Even the impoverished Silures could do better at Caerwent, where the smallest British basilica known measured 180ft (56m) by 100ft (30.5m).

As the basilica and forum of a *municipium*, therefore, the London building is inconceivable unless it is earlier than that of Verulamium. If built early in the reign of Vespasian, say between 70 and 75, well within the limits set by the present archaeological evidence, it can be explained as a false start—a beginning on too modest a scale, before Verulamium set the proper standard a few years later. It must be significant also that neither London's first forum nor the forum of Verulamium conform with the stereotyped British pattern that was set in later Flavian times, eg in Silchester, but in one way or another recall fora in Gaul— Verulamium by its side entrances; Londinium by its elongated form, associated temple and possible side entrance. It would not be surprising if Londinium received the first Flavian forum in Britain, for its population of Roman citizens and sophisticated *peregrini* must have missed this amenity, and Verulamium the second a few years later, when ideas had become more expansive and projects more ambitious.

If, however, new evidence compelled acceptance of the later date proposed by Marsden, a completely different interpretation of this building would have to be sought. It would then be reasonably certain that Londinium in the governorship of Agricola was not yet a *municipium*, and that its future status was still under discussion, as could be inferred from the description of Tacitus—a place not ranking as a *colonia*, but an important settlement—if we transfer this comment from its context of the Boudican revolt to the time of his father-in-law's governorship, regarding it as a notion culled from the historian's memory of Agricola's reminiscences. If Londinium was still legally only a *vicus*, the irregularity of the situation was presumably one of the minor problems with which he was preoccupied as governor, and of which he is likely to have spoken in later life. He was evidently of the opinion that the size and importance of Londinium justified the grant of a charter as a *colonia*, and may well have recommended this to the Emperor. The promotion of a new and unclassified settlement, that had not been planned as a colony of Roman citizens, to this rank without going through the intermediate level of *municipium* would have been a bold and unusual step, and some time for consideration would have to be allowed in addition to the normal delays to be expected from a busy bureaucracy. In these circumstances it is conceivable that the governor yielded to local pressure and permitted the building of a temporary forum in advance of the charter, on condition that it was of such an unassuming character that it could in no way be thought to prejudge the Emperor's decision—a wise precaution, particularly if this happened in 84, when the jealous and suspicious Domitian was already Emperor. The narrow frontage on the main road could be the result of a deliberate striving for modesty, for it would have cost very little more to have extended the south range on to the waste land to the east, to provide a reasonable facade and a less cramped internal piazza.

Another odd feature about this phase of the development of Londinium is the curious change of alignment of the new buildings in the centre of the town by about 2° from the earlier alignment, so that the little forum with its accompanying buildings and roadway is set slightly askew to the earlier line of the east-west road. A similar alignment has been observed in Flavian buildings south of this road in Plough Court. It is a temporary aberration, for with later buildings there is a reversion to the earlier alignment.

The simplest explanation is that the earliest east-west roadway had a sharp kink between Clement's Lane and Nicholas Lane, because a stream flowing south-west had to be bridged there. Subsequently the water was drained or diverted and the stream-bed filled, so that the kink could be replaced by a gentle re-alignment.

Fig. 8   Plan of the great second forum and basilica. *After P. R. V. Marsden*

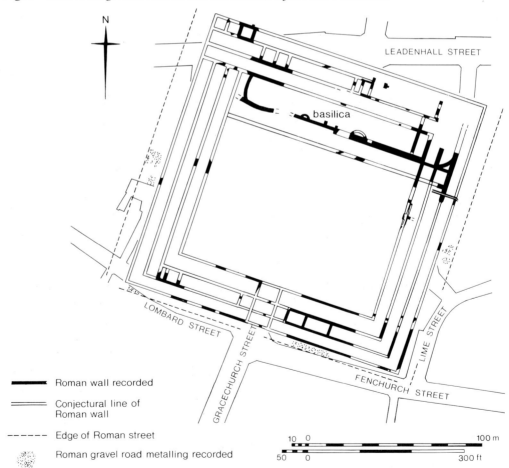

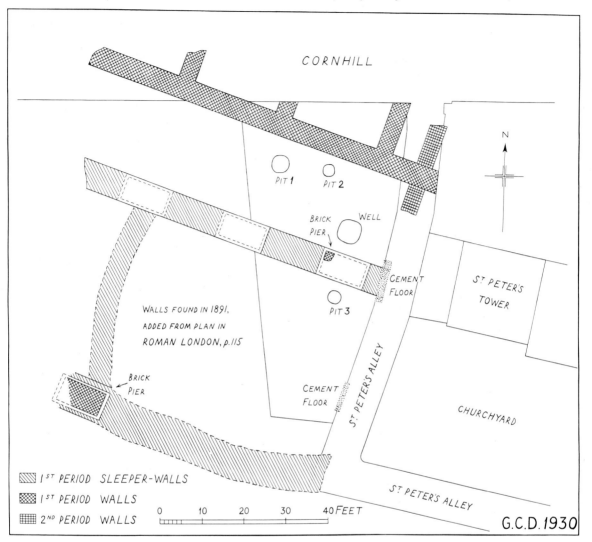

Fig. 9   Plan of portion of basilica, with earlier well and pits, Nos 50 and 52 Cornhill. *Original plan of 1930 by G. C. Dunning*

This introduced a slight irregularity in the street-plan, by making the northern east-west road not quite parallel with the southern in the neighbourhood of Gracechurch Street. The first forum was built on this new alignment and was therefore slightly askew to the approach road from the bridge. This did not much matter as its main facade was not presented to the south. Subsequently, however, the entire city-centre was re-surveyed, with a view to building a much larger forum to which there would be an impressive approach from the river. The east-west road in front of it was therefore brought back to its old alignment at right-angles to the road from the bridge, and the slight deflection necessary to take it to the Walbrook crossing was moved further west.

The great Forum

There can be very little doubt that the next development of this area marks the achievement by Londinium of the status of *colonia*, although we have no historical evidence to support this claim. The whole city centre was replanned, so that the little forum lay in the middle of a new insula. This was 555ft (169.4m) or 570 Roman feet ($4\frac{3}{4}$ *actus*) wide, and was probably perfectly square, though we do not know the precise position of the east-west road that formed its northern boundary, and the great forum and basilica that were subsequently built within the insula extended from south to north for a distance of only 534ft (162.75m) or 550 Roman feet—20 Roman feet short of the dimensions of a perfect square. It is quite likely, however, that the north wall of the basilica stood back by that amount from the adjacent road. The east, west and south sides of the forum, however, extended to the full limits of the insula, so that it was very much larger than the forum of any other city of Roman Britain, though less than three-quarters of the area of the great forum complex at Trier (fig 8).

London's basilica, however, stands alone in the north-western provinces. More than 500ft (152m) long, about as long as St Paul's Cathedral—its precise length is as yet unknown—it is surpassed in Rome itself only by the great Basilica Ulpia (525ft; 160m). It was a vast aisled hall with a central nave and a raised tribunal at its eastern end—possibly at its western end as well. The existence of the southern aisle was doubted until recent observations in a tunnel beneath Gracechurch Street showed traces of its external wall and concrete floor in the correct position. A curious irregularity, suggesting a change of design after the foundations were laid, is a double wall in the eastern half of the basilica's southern side. Massive brick piers stood on the sleeper walls between the nave and aisles. These probably carried an arcade rather than columns, since parts of a concrete structure like an arch, that had probably fallen from the superstructure, were found in Leadenhall Market in 1888. On the northern side of the basilica was a double row of square offices—a reminder that it served as local administrative centre or town hall was well as a court of justice and meeting-place for merchants. The north wall had external buttresses like those of the earlier small basilica, presumably to support engaged columns at a higher level, both for architectural effect and to strengthen the wall.

We know very little of the details of the new forum, save that its southern range also had massive piers, and was divided internally into shops and offices. There were large buttresses on the west wall of the east range, fronting on the inner piazza, but apart from this we know practically nothing of the east and west ranges, beyond the fact that, like the south, they seem to have been divided by four walls into three longitudinal parts, presumably inner and outer arcades or colonnades with a row of shops between them. One of the difficulties about any reconstruction of the great forum is that its walls were extensively robbed to their foundations for building stone, probably in the early Middle Ages. There must have been an impressive entrance from the south, fronting on the east-west road and, almost certainly, facing the approach road from the bridge. A group of piers,

16 Remains of basilica seen when Leadenhall Market was built in 1881–2. Watercolour drawing by Henry Hodge, showing (A) east wall, (B) wall of east apse surviving to higher level behind, and (C) vaults of medieval Leadenhall in rear (view to NW). *Original in Guildhall Library*

some standing on the demolished walls of the first forum, has been interpreted by Philp as the base of a colonnade projecting into the piazza, as in the almost contemporary Forum of Trajan in Rome, but there are other piers that do not fit into this scheme, and the overall picture is obscure. Rather surprisingly the forum piazza was provided with a surface only of white mortar, much later replaced by a surface of pink mortar. Since the ground rose towards Cornhill a massive levelling operation was required before the surface could be laid, and great quantities of brick-earth, sand or gravel were dumped, especially in the southern part of the new forum, so that its massive south wall served as retaining wall as well as frontage. The change in level must have required steps at the south entrance, but no trace of these has yet been found.

The two north-south flanking roads overlay earlier occupation levels and refuse from which Cottrill recovered eleven potter's stamps on samian ware, eight of them from the western road. All were of the first century but several need not be earlier than Flavian.[9] Similarly Dunning obtained pottery of the later Flavian period, including three potters' stamps, in layers of rubbish and brick-earth beneath the concrete (*opus signinum*) floor of the great basilica.[10] These overlay a well which, on pottery evidence, he considered had been filled about 80

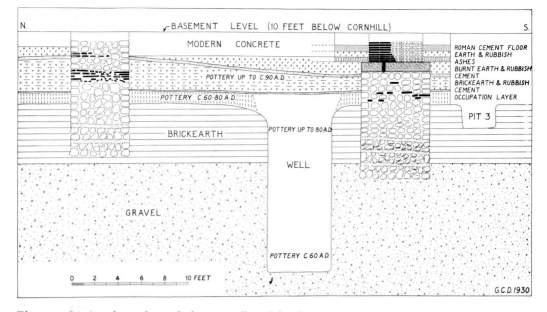

Fig. 10   Section through north sleeper wall with brick pier (right) and northern wall (left) of basilica, with earlier well and occupation level, No 52 Cornhill. *Original section of 1930 by G. C. Dunning*

when a cement floor had been laid over it (fig 10). Unfortunately all this important dating evidence has disappeared, and only summary reports have survived. Nevertheless later revisions in the dating of first-century samian have been minor, and a date in the late Flavian period for the basilica floor is unlikely to have been much affected by them. In recent years good dating evidence has been obtained by Philp for the dumping that followed the demolition of the little forum to provide a level surface for the great forum, and this has been fully published.[11] It includes 14 datable samian sherds, all of the first century, and one of the period 75–90. Coarse pottery from the dump is also published, and is consistent with a date in the late first century, with one or two pieces that are not likely to be earlier than about 90. Although in each case the evidence gives us only a cut-off date, *after* which the roads, basilica floor and levelling dumps were laid, taken all together and considering all three works as part of the same operation, there seems to be little doubt that it took place towards the end of the first century. In particular, with so much samian recorded, the absence of a single early second century piece antedating it should be significant. The evidence has been discussed in some detail, since a later date has been suggested for the great forum. There is in fact definite evidence that the western part of its southern range was built, rebuilt, or completed in a later phase of building, not earlier than the reign of Hadrian, perhaps as a direct result of that Emperor's visit in 122, though the actual work probably took place some years later.[12] A puzzling transitional feature is a group of piers in the central part of the south range, some built directly on the demolished walls of the little forum. These continued in existence well into the second century, when some at least were rebuilt.

It would not be surprising if such a great project as the new forum lost its impetus before completion, particularly as there is reason to believe that some decline in London's prosperity began quite early in the second century, and it may have needed the stimulus of an imperial visit to finish it. There can be little doubt, however, that the new forum was first planned many years earlier, and that building began while the small forum was still standing. There was in fact no need to demolish it until the new basilica and the east and west ranges of the new forum were ready for use. The demolition of the first forum in the 90s therefore implies that the plans for the new forum were probably drawn up not later than the 80s, in the governorship of Agricola or his immediate successor. Such an ambitious project might well have originated in the fertile and imaginative mind of the great Agricola, and if it did he must be accounted one of the founding fathers of Londinium. If, as I have suggested, the little forum was the legacy of a predecessor, Agricola's dissatisfaction with it as a positive embarrassment to his own policy could have impelled him to the opposite extreme. The decision to build the new forum round the earlier one, while continuing to use the latter, itself ensured that the new structure would be large enough to stand clear of its predecessor. The new basilica barely does so, and very little reduction could have been made in the north-south dimension. The width of the forum from east to west and the length of the basilica, however, could certainly have been much less, so that it was evidently fully intended to provide Londinium with a civic centre that would be quite exceptional, particularly in its basilica, which was the Roman equivalent of the City's later Guildhall, with its courts of justice and municipal offices.

The promotion of Londinium to *colonia*, which is surely indicated by this great building, can best be accounted for, not by London's commercial prosperity, but by the decision, which can only have come from the Emperor himself on the advice of the governor, to recognise it as the capital of Britain, in place of Camulodunum. As we have seen, the procurator had from an early date found that it was the most convenient centre for the financial administration, and the governor must have found himself increasingly obliged to use it as a meeting place that was easily accessible from all parts of Britain and from the Continent. For this reason he may well have decided that it was the most convenient winter quarters for himself and his staff officers when they were not actively campaigning and could devote attention to the affairs of the province as a whole. Where, for example, did Agricola spend the winter of 78–9, when he launched his policy of Romanisation, and must have called together representatives from all parts of the province? London is likely to have become the capital *de facto* before it was recognised as such. It was then presumably given a charter as an 'honorary' *colonia*, since it was never a 'colony' in the technical sense, meaning a planned settlement of Roman citizens. All provincial capitals were *coloniae*, however, and London could not be an exception. There must have been a fair number of

Roman citizens among its residents—men like Aulus Alfidius Olussa who was born at Athens and died in Londinium at the age of 70, almost certainly before 100.[13] It may well have provided the occasion also for the grant of citizenship at least to the more important *peregrini* who were permanent residents, and there were no doubt many other legal and administrative questions to be settled before Londinium could receive its charter and consitution as a *colonia*.

The Governor's Palace (*Praetorium*)

The provincial capital required a proper residence for the governor, and this was built on the steeply sloping hillside above the Thames just east of the mouth of the Walbrook. A similar position overlooking the Rhine was chosen for the *praetorium* at Cologne. Unfortunately it has been possible to excavate archaeologically only part of the east wing in Suffolk Lane and in very confined areas in the northern part of the building. The rest has been recorded piecemeal during builders' excavations and in such limited rescue excavation as was possible on sites where building work was already in progress. Great credit is due to Peter Marsden for carrying out this work, mostly single-handed in difficult conditions, and for his subsequent careful research in assembling earlier records and putting together the pieces of the jigsaw to form a comprehensible building (fig 11).[14] What emerges is a complex structure about 140 yards (130m) long, extending on terraces between the Roman riverfront and the east-west road beneath Cannon Street. It was probably planned as an impressive symmetrical building with its widest frontage facing the river, but various irregularities were imposed by the nature of the terrain. We have no knowledge of the west wing, which underlies Cannon Street Station, and of which a substantial part probably still survives beneath the railway arches.

The palace was built around a central garden court, a great part of which was occupied by an elongated central pool on a massive concrete foundation. Adjoining its north side was a small pool enclosed by an apse, and symmetry would demand a second similar pool to the west beneath the railway station. A masonry base in the small pool suggested that a statue stood there in an alcove, so that the pool complex may have been a nymphaeum. Other masonry foundations in the garden court probably also supported statues or ornamental features.

To the north of the garden terrace was a great hall about 80ft (24.38m) long and 43ft (13.1m) wide internally, with massive foundations of very hard ragstone concrete, $6\frac{1}{2}$–10ft (2–3m) thick and evidently intended to support a very lofty superstructure. Two small surviving portion indicated that this was built of tiles. The compartment was centrally placed and was presumably the main reception hall. Adjoining it to the east was a hall with similarly massive foundations, of which we know little beyond the fact that it had a projecting apse to the south, and so presumably served as a court-room with a tribunal or dais. Portions of other walls to the north under Bush Lane and west of it indicate that a range of probably smaller rooms extended north to Cannon Street on a higher terrace.

The east wing, lying immediately east of the garden court, comprised a series

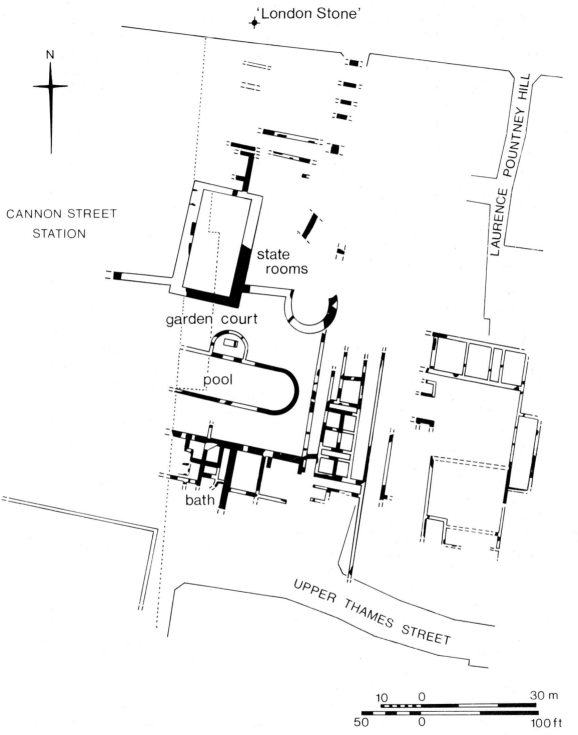

Fig. 11   Plan of Roman palace in Cannon Street, with possibly separate public building to east. *After P. R. V. Marsden*

of small rooms in pairs with two larger rooms to the north. There was a corridor on each side, and two narrow corridors between groups of rooms probably contained stairways to an upper floor. It is an arrangement similar to that of a *mansio* or inn, and therefore suggests that these were quarters for visiting officials, though they would have served equally well as administrative offices. The larger rooms at least seem to have been heated by flues for hot air, and there was a drainage system beneath the floor. The east wing continued further south at a lower level and may have projected beyond the main facade of the building.

The south wing was wholly on the lower terrace and seems to have contained residential quarters with service rooms adjoining them. It was subsequently modified with the addition of hypocausts, probably for a small bath-house. No evidence for the actual river frontage has been found in recent years, but the observation of a massive east-west wall and a large column base in Little Bush Lane in 1846 suggests that there may have been an impressive colonnade. Finds of timber beams, some superimposed horizontally, in test holes beneath Upper Thames Street, indicate that there was a wooden wharf to the south of the building, comparable with those found further east. This would have covered the soft silt near the river-side, which must have been here approximately on the southern edge of Upper Thames Street.

Immediately east of the palace traces were observed in a builder's excavation of a substantial Roman building to the east of Suffolk Lane.[15] The fragments recorded suggest four ranges of rooms around a central area that is likely to have been a garden or courtyard. Its dimensions, more than 180 by at least 125ft (55 by 38m), and its position in close proximity to the palace and on an equally favourable site overlooking the river, strongly suggests that it was an official building, and it may have been merely an extension of the palace. There is a gap of about 15ft (4.5m) between the known walls of both buildings, but this was occupied by mortar floors and cannot have been a roadway.[16] It must therefore be assumed that both were part of the same governmental complex, though the self-contained plan of the eastern building and its apparent separation at least by a corridor suggest that it may have had a different function.

A high officer who might have required separate accommodation in Londinium at about the time the palace was built was the imperial juridical legate (*legatus iuridicus*), whose presence there is rather doubtfully attested by a fragment of an inscription commemorating Trajan's victory in Dacia in 102 or 106.[17] This was an appointment first made by Vespasian with the purpose of relieving the governor of the legal tasks of the province. The procurator also would have needed a residence and headquarters in London, possibly a successor to the stone building in Lombard Street that was demolished when the first forum was built. It is unlikely that this structure could have been its immediate successor, however, since it is more likely to have been built after the main part of the palace than before it. The natural sequence of building would have been first the *praetorium* in the area east of the Walbrook, and then this extension which respects its site and seems to be an addition. The squeezing of the palace into a vacant site between an existing building and the mouth of the Walbrook seems less likely, though this might account for the distortion that introduced irregularities into its plan (fig 11).

Unfortunately there is no evidence for the date of the eastern building, but the *praetorium* itself overlies or cuts through a fair number of deposits containing nothing later than the Flavian period. As with the great forum and basilica we have evidence giving us only the date after which the construction took place, but there is sufficient of this to suggest rather strongly that it was built not earlier than 80 and not later than the early second century. As with the large basilica, a date in the last decade of the first century seems likely.

Subsequent demolition and site clearances have left little trace of the more decorative features of any of these buildings. A mosaic floor was found with the remains of a large hall west of Bush Lane, during the rebuilding after the Great Fire of 1666, and a drawing by Aubrey of a fragment of it has been preserved in the Bodleian Library.[18] Remarkably, the suggestion was made even then that this might be part of the governor's palace—a lucky guess rather than an informed judgement. The hall must be the great state room east of Cannon Street Station, but this had a plain mortar floor, so the mosaic presumably came from a neighbouring room. Another fragment of patterned mosaic, which had a guilloche border, was seen in the edge of the builder's excavation in the western range of the eastern building, just east of Suffolk Lane, where part of it may still survive. Scattered tesserae of various colours testify to the former existence of mosaic floors in other rooms of the palace, though plain mortar and opus signinum floors were common. Fragments of painted wall-plaster in red, green, yellow, blue and black were found, some with traces of fresco painting, but none was large enough to indicate the design. Scraps of Purbeck marble and a piece of white-painted stucco were also presumably derived from the walls.

A point of particular interest is the apparent association of the mysterious 'London Stone' with the Cannon Street palace. This historic landmark seems to have been regarded in the Middle Ages as the very heart of the City of London, and has been surmised to be the central milestone from which distances were measured in Roman Britain, the British equivalent of the *Milliarium Aureum* at Rome. All that survives of it is its rounded top of Clipsham limestone, now set in a recess in the wall of a bank on the north side of Cannon Street. Until 1742, however, it stood as a deeply embedded stump of stone on the south side of the street, in the middle of the roadway of the present widened street. Sir Christopher Wren apparently saw foundations below it during the rebuilding after the Fire, and was convinced by these that it was not a mere pillar but something more elaborate, which he suspected was somehow connected with the pavement and walls of the Roman building he had seen to the south.[19] Marsden's reconstruction of the plan of this strongly suggests that he was right, for London Stone stood almost exactly on the line of the central axis of the palace. If therefore this building had a large gateway fronting on the Roman street, as was almost certainly the case, the Stone would have stood on its centre, or more probably

17 Effigy of legionary soldier, probably a junior officer (optio), carrying writing-tablets; limestone relief from tomb, re-used as building material in late Roman bastion, Camomile Street. Height 4ft 4in (1.3m). *Museum of London*

immediately in front of its central point adjacent to the Roman roadway, precisely where an important Roman monument might have been placed; though we shall probably never know whether it served as a milestone and measuring point or was merely commemorative. The Roman origin of London Stone now seems very likely, therefore, but its surviving apex could well be of later date, for Clipsham limestone does not seem to have been generally used in Roman times.

The Roman Fort

The adoption of Londinium as the capital required not only a residence for the governor but quarters for a considerable military establishment. This included not only soldiers for escort and guard duties, grooms and other military servants, drawn from the auxiliary forces, but also officers and men seconded from the legions for special staff duties as the executives of the military government. Among these at a much later date was a legionary of *Legio II Augusta* named Celsus, who was seconded to serve on the governor's staff as a *speculator*, a sort of military policeman mainly concerned with the execution of justice. He died in London, where his tombstone was set up on Ludgate Hill by several of his comrades, at least one of whom held a similar staff appointment.[20] Officers who were seconded brought with them their personal assistants (*beneficiarii*), such as G. Pomponius Valens, the *beneficiarius* of a tribune, who came originally from Colchester and likewise died in London. [21] A fine relief effigy from a soldier's tomb, found re-used as building material in a late Roman bastion of the city wall, represents a legionary or junior officer (*optio*) who had presumably been seconded for staff duties, since, although he wears a sword, he carries also a bundle of writing tablets (**17**). Secondments for the governor's staff would have been drawn from all the legions in Britain, and significantly three of the four that formed the permanent garrison from the early second century are represented by funerary inscriptions from London. The auxiliary troops in the capital are likely to have been more numerous, but there is only one auxiliary tombstone from London and no inscriptions relating to them have been found. The reason, no doubt, is that less provision was made for their burial expenses, and in a city where suitable stone had to be brought from a distance and was therefore expensive, auxiliary soldiers had to be content with wooden tombstones which have not survived.

Accommodation had to be found for military personnel, both for staff stationed in Londinium and for others passing through the city or temporarily visiting it to receive instructions or deliver reports. A permanent barracks was therefore required, and this was probably the main function of the stone-built fort constructed early in the second century on high ground west of the valley of the Walbrook and north of the industrial and residential development that had already taken place along the roadway to the west. It was built well away from this in an area that had hitherto been sparsely occupied.

The outer walls were nearly 4ft (1.2m) thick, and built of the usual ragstone from Kent, with faces of squared blocks laid in courses, between which was a fill

18   South-west corner of Roman fort, Noble Street, showing foundations of corner turret (A), intermediate turret (B), fort wall (C) and later thickening wall (D) (view to SW). *Museum of London*

of random lumps of ragstone set in mortar, forming a very hard rubble concrete. The fort, which was of the typical 'playing-card' shape, was provided with the normal defensive attributes of external ditch, internal bank and turrets placed internally at the rounded corners and in intermediate positions. The foundations of its south-west corner wall with turret and of an intermediate turret to the north can be seen west of Noble Street (**18**). Though less than a quarter of the size of the great legionary fortresses, it was much larger than the normal auxiliary fort, covering an area of about 12 acres (nearly 5ha). There were the normal four gates, centrally placed in the shorter north and south sides and just south of the centre of the east and west sides. Only part of the west gate has been found (**19**), and the bases

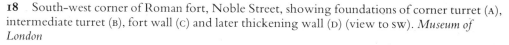

19   West gate of Roman fort, northern half, as excavated, showing north guard room (A) with doorway (B), gravel metalling of central roadway (C), and gate-post socket (D) (view to N). *Museum of London*

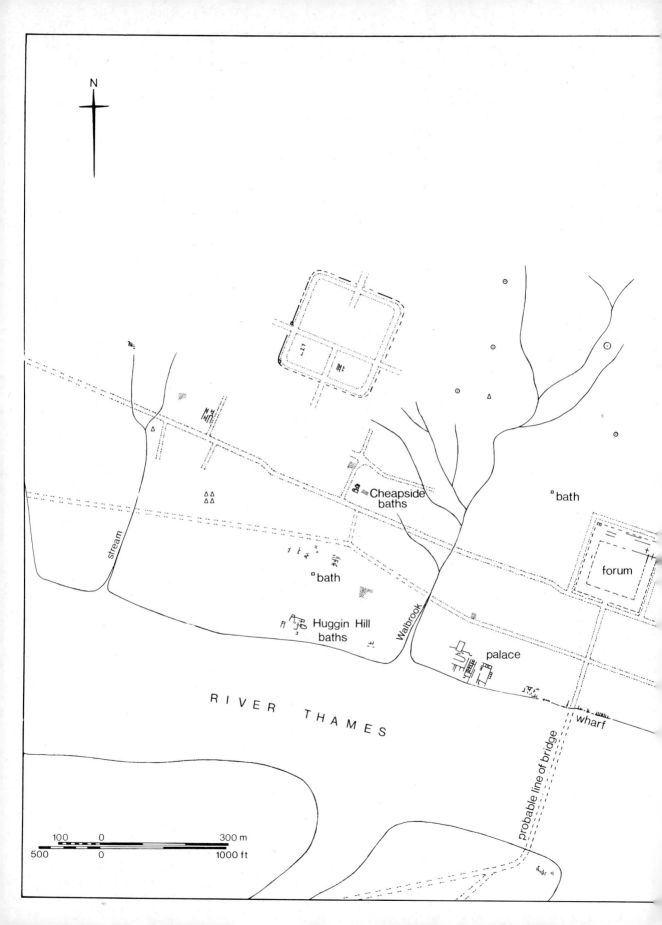

N

Cheapside
baths

°bath

°bath

forum

Huggin Hill
baths

Walbrook

palace

stream

R I V E R   T H A M E S

probable line of bridge

wharf

100   0   300 m

500   0   1000 ft

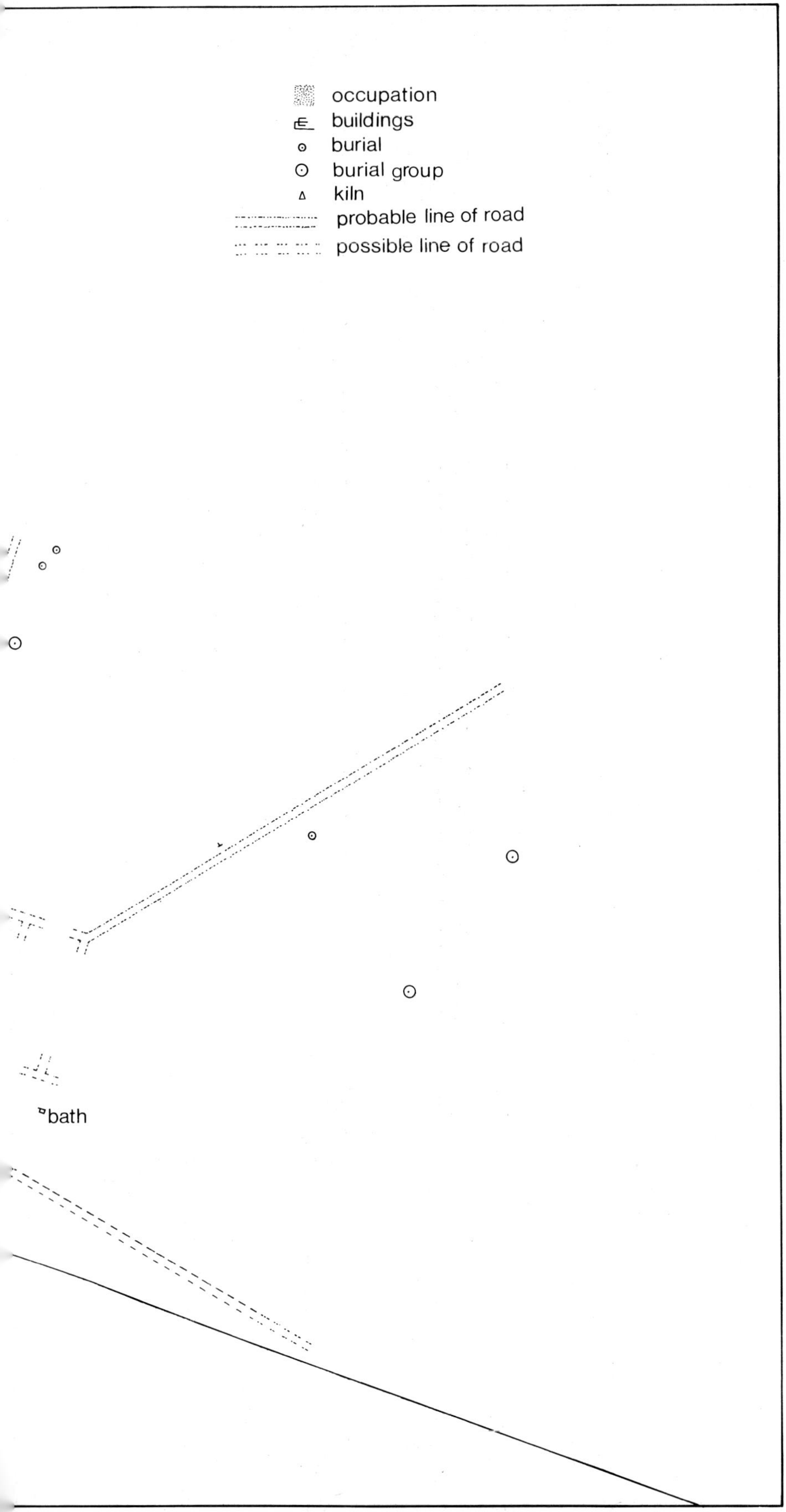

occupation

⊨ buildings

o burial

⊙ burial group

△ kiln

---·---·--- probable line of road

··· ··· ··· ··· possible line of road

□bath

Fig. 12 Map: features of Londinium late first–early second century. *C. Unwin*

of its rectangular north tower and central piers have been preserved under the post-war roadway of London Wall. The position of the south gate was identified by the foundation of one surviving gate-jamb and by the closely set post-holes that supported a bridge from it over the external ditch, although no trace of the actual gate-house had survived. The north gate subsequently became the Roman and mediaeval gate in the later city wall called Cripplegate. Before the identification of the fort by Professor Grimes as a result of his post-war excavations,[22] Cripplegate had been something of a mystery, since unlike the other ancient city gates it has never given access to a major road. It is now known to be a remarkable topographical survival, antedating the city wall itself and therefore the oldest of its gates. Because of its later convenience Cripplegate was rebuilt several times, but it owed its origin simply to Roman military conservatism; a standard fort had a gateway in each side even if it led nowhere in particular. The roadways were similarly standardised—a *via praetoria* that led from the main gate (in this case the south gate) straight to the headquarters building (*principia*), making a T-junction with the *via principalis* that crossed the fort between its two lateral gates and on which the *principium* fronted. Both survived in the mediaeval and recent street-plan of the City, with some slight divergence from their original lines—the *via praetoria* as part of Wood Street and the *via principalis* as Silver Street and Addle Street, both of which fell victims to post-war replanning, so that only the western end of Addle Street now survives in its original place. A fort also had a perimeter road (*intervallum* road) that followed its sides, on the inner side of the earth bank that was thrown up against its wall. Traces of this, with the usual gravel surface and side-gullies for drainage, were found on the west side of the London fort.

Few traces of internal buildings survived the post-Roman building in this area, but excavations south of the *via principalis* in the western part of the fort produced evidence of a comparatively narrow building with long axis north to south and a corridor on its east side. It was like a barrack block but had unusually large rooms and seemed to be of a higher standard than a normal barracks, with plastered walls and a floor of plain red tesserae. No doubt headquarters staff, then as now, expected superior accommodation. Two other barrack blocks with north-south long axes were found east of the *via praetoria* on the site of St Alban Wood Street. They faced one another, with corridors or verandahs overlooking a gravel road, 13ft (4m) wide, which lay between them. They were divided into fairly uniform rooms, 21–2ft (about 6.5m) each way, larger than those in a normal legionary barrack block, but considerably smaller than the rooms in the block to the west, which was presumably reserved for higher ranks. Insufficient remained of the barrack blocks east of Wood Street for any comparison of quality.

Good dating evidence came from earlier pits underlying these stone buildings, suggesting that they were built in the early second century, and this conforms with evidence from other parts of the fort. The full dating evidence has not yet been fully assessed, but it is clear that the provision of a large stone fort has little to do with the defence of Londinium, but is yet another manifestation of its

Fig. 13 Dedicatory inscription to the divinity of the Emperor, in the name of the Province of Britain, found re-used as building material in Nicholas Lane and subsequently lost. *Original drawing by C. Roach Smith*

transformation into the provincial capital. This involved public building on a huge scale that could hardly have been completed in a decade or two. No doubt careful consideration was given to priorities, and resident troops could for a while have been accommodated in billets or a temporary camp—though there is no evidence that the latter was on the site of the stone fort, as might have been expected.

The Provincial Cult in Londinium

Another building that would certainly have been required in the capital was an impressive temple for the state cult of Emperor worship. We do not yet know its site, and our only clue to its whereabouts is a portion of an inscription on a large slab that had been re-used as the corner-stone of a building of ragstone, chalk and flint in Nicholas Lane, between the two main east-west roads and west of the bridge. It seems likely that a large and heavy stone would have been re-used somewhere near the building from which it came, so there is a fair probability that the temple for which it was made stood not far away. The size of the letters, 6in (15cm) high, is surpassed among the known inscriptions of Roman Britain only in the monumental slab from the Wroxeter forum ($6-9\frac{1}{8}$in). Wherever the temple stood, it was evidently on a scale comparable with the great public buildings of the province. The inscription, now unfortunately lost, but carefully recorded in drawings by Roach Smith and others, read NVM C ——/PROV——/BRITA——: *Num(ini) C[aes(aris) Aug(usti)] Prov[incia] Brita[nnia]* 'To the Deity of the Emperor the Province of Britain (set this up)' (fig 13).[23]

It is significant that the dedication was made, not by the local *curia* or even by the governor, but in the name of the province of Britain, undoubtedly through the agency of the Provincial Council, the one body that represented all the tribes of the province. This strongly suggests that Londinium had become the religious capital as well as the administrative capital, and was now the centre where the

Council met for its prime purpose of organising and financing the annual ceremonies of the state cult. This view is supported by another London inscription, which tells us that Anenclutus, a high-grade slave who was in the service of the Provincial Council, buried his young wife at Londinium, probably in the late first century.[24] The transference of the headquarters of the state cult to the new capital was of course a logical development, although the temple of Claudius at Camulodunum continued to be maintained, as might be expected, for imperial prestige demanded no less.

Public Baths

No city, much less the capital, was complete without its public baths, which played an important part in the social life of its citizens. Londinium had more than one, and it is quite possible that the site of its principal baths remains to be discovered. A small plunge bath in Threadneedle Street probably formed part of a private bath-house, like one belonging to a late Roman house in Lower Thames Street, for in later times it became fashionable for the wealthy to have their own bath-houses. Larger plunge-baths or tanks found in Cannon Street, Monument Street, Lime Street and Mark Lane, however, could have belonged to public

Fig. 14   Plan of Roman public baths, Huggin Hill. *After P. R. V. Marsden*

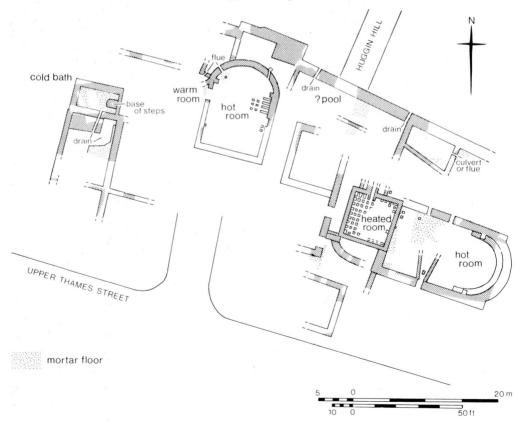

bath-houses on which we have no further information.[25] The one in Lime Street, particularly, lies immediately east of the forum, where a public building would be more likely than a private mansion, and there is evidence for an early date, when visits to the public baths were a social necessity and private baths in cities were almost unknown.

The one public bath-house that we know a great deal about, thanks mainly to Peter Marsden, was built on the slope above the river just north of Upper Thames Street, extending across Huggin Hill (fig 14).[26] This was a position where natural springs emerged from the hillside at the junction of the London Clay and the overlying gravels, so that there was a constant supply of water. The bath-house was placed just below the spring-line and chambers that appear to have been reservoirs were built on its northern edge. The steep slope made it necessary to terrace the hill-side with a massive northern retaining wall, part of which is still visible just west of Huggin Hill. Just south of this was a domed hot-room (*caldarium*) with an apsidal north wall, heated by a hypocaust. A terra-cotta pipe through the curved wall would have carried water to a sunken pool within the apse. Water from this thrown at intervals on the hot floor would have ensured that the room was constantly filled with steam, for the most important part of the procedure was what we now call a Turkish bath. The bather then cooled off in an adjacent warm room (*tepidarium*), probably to the west, where a single tile floor support, observed in an area that could not be investigated, suggests there was another hypocaust-heated chamber. He could then take a final cold plunge in a bath (found about 40ft (12m) west of the hot-room) which would have been in the cold room (*frigidarium*).

East of Huggin Hill, another complete and separate bath system was later added, with new and exceptionally large hot-room, the apsidal end of which was in the east. A square unheated room already built to the west of it was converted into a warm-room by the addition of a hypocaust. It seems likely that the intention was to provide separate bath-houses for men and women, probably in response to the prohibition of mixed bathing by Hadrian,[27] and the extension may have been the direct result of his visit in 122. Such evidence as we have from the foundation trenches of the original structure suggests that it was built in the late first century.

The Huggin Hill baths were clearly one of the great bathing establishments (*thermae*) of Londinium, but the other bath-house of which we have a fair knowledge is of the smaller kind (*balneae*) that provided bathing facilities either for the general public or for the exclusive use of a section of the community. This was observed and recorded by I. Noël Hume on the north side of Cheapside during excavations for the Sun Life Assurance building in 1956.[28] It was seen only in pieces as it was destroyed, but before the builder's excavation began the foundation at least must have been substantially complete (fig 15). Here also there seem to have been two phases of construction, the first conjecturally of the late first century—it is unlikely to be earlier in this area and can hardly be much later—with substantial rebuilding and modification early in the second century.

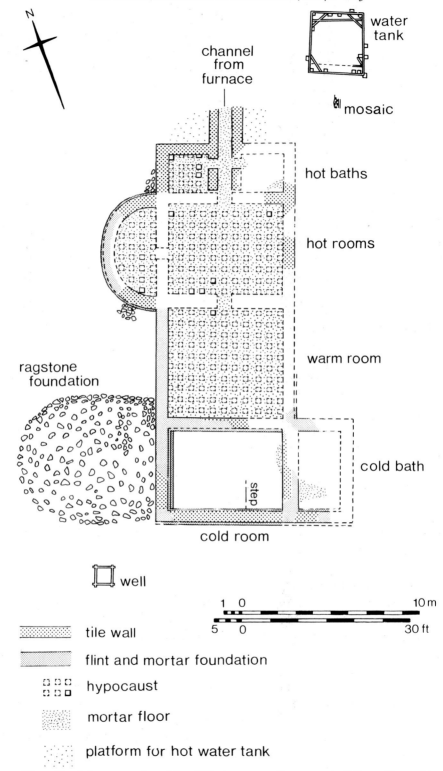

Fig. 15 Plan of bath-house on site of Sun Life Assurance Company building, Cheapside

In both phases the sequence of hot room, warm room and cold room was from north to south, with cold plunge adjoining the eastern end of the *frigidarium*. The alterations included the construction of two small heated compartments, perhaps to contain hot baths or douches, at the north end of the *caldarium*; also a massive foundation was laid to the west of the *frigidarium*, possibly for a 'Spartan Room' (*laconicum*), a chamber providing dry heat as in a modern Swedish bath, or perhaps merely for an open-air swimming pool.

The Cheapside baths are of the simple linear form commonly associated with military establishments, and are comparable in scale. There is therefore a distinct possibility that they belonged to the Roman fort and were for the exclusive use of its occupants. A north-south road immediately west of the baths skirted the east side of the fort and would have led directly to its east gate, so that access would have been easy, though the distance is somewhat greater than would normally have been the case between a fort and its bath-house. We know of no other baths for the fort, however, and the position, as always, was determined by the supply of water. The Cheapside baths lay immediately south-west of a small tributary of the Walbrook, which was covered at an early date, but continued as a submerged spring. A large wooden water tank was constructed on its course, just north-east of the bath-house, in a convenient position to serve as a reservoir for its water-tanks.

Nevertheless, there were similar submerged streams further north and much nearer the fort, so this bath-house is unlikely to have been built to serve it, though it may subsequently have been taken over by the military as a convenient facility that was already in existence. This may in fact have been the occasion for the modifications that were made to it early in the second century. The proximity of the main Roman road to Silchester and the west suggests that this bath-house may originally have belonged to a large inn on the western outskirts of the city, in which case it probably owed its origin to private enterprise. That it was built before the fort is strongly indicated by the position of the north-south road that skirts it. Its line lies a little to the east of the north-south road skirting the fort, with which it must have connected by a slight kink. This irregularity is explicable only if it was laid out as part of an earlier development.

Public works in Londinium

With the probable exception of the Cheapside bath-house, all the buildings discussed in this chapter were the products of public initiative and were for public purposes. They completely transformed the face of Londinium and were to have a long-term effect on the topography of the city. Public building was normally the responsibility of local government, exercised by the local *curia* or senate, although at this period it was being actively encouraged in Britain by the provincial government as a matter of policy, by means of financial and technical assistance. There is reason to believe that in London government was much more closely involved through its decision to create a new provincial capital. It was directly concerned with the palace and fort, and probably found it convenient to control the public building programme as a whole, since it was an ambitious project requiring careful planning and allocation of material and labour with due regard to priorities. The ragstone quarries of Kent had to be exploited on a much larger scale and the facilities for transport developed—a responsibility that would naturally fall to the procurator of the province and his subordinate *procuratores*. Tiles and bricks also had to be manufactured in great quantities, and fortunately raw material lay to hand in the brick-earth deposits overlying the local gravels. A state brick-works was accordingly established at Londinium, solely—as far as we are aware—to satsify the needs of the city's building programme. Its products were stamped PP BR, P PR BR, P BR, or some slight variant of these abbreviations, often with the addition of LON for *Londinii* ('at London') (20). The authority of the provincial government is clearly indicated by P BR or PR BR, for *Provinciae Britanniae* ('of the Province of Britain'), and the additional P, which often occurs at the beginning of the stamp, is more likely to stand for the *procurator* than for any other government official. This combination of letters may well have been equally familiar on more perishable materials that have not survived—perhaps as familiar as their more recent equivalent, PWD ('Public Works Department') in the

20   Tile from Dowgate with stamp P.PR.BR

former colonies of the British Empire. We do not know the location of this state brick-works; it may well have established tileries in several of the areas west of the Walbrook where there was a deposit of brick-earth worth exploiting—as in the neighbourhood of Carter Lane and St Paul's.

The destination of these tiles is more certain than their source. Peter Marsden has made a useful study of their distribution, showing that a number have been found on the site of the great basilica, a number on the site of the palace, several in the fort and its immediate neighbourhood, and one (on a roof-tile) on the site of the Huggin Hill Baths.[29] In addition, a number have been found in the somewhat mysterious area west of the Huggin Hill baths, where there is clear evidence of major public works with terracing at a later period, involving the demolition of ragstone and tile buildings that are likely to be of the period of the stamps (late first–early second century). This is an area remarkably lacking in domestic debris, and in later times it seems to have contained a religious precinct with which places of entertainment may have been associated. This may have been its character from its first development, which could well have taken place in the great period of public works between the reigns of Domitian and Hadrian.

It is also worth noting that a single tile-stamp of this kind was found near the junction of Cannon Street and Queen Victoria Street, where there was also a Roman plunge-bath $14\frac{1}{2}$ft (4.4m) long, and that just south of this immense walls, some with fresco paintings, were found in 1845 during the construction of Queen Victoria Street.[30] These finds rather strongly suggest that the Huggin Hill *thermae*, large as they were, formed only part of a much greater bath complex that extended to the north on higher terraces as far as Cannon Street. We have of course no evidence for the date of the finds to the north, but the association of the tile stamp would suggest that they were contemporary with the Huggin Hill baths and could hardly belong to a completely separate establishment.

Not all the tiles used in public buildings in London were made by the state brick-works, however, and a remarkable recent find in the excavated material from the fort has been a tile-stamp of the Channel Fleet (*Classis Britannica*), the only one ever found in London. This does not of course necessarily mean that sailors were concerned with the actual building of the fort or that they were ever stationed there, though the presence of a naval detachment would be likely if ships were allocated for the personal use of the governor. However this may be, the stamp seems to indicate that at least one load of tiles was brought from the south coast to assist in the building programme at London, perhaps as ballast for a ship due to call there. It is a small reminder that major public works in the capital could draw at need on the resources of the province as a whole, and undoubtedly did so for skilled labour as well as building material.

5

Londinium in its Heyday

The Port

Underlying the aggrandisement of Londinium described in the last chapter was a great surge of commercial vitality of a strength and impetus that London was not to know again for more than a thousand years. It clearly began before the policy decision was taken to create a major Roman city—a decision which it must surely have influenced—and had passed its peak before that policy could be fully implemented. It was clearly based primarily on the Thames-side port which, with its accompanying road system, was found to be indispensable. The Roman mission was to bring the benefits of Mediterranean civilisation as quickly as possible to the barbarous British, and there were easy profits to be made in doing so. An appetite for the luxuries and sophisticated products of a superior technology was soon aroused, and the port of Londinium provided a ready means by which they could be poured into Britain and by which the valuable products of an undeveloped country, rich in minerals, sheep and cattle, could be withdrawn.

We know a little about the facilities provided by the port of Londinium at the time of its greatest prosperity, which seems to have begun in the 60s, quite soon after the suppression of Boudica's revolt, and long before officialdom had made the decisions about London's status that were to transform the centre of the city. The port had already been flourishing before the revolt, importing wine from Italy and Rhodes, fish-sauce (*garum*) and olive oil from southern Spain in their characteristic amphorae, terra-cotta lamps and other products that were essential for the Mediterranean way of life, as well as the ubiquitous red glossy samian pottery from the factories of South Gaul. These imports soon revived after 60, and increased to a great flood during the Flavian period, when the port of Londinium seems to have reached its peak of activity.

For this substantial wharfs were required, and well-preserved stretches of a wooden waterfront have recently been found both below the probable site of the Roman bridge, between Fish Street Hill and Botolph Lane, just north of Lower Thames Street, and above it at Miles Lane, north of Upper Thames Street, where

21 Timber waterfront of later first century (in use c80–100), between Pudding Lane and Fish Street Hill, cut by wooden drainage gully of (?) second century (view to N). *Museum of London*

it lay 110 yards (100m) north of the present riverside.[1] The front wall consisted of massive squared timber baulks laid horizontally and braced to a back wall by horizontal timbers mortised to them (**21**, fig 16). Pottery evidence indicates a date in the early Flavian period, but a more precise date will in due course be available from tree-ring analysis. At Pudding Lane the wharf was infilled with clay, gravel and refuse, and two masonry warehouses were built a few yards to the north. These seem to have had an open colonnaded or arcaded facade towards the river, as may also have been the case with the most easterly building (fig 16, Building A) north of the river-front at Miles Lane. The Flavian wharf at Pudding Lane had replaced an earlier timber landing-stage of more open construction in the same position, and was itself superseded when a new waterfront was built further south, and land was reclaimed by dumping south of the first-century river-front. On pottery evidence this happened very early in the second century on both sites. The subsequent waterfront presumably lies mostly under Thames Street, but was probably seen just south of the street frontage further east on the Custom House site. Here there were horizontal east-west timbers with a plank facing held by

vertical posts. A backing of clay contained late first- early second-century pottery, and the excavator interpreted the structure as a waterfront not later than about the beginning of Hadrian's reign.[2] A further extension to the south and reclamation took place in late Antonine or Severan times, when a massive waterfront was constructed (see pp148–53).

The floods of imports that arrived at the quays of Londinium in the half-century after 60 included manufactured goods of many kinds: bronze table-ware and serving-flagons from south Italy, terra-cotta lamps from north Italy, mill-stones from the middle Rhine (also imported before 60), mass-produced pipe-clay figurines from Central Gaul and the Rhineland and fine glassware from Italy and the east—one fine double-handled cup from a pit of 60–80 near the Walbrook is rich in antimony like glass from Mesopotamia. Other early imports from the eastern Mediterranean are curious small carrot-shaped amphorae with wide mouths, now identified as Palestinian in origin, which may have contained dates. The imports of South Gaulish samian ware which had been pouring into the port of Londinium under Nero mounted to a flood under the Flavian emperors. Most of it no doubt travelled further into Britain and helped to enrich the London merchants, but a great deal remained for local use. It has been estimated statistically that the surprisingly high proportion of 27.5% of *all* pottery from first century Londinium is samian.[3] In the earlier period of the port's activity there were small imports of other fine wares, no doubt brought in with more important commodities. They included ornamented and rough-cast cups and beakers from Lyons, lead-glazed flagons and drinking vessels from St Rémy in Central Gaul, and dishes or shallow bowls of 'Pompeian Red Ware' probably from Campania. In the late first and early second centuries they were replaced by colour-coated wares from Central Gaul and the Rhine/Mosel region, which were later to become the principal sources of imported pottery. Central Gaulish samian also replaced the South Gaulish early in the second century, but never achieved the same volume of imports, while East Gaulish samian, which began production at a somewhat later date (about 125), is scarce in London. A minor import that was almost certainly the result of a special order was a piece of green-veined Pyrenean marble, apparently for the decoration of the Cannon Street palace where it was found. For the most part, however, the architect was content with Purbeck marble panels and veneers, fragments of which were also found on the site. The occasional occurrence in London of Roman jewellery, such as emeralds, probably from Egypt, in a fragment of necklace found in a Roman drain in Cannon Street, and amber beads from the Baltic found in the Walbrook, is an indication of the presence of wealthy ladies rather than trade, for these were probably brought to Londinium as the possessions of individuals. The presence of a well-to-do class that was used to the luxuries of civilisation, however, must have played its part in

22   South-western corner of later first century waterfront on east side of Fish Street Hill, 1981, ? under the bridge, of which a possible timber pier is visible in the background (see also **9**, p29) (view to s). *Museum of London*

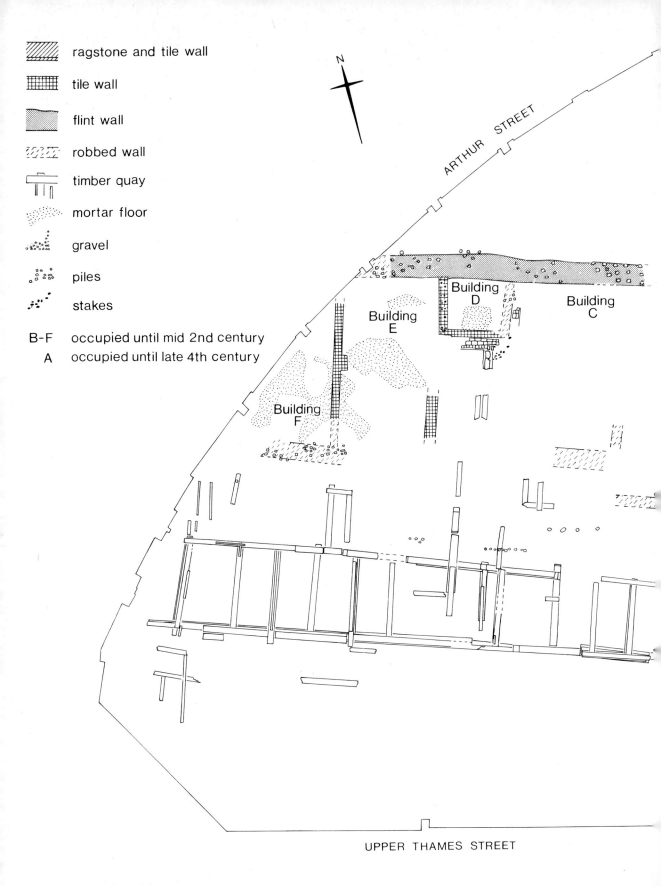

ragstone and tile wall

tile wall

flint wall

robbed wall

timber quay

mortar floor

gravel

piles

stakes

B-F   occupied until mid 2nd century
  A   occupied until late 4th century

N

ARTHUR STREET

Building D

Building E

Building C

Building F

UPPER THAMES STREET

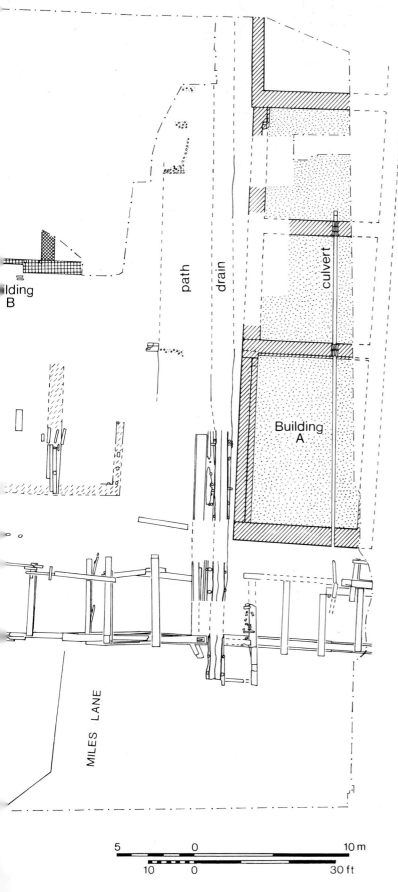

path

drain

culvert

lding
B

Building
A

MILES LANE

5   0   10 m

10   0   30 ft

Fig. 16   Plan of later first–century
waterfront, with buildings behind,
Miles Lane. *After L. Miller*

stimulating imports, by setting an example in fashion and Romanised 'high life' that would be emulated by British provincials.

As might be expected, we have little direct evidence of the exports that passed through the port in return for these imports. The traditional pre-Conquest exports of Britain recorded by Strabo were corn, cattle, hides, gold, silver, iron, slaves and hunting-dogs. At this period, however, most of the surplus corn and hides at least must have been absorbed by the needs of the army in Britain, and the increased production of iron was probably also directed mainly towards military and naval requirements, though there may have been some surplus for export. The slave-trade must have grown during the period of conquest and expansion, for it was the accepted means to dispose of prisoners-of-war, but with the stabilisation of the frontier this valuable export must have dwindled. An iron shackle found in the Walbrook with the tools of many local crafts and trades, probably deposited for votive purposes, suggests that the slave-trade was included among them. Gold, silver and lead were already being exploited, probably as an imperial monopoly under the direct control of the procurator. A small iron stamp in the Museum of London collection, from its condition found in the Walbrook or Thames, has the letters M. P. BR., probably standing for *Metalla Provinciae Britanniae* ('Mines of the Province of Britain'). It was presumably used for marking ingots of one of these soft metals by officials who checked them at Londinium before export. It is a much smaller stamp than is usually found on lead, and is more likely to have been used on gold from the Dolaucothi mine in South Wales or on silver extracted from the lead of the Mendips or Derbyshire. At a later period woollen cloth in the form of cloaks and rugs was an important export, but it is unlikely that the industry was sufficiently organised to provide much surplus for export by the early second century. Minor exports that almost certainly passed through Londinium in the first century, however, were British oysters and basketwork, both of which were obtainable then in Rome, as we know from literary sources.

Letters from Londinium

Trade in actual commodities was not the only source of wealth in Londinium, and from the beginning there were those whose principal concern was the profitable investment of money. Significantly, one of the half-dozen fragmentary letters we have surviving from Roman London deals with a financial transaction, probably the terms of repayment of a loan. Like all except one of the others, it survives as the scratchings of a stylus on the soft pine-wood of a writing tablet, originally covered with a wax writing surface, through which the point of the stylus had pressed sufficiently hard to mark the wood beneath. The cursive Latin script has been translated '... which money by the terms likewise of the claim shall be paid to me by Crescens [presumably an agent acting as intermediary] or by the person concerned ...' (fig 17.2). Like several other writing tablets with readable lines it was found in 1927 in the stream-bed or flood deposits of the Walbrook in Lothbury, where the wood was preserved by the water-logged nature of the soil.[4]

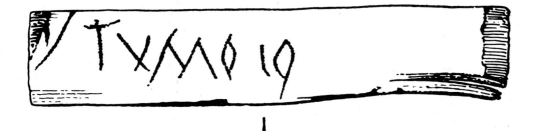

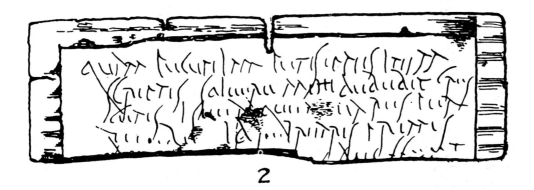

Fig. 17 Fragments of wooden writing-tablets, with legible scratched impressions of writing, from the Walbrook at Lothbury. *Drawings by R. G. Collingwood*

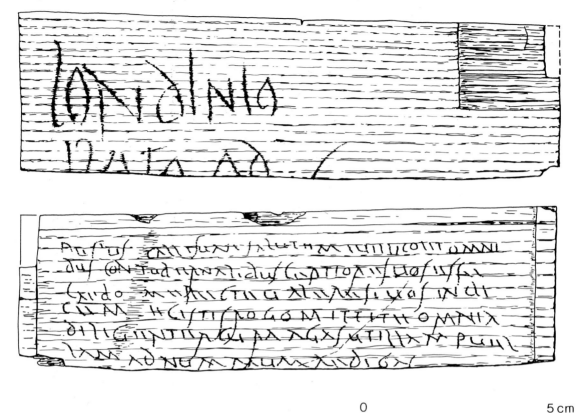

Fig. 18   Portion of wooden writing tablet with scratched impressions of part of address
'*Londinio*' and letter from Rufus, son of Callisunus, to Epillicus; from the Walbrook, probably at
Lothbury. *After I. A. Richmond*

One of the others can be dated to the period 84–96 by a reference to the
Emperor Domitian. This is an oath 'by Jupiter Best and Greatest and by the
Genius of his Imperial Majesty Domitian Conqueror of Germany, and by the
Gods of our fathers ...'. On the back of the tablet which formed the outside of a
double- or treble-leafed package, it was addressed [*Po*]*stumo Lo*[*ndinii*] 'To
Postumus at London' (fig 17.1). This is part of a legal contract, no doubt relating
to a business transaction, that was presumably written and sealed in the presence
of witnesses. It seems likely that the entire group is of about the same date, when
the prosperity and activities of Londinium were at their height.

The longest passage that we have in any of these letters may relate to the
recovery of a debt from a defaulting borrower by the seizure of property (fig 18).
It can be translated as follows: 'Rufus, son of Callisunus, sends greetings to
Epillicus and all his fellows. I believe you know that I am very well. If you have
made the list please send it. Do look after everything carefully so that you squeeze
the last penny from that girl.' The alternative, more literal, translation of the last

phrase (*'ut illam puellam ad nummum redigas ...'*) 'that you turn that girl into cash ...', would make it a direct reference to the London slave-market. In that case presumably the slave-girl was included in the property that was being taken over. It is impossible to judge the precise contemporary meaning of a colloquial phrase, but it could be argued that the preceding words *'omnia diligenter cura agas ut ...'* ('look after everything carefully so that ...') lead more naturally to the first alternative.[5] If correct, this suggests rather strongly that the list requested was an inventory of property taken over in settlement of debt. It is of considerable interest that the writer of the letter from his nomenclature is not a Roman citizen but a wealthy *peregrinus*, probably of Gaulish origin, as his father's Celtic name suggests. The head servant to whom he writes, and who seems to be in charge of his affairs in London, also has a Celtic name, Epillicus, and is evidently a Gaul or Briton. Latin, as might be expected, was the natural language for business correspondence, whatever the origin of the writer. On the back of the tablet is the address *'Londinio'* with the upper part of a name.

Most tantalising of all these fragmentary letters is one that evidently refers to at least two activities in Londinium, retail trade and ship-building—and possibly to a third, bureaucratic control. There are disjointed references to selling something from a shop, building a ship, making a steering-oar (*clavum*) and granting authority to do something, including probably the making of the steering-oar (fig 17.3).

There is also a reminder of the continuing presence of bureaucracy from another writing-tablet found in the Walbrook. This has no visible writing, but a branded stamp proclaims it official stationery, 'issued by the Imperial Procurators of the Province of Britain' (PROC AVG DEDERVNT/BRIT PROV).

The only other letter found in London that has yielded readable phrases is of quite a different type. This was found in a timber-lined pit of the early second century on the site of Temple House, Queen Victoria Street. It consists of a thin strip of wood cut in the centre to form two leaves, which were presumably tied together. The writing, which was in carbon ink, was in two columns, one on each leaf; it unfortunately disappeared during the treatment of the wood, but portions could be read on infra-red photographs taken while it was still wet. This was a letter written from Durobrivae (Rochester or Water Newton—more likely the former) and concerns a boy, probably a slave, who had run away, apparently absconding with something with which he had been entrusted, possibly in a wagon.[6] It throws no light on activities in Londinium, though the city is mentioned by name with reference to the writer's departure for Durobrivae.

The last letter is, however, a reminder that there must have been a great deal of travel and transport of goods between London and the other cities of Roman Britain by road, and no doubt many people in Londinium were fully occupied by internal trade. Pottery stamped by makers of this period at Brockley Hill, Middlesex, and other potteries in the region of Verulamium for example, has been found in Richborough and Chichester, and must have come there via Londinium. It may be suspected also that middle-men in London took their profit from the distribution of the salt produced in the Thames estuary to the inland towns. There must also have been opportunities for marketing agricultural produce, cloth, skins and leather in a place from which they could so readily be distributed in all directions.

Crafts and industry

Ship-building, for which so surprisingly we have actual documentary evidence, was an industry likely to be found in any port, and would have developed naturally from the servicing and repairs inevitably required by visiting ships. Many other service industries also developed naturally from the local needs of a prosperous community, and some no doubt in due course contributed also to the stock of goods available for trade. A remarkable archaeological phenomenon, to which reference has already been made, is the quantity and variety of craftsmen's tools that have survived in almost perfect condition in the earlier levels of the stream-bed of the Walbrook, where they are accompanied by coins covering approximately the first hundred years of the city's existence, for the series barely extends beyond the middle of the second century. Woodworkers' tools include chisels, gouges, bits, awls, a double-handled draw-knife and neat little folding bronze rules for measuring. With the addition of modern wooden handles and some sharpening, most of these tools would still be serviceable today. Metal-workers' implements include an anvil, pincers for handling the hot metal, hammers of various kinds, an axe-shaped chisel and an iron tool for producing gadroon ornamentation on bronze or silver vessels. There are also stone-masons' picks, chisels, points and a lewising-tool for cutting grooves in masonry blocks for the attachment of a lifting device. Plasterers' tools include trowels, spatulae and the typical 'small tool' for work in awkward corners. There are also large iron dividers of the kind used for builders' measurements. Not all the crafts represented by the tools from the Walbrook are urban; they include two ploughshares, mattocks, hoes and pruning-hooks, presumably deposited—the ploughshares, at least, can hardly have been accidentally lost—by men who may have lived in Londinium but gained their livelihood from the countryside, a form of commuting still familiar in Italy. More to be expected, perhaps, are the tools of the waterfront and docks that have also been found—the boat-hooks, crane-hook, dockers' hooks for handling bales, and jemmy for opening packing-cases (23). These, it should perhaps be mentioned, came not from the mouth of the Walbrook near the docks themselves, but from the Bucklersbury House site where the stream was only 12ft (3.7m) wide and navigable only by the smallest of boats, so there is no possibility they were lost in use. A more esoteric craft represented among the Walbrook tools is that of the surgeon. Mostly in bronze, which seems to have been considered a more suitable material than iron for this purpose, probably because it could be shaped more delicately, these implements include scalpels, probes and spatulae, one of which is deliberately bent, perhaps for use as a tongue depressor. I have also seen an undoubted catheter in bronze tubing found at Bucklersbury House, but unfortunately this vanished at once into private

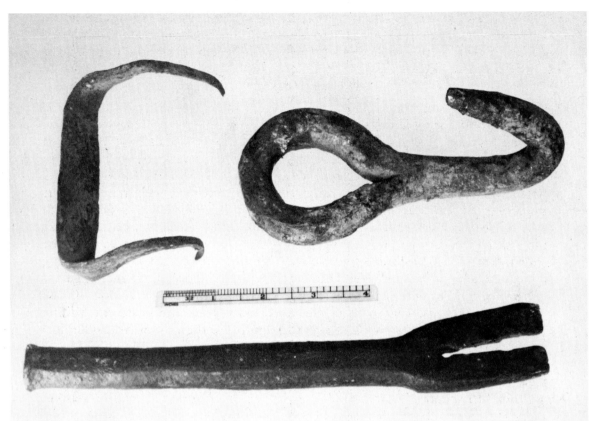

23 Roman dockers tools and crane-hook, from the Walbrook, site of Bucklersbury House, Walbrook. *Museum of London*

possession, from which it could not be recovered for proper recording.

Very much more numerous than any other tool in the Walbrook series, however, is the stylus for writing on wax tablets, the characteristic implement of the clerical worker, who must have played almost as large a part in the life of Londinium as in the modern City of London. More than 100 of these little implements, pointed at one end for writing and with a chisel edge for erasures at the other, were recovered by the staff of Guildhall Museum from the bed of the Walbrook on the Bucklersbury House site alone, and this must have been a small proportion of the total number. It must be emphasised that they did not occur in groups or bundles as jettisoned stock but, like the other tools, had evidently been dropped in the stream individually. It is difficult to account for the great number and variety of these finds in the bed of the Walbrook, except on the assumption that it was a common custom in first- and early second-century Londinium to devote a tool of one's trade or a sample of one's wares to a local deity by throwing it into the stream.

Whether any of these tools were made locally is quite unknown, but it is by no means improbable, since iron was readily available from the Weald and in more limited quantities from local ironstone. Apart from Stane Street, there were two important roads from London through Sussex towards the future sites of Lewes and Brighton, so that there was no problem about the transport of pig-iron by wagon to Londinium.[7] Both of these roads were metalled with iron slag in the Wealden area, so their connection with the iron industry is clear. Analysis of industrial slag from three sites recently excavated in Southwark—Toppings Wharf by the river, 1–7 St Thomas Street and 210–211 Borough High Street—has shown that iron-smithing was carried on there.[8] More than 10kg of iron slag came from Roman levels on the last site. It is most unlikely that there was smelting from the ore on any of these sites, however, and it is believed that these relatively small quantities of slag were produced in making iron artefacts, either incidentally by the combination of particles of iron oxide with siliceous material in the hearth-lining, or through the use of sand to clean heated surfaces of iron in the process of hammer-welding.

Significantly, each of these sites also produced evidence of bronze-working, with indications that it was for the production of small objects. A crucible with beads of copper and bronze in the slag on its inner surface was found in St Thomas Street; a bronze bar that was probably the primary material as received by the manufacturer, an unfinished bronze handle or loop for suspension and slag with bronze particles came from the site in Borough High Street: and a burnt area adjacent to a hearth at Toppings Wharf contained both iron and bronze particles, while elsewhere on the site were found pieces of bronze that were obviously spilt metal from casting. A glance through the knives, tools and styli from the Walbrook in the Museum of London will show that bronze was sometimes combined with iron in the same implement as handle, decorative band or loop for suspension, and it would not be surprising if some of these came from contemporary local workshops where both metals were used. In Southwark the metal-working seems to have commenced before 70 and continued into the earlier part of the second century, covering the period when most of the tools were dropped into the Walbrook.

Within the city of Londinium itself, evidence of bronze-working, considered to be of Roman date, was found in a builders' excavation in Crosby Square,[9] and there is slag indicating blacksmiths' work from the recently excavated GPO site north of Newgate Street and east of King Edward Street. Here, as in Southwark, industrial activity continued from Flavian times or earlier well into the second century. It was recommenced after a great fire that can be dated elsewhere to about 125–30, but came to an end some years later in the Antonine period.[10]

It seems fairly certain that metal-working in London was not limited to tools and objects of utility but was concerned also with personal ornaments such as brooches, used by both sexes as dress and cloak-fasteners. Lumps of crude green enamel were found in Nicholas Lane and balls of blue frit, probably for making enamel, were found in a second-century dump on the marshes south-east of the industrial site in St Thomas Street, Southwark. These suggest that enamelled bronze brooches and other ornaments, of the kind imported from Gallia Belgica, were also made locally.

The Southwark dump also contained fragments of crucibles, on which traces of gold could be detected, and pieces of thin clay tube rather like the stem of a tobacco-pipe, which may have been part of a blow-pipe used in metal-working.[11] A goldsmith was also at work in the 80s on the site that was later to be occupied by the Cannon Street Palace. This raises the question whether he was employed by the provincial government, on a site that it already owned, as an agent of the imperial monopoly. He was engaged in the refining of gold, as is shown by the fragments of crucibles with tiny globules of gold on their inner surfaces and pieces of clay luting used to seal the lids to the crucibles, found in his deposits of rubbish. The process was one that was still in use in the sixteenth century and is described in a treatise of that period.[12] Alternate layers of brick-dust or a similar absorbent material and the unrefined gold were placed in the crucible. A natural organic acid such as urine was then poured in, and the lid was hermetically sealed to the crucible by a clay luting. Prolonged heating followed, during which impurities in the gold were dissolved in the acid fumes and were absorbed into the surrounding brick-dust. An interesting feature of the fragments of luting found is that they had been impressed with small oblong dies or moulds, presumably used as a security seal to ensure that nobody tampered with the valuable contents during the lengthy period of heating. One impression repeated several times represented in relief a lion confronted by a boar, and a fragment of another apparently represented the tail of a hippocamp. The lion and boar impressions, although practically identical, were apparently not all from the same die, though it is difficult to be quite sure of this as the fine detail of the die was lost in the impression owing to the coarseness of the clay. It seems most unlikely that this was the purpose for which the dies had been made, since something equally distinctive but much coarser would have served the purpose as well or better. They are the wrong shape and too large to be document seals, and the most likely explanation is that they were moulds used by the goldsmith for making ornamental plaques of some kind, and were conveniently to hand when he required a security seal. Professor Hatt considers that the representation of a fight between a lion and boar, which also occurs on South Gaulish decorated samian bowls, has a religious significance, perhaps representing a conflict between Teutates (the boar) and Taranis (the lion), and points out that the same subject occurs in a votive bas-relief in the sanctuary of Le Donon.[13] This might suggest that the moulds were used in the production of votive plaques, though not of the usual form, or amuletic jewellery. They might equally well have been used as a unit of design in a diadem or even a decorated vessel. Since the dies were intaglio they must have been used either for some form of casting or for embossing very thin sheet metal that could be rubbed into the die.[14] The fact that this goldsmith seems to have been concerned with making jewellery as well as gold-refining does not rule out the possibility that he was working for the state, for he may have been doing free-lance work as well, with or without permission.

The evidence for glass-making in Londinium is at present dubious, and the only apparently convincing find of this nature was inadequately recorded. In 1878 a collection of glass fragments was exhibited to the British Archaeological Association with a mass of green and white glass slag that weighed nearly ½cwt (25kg), two small masses of blue glass adhering to fragments of pot or crucible, and an iron bowl 'for pressing and moulding the ornamental portions of glass vessels, presenting a pattern very similar to those from Cyprus', all from a site in Clement's Lane.[15] The possibility remains that the slag, iron mould and blue glass in a crucible related to bronze-working, the blue glass being used for enamelling, and that the presence of fragments of glass vessels on the same site was fortuitous. The vessels described are of high quality—a basin with filigree lines of white, a fragment imitating chalcedony, and a bowl with cut facets—and were almost certainly imports, though when broken they could have been collected by a glass-maker for use as cullet. The first glass-making in Britain is likely to have been of a humble nature and for utilitarian purposes. It is possible that there was difficulty in obtaining suitable sands locally even for this, for window-glass is by no means common among the finds of Roman London.

Evidence of leather-working was found by Professor Grimes west of the Walbrook in Queen Victoria Street. Here there was a succession of hut-floors or working-floors, on one of which portions of a skin survived, held down by the pegs used to stretch it for cutting up, and there were numerous fragments of leather waste, including parts of shoes.[16] Cut leather waste was found in Roman levels at Founders Court, Lothbury, beside the Walbrook, and unfinished shoes, particularly slipper-like sandals (carbatinae), have also been found in the Walbrook valley. The convenience of a good water supply probably attracted the leather-workers to the neighbourhood of the stream, though the survival of their products in water-logged deposits alone may give a distorted picture of their actual distribution, and much of this waste was incorporated in dumps of material to raise the stream-banks.

Tile-making, as we have seen, was an industry that made use of the local brick-earth, probably mainly to meet the demands of the London building programme, and was partly at least under state control. It is a product of a brickyard, presumably local, that has provided one of the more human documents of Londinium—a message scratched on the tile before firing, saying in colloquial Latin that Austalis has been going off on his own every day for a fortnight. It testifies both to literacy and the use of Latin in the brickyards, and is our only surviving joke from Londinium—for Austalis was obviously being teased for his mysterious disappearances, perhaps to see a girl.

It was the presence of this useful local loam or brick-earth overlying the gravels that gave rise to the pottery industry of Londinium, though finer clays were probably soon brought from elsewhere by river barge as the potters became more ambitious. The first recorded and most remarkable discovery of pottery kilns in London was made in 1672, during excavations for the foundations of the north-east part of the north transept of Wren's new St Paul's Cathedral. At a depth of 26ft (7.9m), it is said, four dome-shaped kilns were found arranged cross-wise, apparently with a common flue-channel.[17] One of the four survived almost intact, with its dome-shaped roof. According to John Conyers, a contemporary observer, 'it was 5ft from top to bottom and of the same width, and had no other matter for its form and building but the outward loam, naturally crusted hardish by the heat burning the loam red, like brick; the floor in the middle supported by, and cut out of, loam, and helped with old-fashioned Roman tyles' shards, but very few, and such as I have seen used for repositories for urns, in the fashion of and like ovens. The kiln was full of the coarser sort of pot, so that few were saved whole, viz., lamps, bottles, urns and dishes.' Some drawings of pots of the later first and early second centuries are contained in the MS account in the British Museum, but they are of various kinds that would be unlikely to be found together in the same firing, and as the drawings seem to represent complete pots—probably the only ones that would then be kept—some or all of them may have come from the neighbouring cremation burials which were also found at that time.

An eighteenth-century writer informs us that pottery moulds with 'Figures of Men, of Lions, of Leaves of Trees, and other Things' were also found nearby.[18] If this account can be trusted, potters in Londinium were trying to copy the fine moulded samian ware from Gaul, as we know was being done at a later date at Camulodunum. No confirmation of the manufacture of a London version of samian has ever been found, however, and the one sherd of British 'samian' that has been identified in London, an apparent kiln-waster found in Aldgate at the eastern extremity of the city, was almost certainly made by a potter who worked at Pulborough in West Sussex, where fragments of his moulds have been found.[19] Since through lack of skill most of his work is over-fired with a tendency to blister, it is conceivable he attempted to market sub-standard ware in London, or at least sent a sample there. In the absence of any confirmatory evidence it cannot be assumed that he ever worked in Londinium.

The stoke-hole, vents and parts of the centrally supported oven floor of an updraught kiln were recorded by Marsden in 1961 about 200 yards (183m) to the north-west of the St Paul's kilns, immediately east of the bed of a stream that had obviously provided the potters with their essential supply of water. Sherds of a coarse sandy ware were found in the kiln. These were fragments of jars and possibly a jug of the late first or early second century, and it can reasonably be assumed they were local products, though not necessarily fired in the kiln where they were found.[20] It seems likely that the pottery industry extended also to the north side of the Newgate Street road, where the stream bifurcated. Between its two branches were pits which had been dug for brick-earth and subsequently used as dumps or stores for material that may have been connected with potting. One contained a quantity of prepared clay, which had been dug out on one side, and several others contained fine sand. A hole filled with wood-ash observed in the section of the builders' excavation and believed to have been a flue, could have been part of a kiln.[21]

It has been suggested that there was another pottery-producing district in the northern part of the city between the fort and the Walbrook, in the neighbourhood of Coleman Street and Moorgate, an area of which we have little archaeological knowledge. The hypothesis is based on a great dump of pottery, including many 'wasters' (pots spoilt in firing), found on natural brick-earth just west of a tributary of the Walbrook, during the rebuilding in 1936 of 1–4 Copthall Close.[22] It is considered that the wasters, which could not have been sold, are unlikely to have been taken far from the kiln where they were produced. The undoubted kiln waste consists mainly of plain grey wares—chiefly jars and bowls—but there are also probable wasters of fine mica-dusted ware and the so-called 'London ware'. The former has a micaceous slip with the purpose of giving it a faint glitter when light is reflected from the grains of mica, so that it has a slightly metallic appearance. The micaceous clay is not local and is likely to have been imported. The supposed wasters, mostly dishes, were not distorted, but some were blistered and others had rising bases due to sagging when the vessel was fired upside down. In a fine ware these faults could have made the vessel unsaleable. The 'London ware', as its traditional name implies, has always been associated with the London area, but was made in various places, including the North Kent marshes, and these probable wasters of the ware, associated with the undoubted kiln dump of grey pottery, are the only indication that it may also have been made in Londinium itself. 'London ware' is a hard grey pottery with a fine black burnished surface that is often made in imitation of samian forms, especially bowls, but is ornamented with a simple decoration of incised lines and compass-drawn half-circles. The supposed wasters are under-fired and discoloured to light grey, red or brown. 'London ware', like mica-dusted ware, seems to have been produced between about 90 and 130, when strong efforts were being made by Romano-British potters to compete with imported fine wares.

It may be suspected that tile- and pottery-making were practised on a very small scale within the city itself, since a major industry is normally accompanied by the dumping of kiln waste in great quantities, and there is little evidence of this in the City of London, even in the supposedly industrial areas. The manufacture of pottery had certainly become a major industry within 30 miles or so of Londinium, and more tileries on the scale of one recently found in Canons Park, Edgware, undoubtedly remain to be discovered within that area. In the city itself and its immediate environs, however, both industries were probably of minor importance.

The Hadrianic fire

G. C. Dunning was impressed by the great quantity of burnt daub with a very considerable amount of samian pottery blackened by fire on the site of Regis House, King William Street. Most of the closely dateable samian was of the period 120–130 and strongly suggested that the fire had occurred about that time. He subsequently found that there were ten sites east of the Walbrook where there were burnt levels indicating a second century fire, extending from St Swithin's Lane in the west to the site of All Hallows Barking Church, Great Tower Street, in the east. West of the Walbrook the evidence was then less impressive, but there were four similar sites extending from Cannon Street in the south to King Street in the north, all east of the King Street–Queen Street roadway. Dunning extended the suggested area of the fire by plotting the finds of burnt samian of the relevant date in the museum collections. These not only filled in the interstices between the known sites where there were burnt levels, but extended the possible range of the fire dramatically to Aldgate in the north-east and Paternoster Row in the west. From all this he deduced that there had been a great fire in Londinium in the reign of Hadrian, comparable in its devastation with the Boudican fire of 60, the fire of 1666, and the fires of 1940–1.[23] In 1965 four more sites with burnt levels probably of the second century could be added.[24] These, however, affected the general pattern very little, except by confirming the presence of burnt buildings immediately east of the Walbrook in an area where the fire had previously been indicated only by burnt samian—of dubious evidential value in the valley of the Walbrook, where there was continual dumping to raise the banks.

Recently Geoff Marsh has made a further study of the Regis House samian and of Dunning's MS site-notes, as part of a wider survey of the samian collection in the Museum of London, and has reached the conclusion that the finds came from a pottery warehouse which was burnt on the site, and were not dumped there as Dunning thought. He suggests that the ragstone wall, on the west of which the burnt debris was piled, was the east wall of one of a series of long narrow buildings similar to those found a little further west in Miles Lane. These were all built on a massive structure of interlocking oak beams, evidently part of a major scheme of embankment like those on the waterfront further east. Marsh suggests a date soon after 80 for this construction on the bulk of the samian evidence, disregarding two or three later stamps which he believes to be intrusive from the warehouse deposit. If so, it is presumably contemporary with the Flavian waterfront found east of Fish Street Hill. The foundations of the Regis House building were cut into a thick deposit of oyster shells, which here seems to have formed the surface of the embankment. The warehouse is therefore presumably of somewhat later date, though the only dating evidence is that it was in existence at the time of the fire. This Marsh would date from the Regis House samian to 120–5, probably just before 125, on the basis of current views on dating these imports. The case he makes for the pottery being the stock of a warehouse is convincing. The burnt deposit, which also contained broken roofing-tiles and wall plaster, produced fragments of at least 600 decorated samian vessels and over 115 stamps that represented at least 35 potters, with only a dozen or so vessels of coarse ware. Most of the samian came from a single manufacturing area of central Gaul—Les-Martres-de-Veyre—and must surely represent the last cargo received before the fire. Moreover, several pieces are fused together, as if they were burnt while stacked in piles. Melting of this kind could only have occurred in an intense heat of more than 1200°C. The site lies immediately west of the bridge approach road, which may be represented by gravel deposits found on the east or outer side of the wall. The proximity of the bridge to such a great conflagration strongly suggests that it was also burnt, and its burning timbers may well have contributed to the intensity of the fire at the warehouse.[25]

In more recent excavations, much evidence of burnt buildings of the early second century and probably of Hadrianic date[26] has been found in Milk Street, Watling Court in Cannon Street west of Bow Lane, and on the GPO site immediately east of King Edward Street. All are further west than the burnt levels previously recorded, although they are within the area covered by the distribution of the burnt samian, and therefore provide striking confirmation of its general validity as an indicator of the area affected. As a result of these excavations, an extensive early second-century fire in the western half of the city can now be regarded as an archaeological fact, and it will be surprising if more detailed work on the dating evidence fails to confirm that it took place in the third decade of the century as indicated by the burnt samian elsewhere. The whole problem of the fire has recently been intensively studied by S. Roskams and L. Watson.[27] The question is complicated by the uncertainty of dating evidence on many sites, particularly those known only from rescue work and observation during builders' excavations—the great majority; by the fact that burnt debris was often cleared and dumped elsewhere; and by the certainty that there were also other lesser fires during the later first and second centuries. There was, for example, a later second century (Antonine) fire on part of the site at Watling Court, and a fair amount of burnt Antonine samian of about 160–80 has recently been detected by G. Marsh in the old collection in the Museum of London; so some of the burnt sites attributed to the Hadrianic fire may well relate to this. Nevertheless, Dunning's hypothesis that there was a great conflagration that destroyed most of Londinium in the reign of Hadrian between 120–30 has received ample confirmation. The evidence is now more conclusive from the west of the Walbrook, where it was weaker when Dunning wrote his paper. East of the stream, however, are many well dated deposits of dumped Hadrianic fire debris and less closely dated second century burnt levels *in situ*. It still seems likely that the area affected extended from Newgate Street to the Tower. The fort, probably already in existence, seems to have escaped, perhaps thanks to the efficiency of military fire pickets, and there is no certain evidence of damage to the basilica and forum, the palace or the Huggin Hill baths. These, however, were stone-built, and the survival of their lower walls unscathed does not necessarily mean there was no damage to more combustible parts, such as wooden fittings, at a higher level. The smaller Cheapside baths were certainly substantially rebuilt and altered in the later part of their existence—ie probably in the early second century—and this could have been the result of damage from the fire that certainly raged in the neighbourhood. It was the timber-framed wattle and daub buildings, many of which almost certainly had thatched roofs, that suffered complete destruction, however, and among these the fire, in any sort of wind, would have spread rapidly. There is no known political event with which it can be associated, and in all probability it was the result of accident, like the fire of 1666. In one significant respect it differed from the Boudican fire of 60, which seems to have destroyed houses already emptied of their contents, and was therefore anticipated. The Hadrianic fire, on the other hand, seems to have taken people by surprise. In the burnt debris overlying the floor of a house on the east side of the Walbrook, for example, half-a-dozen complete or almost complete pots were found abandoned while in use, one containing carbonised grain.[28]

The growth of Londinium

The area covered by the Hadrianic fire has in the past been used as an indicator of the growth of Londinium by the early second century, in comparison with the much smaller area that until recently was the known extent of the Boudican fire 60–65 years earlier.[29] In the last few years, however, evidence of a mid-first-century fire that is almost certainly that of 60 has been found on two outlying sites to the east and west, at Aldgate and in Newgat Street (see pp51–2). On the GPO site, north of Newgate Street, as we have seen, there was delay of some years before rebuilding took place after the disaster of 60. Eventually two gravel pathways were laid out, presumably early in the Flavian period, as if to divide the site into rectangular building plots. On these plots substantial timber-framed buildings were subsequently constructed with sills set directly on the ground. The infill of the walls was of mud brick, the bricks for which were made on the spot from brick-earth quarried from a large pit immediately to the north. This was subsequently filled with organic and domestic refuse by the occupants of the buildings. Smaller pits were filled with industrial waste, not yet fully investigated. Both houses had a common party wall towards the street, but were separated towards the rear. It seems that they were built as part of a development scheme which in all probability extended over a larger area, but internally they were individually planned to suit the requirements of the occupier. Eventually the western building was removed and the west wall of the eastern building was modified to serve as an external wall.

Probably early in the second century two new timber-framed buildings with an alleyway between them were constructed over the whole area, though it is suggested because of the varying sizes of the brick-earth sills that the alley was covered at first floor level, so that the load of the eastern side of the western building was borne by the west wall of its neighbour. In that case they would have presented a continuous facade to the street, probably as a pair of shops. Behind these were large rooms, some of which contained substantial hearths, believed to be for industrial purposes. Smaller rooms to the rear also contained hearths, probably for domestic heating (plan, fig 19, **24**). A gravelled lane immediately to the east gave access from the main road to the rear of the buildings. They seem to have been planned for both commercial and industrial purposes, perhaps in order that goods made in the work-shop area behind could be sold in the front shop.

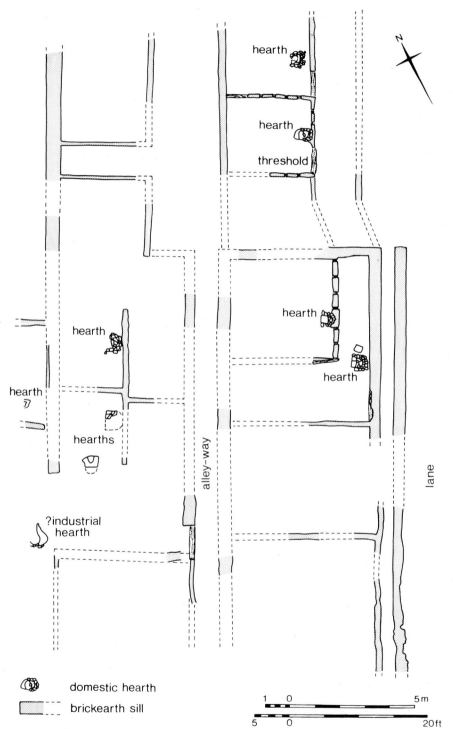

Fig. 19   Plan of timber-framed houses with brickearth sills, destroyed in the Hadrianic fire of c 120–125, excavated on the GPO site, Newgate Street, 1975–9

Living quarters were either in the small rooms behind or at first-floor level, or both. It is to be hoped that further study of the finds from the site will throw more light on the activities carried on in the work-shops. Later some modifications were made to the northern end of the western building, which was extended and separated from the eastern one. Both buildings were then destroyed in the Hadrianic fire, and the debris from them overlay the bases of their walls and helped to preserve them. The burnt material was however soon levelled off and new buildings to the same plan were constructed on the ruins of the old, apparently with very little delay. They were clearly intended for the same purpose, for a new large industrial hearth in the western building was placed in almost exactly the same position as its predecessor. It seems probable that they were even occupied by the same people. Since the outline of the burnt buildings had been completely obliterated by the thick deposit of debris, a record with measurements must have survived, so that their plan could be laid out anew in precisely the same place. The immediate recovery after the Hadrianic fire is in marked contrast to the delay in rebuilding after 60, and is a clear indication of continued vitality and confidence.[30]

This industrial area was probably now included within the official limits of the

24   Clay wall-sills and tile hearth, probably domestic, at rear of building destroyed in the Hadrianic fire, GPO site, Newgate Street (view to SE). *Museum of London*

city, which had almost certainly been extended in Flavian times as part of the ambitious development of Londinium as a capital city, described in the last chapter. The old inner cemeteries had long passed out of use, not later than early Flavian times, and possibly at the time of the Boudican revolt. On the west they were superseded by a cemetery in the neighbourhood of Warwick Square and west of the probable industrial zone, though within the line of the later city wall. The new city boundary may have been fixed on the line of a stream that continued to flow, presumably through culverts beneath the Newgate Street road.

Similarly on the eastern side of the city the old inner cemetery had passed out of use, superseded by the outer one in the neighbourhood of Haydon Square and the Minories, which had been established almost as early but was to continue as a burial ground into later Roman times. Here the new boundary was probably already extended to the line of the later city wall. We still know very little about the development of the south-eastern part of the city, but so far there seems to be no evidence that it was occupied in 60. On the site of All Hallows Church at the eastern end of Great Tower Street there was a sequence of occupation levels, probably representing a succession of clay and timber houses, but it did not begin until Flavian times. As in Newgate Street it was interrupted but not concluded by the Hadrianic fire. It seems likely that in this area the extension of the boundary marked a real expansion in occupation. At Aldgate considerable disruption must have been caused by the construction of a new road out of the city to Old Ford and Colchester. This presumably took place in Flavian times, when the alignment of the adjacent buildings was made to accord with it. It can only have happened when major alterations were being made to the city street plan, such as occurred when the new insula for the great forum and basilica was laid out late in the first century. It presumably met the street grid on the line of a new east–west street laid out north of the basilica, but whether it could also have continued on its diagonal course into the heart of the city remains very doubtful.

When the Emperor Hadrian visited Londinium in 122, the Roman city he saw had not yet achieved its greatest size. It was still to be extended a little to the west, as we have seen, and also to the north, where likewise there are second-century burials inside the line of the later city wall. It was also to receive additional great public works—most notably the wall itself. It may, however, have already acquired its fine new stone fort, and had at last completed—or was about to complete—one of the most impressive fora to be seen in the western provinces. It had already been equipped with the public baths that were an essential part of urban civilisation, though perhaps they did not yet offer all the facilities the Emperor thought appropriate, for the Huggin Hill baths were extended about this time, probably to provide a separate bathing suite for women. Above all, the city had a river-side palace with a splendid view of the Thames and its bridge, in which a visiting emperor could be accommodated in a style that befitted the capital of one of his provinces. Londinium had already reached or passed the peak of its vitality, the continuing vigour of which was to be demonstrated by the

25   Bronze head of the emperor Hadrian, larger than life-size, possibly commemorating his visit
in 122; dredged from the Thames near London Bridge, 1834. Height c 16½ in (42cm). *British Museum*

speed of its recovery from the disastrous fire. Whether its trade was quite as flourishing as it had been 25 years earlier is a matter of doubt, however. Certainly much less samian pottery was being imported, due perhaps to a decline in production rather than demand, and coin finds indicate that much less new money was coming into Londinium. The great quantity of coins dredged from the Thames near Old London Bridge between 1834 and 1841, and recorded by Roach Smith, should provide a fair sample of the currency of Roman London.[31] They include 391 coins of the Flavian emperors and only 166 of Nerva. Trajan and Hadrian, whose reigns span a somewhat longer period. The significance in economic terms of a reduction of the casual losses of new small change from the mint is uncertain. It may mean that less money was coming into London, that there were fewer people about to lose it—or both. In a commercial centre it seems more likely to indicate decline than continuing prosperity, but may reflect a subsequent Antonine decline rather than one that had already begun in the reign of Hadrian, when a high proportion of the coins in circulation would still have been of the Flavian period.

6

The Hinterland of Londinium

The Roman roads

Londinium was a tiny part of what is now London, for the Roman city itself was even smaller than the famous square mile of the City of London that now occupies its site. The present City, with its minute residential population of 7000 and its enormous army of day-time workers, is almost identical in its limits with the mediaeval city, which had grown beyond the Roman walls. The shape of the Roman city and the position of some of its streets have, however, survived in the modern topography of the City. Striking examples of this are Newgate Street and the northern part of Wood Street, whose positions were fixed by the Roman and subsequently mediaeval gates of Newgate and Cripplegate. Similarly, there must have been a Roman street on Ludgate Hill leading to Ludgate, a major thoroughfare that was diverted when St Paul's was founded in the early seventh century; and another at Aldgate that linked the road to Colchester with the Roman street grid. The situation at Aldersgate and Bishopsgate is more obscure; there clearly were Roman streets passing through them both where Aldersgate Street and Bishopsgate now lie, but we do not know how closely they follow the modern street-line. With the exception of Cripplegate, which was merely the north gate of the Roman fort, all these gates led to major Roman roads which have affected the shape and development of London beyond the walls. Parts of these roads have survived as modern highways, though in many other places the present roads have departed from their original Roman alignments for reasons that are quite unknown. In some areas where there was intensive building from an early date, as in north Southwark, this was probably due to encroachments by property-owners on the line of the road, resulting in gradual diversions which eventually established a new alignment. In areas that were rural until recent times, it must be assumed that whole stretches of the ancient roads were lost to view in the Dark Ages, while other stretches of the same roads remained visible and in use. Most attempts to identify the lines of Roman roads have necessarily been based on surviving topographical features, in the knowledge both that these highways were normally constructed in straight alignments and that one of them must have

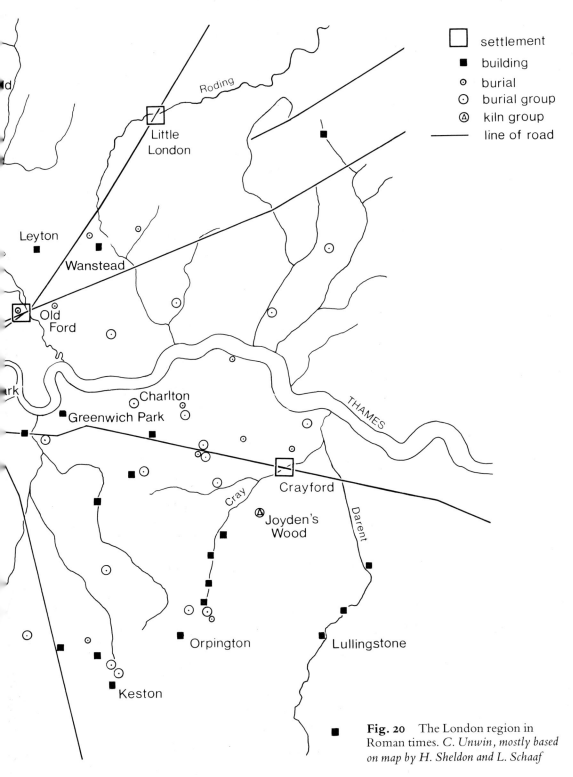

Fig. 20 The London region in Roman times. *C. Unwin, mostly based on map by H. Sheldon and L. Schaaf*

passed through the area in question. In a built-up area like Greater London this can only give us an approximation of the truth, unless it can be confirmed by archaeological observation. In theory, the confirmation of the alignment of a linear feature that has departed from the existing road should present no problem if opportunity for excavation occurs. In practice, however, this has proved to be one of the least rewarding of all archaeological tasks, partly because outside the long-occupied areas of the City and north Southwark Roman roads in Greater London are not far below the surface, and are therefore likely to have been destroyed without trace, and partly because the discovery of remnants of a featureless gravel deposit in a region where gravel abounds may prove little or nothing. Only a succession of such finds may establish a road alignment beyond doubt, and this is likely to be achieved only in an area that is being subjected to intensive archaeological study.

Not surprisingly our most definite knowledge of Roman roads in London comes from north Southwark, where more archaeological work has been done than in any part of London outside the City. Here, as already discussed (pp28–31, fig 2) there is evidence for a road of early date linking London Bridge with the Westminster crossing—a road that has left neither modern descendant nor evidence of its existence in the later topography. Moreover, the Southwark archaeologists have traced the precise course of the road leading from the junction of Watling Street and Stane Street in the neighbourhood of St George's Church to the bridge. It underlies Borough High Street itself only in two fairly short stretches, but crosses diagonally from the east side of the High Street at 201–211 to the west side at 106–114, swinging in a curve to underlie the High Street again at its junction with Southwark Street. It now continued in a straight line to its junction with the other road near the bridge, but a divergence to the east by the High Street has caused it to underlie the frontage on the west side of the modern street again opposite St Thomas Street.[1] A similar relationship between a Roman road and its modern descendant may be expected elsewhere. With this proviso we can identify with fair confidence many stretches of highway in Greater London with the roads laid out by the Romans.

Watling Street itself, leading from the Channel ports in Kent to the Thames crossing, and probably the first road to be constructed, is lost in obscurity in its final approaches through inner London to its junction with Stane Street at St George's Church. The final stretch in the neighbourhood of Great Dover Street is in fact not the original alignment at all, but a diversion to the north consequent upon the building of London Bridge about 50. Originally it must have continued further south at or near the Elephant and Castle in a direct approach to the original Lambeth–Westminster crossing between Westminster Bridge and Lambeth Bridge. This is a case where neither modern street-lines nor straight lines drawn on maps will give us even an approximation to the truth, which can only emerge, painfully and slowly, from a long series of archaeological observations. It is clear that the whole area south of the great curve of the Thames at Deptford was marshy and intersected by creeks. The mouth of the Ravensbourne river in particular presented a major obstacle and made necessary a wide detour to the south in the approach to the Thames crossing. How closely this is followed by the modern roads which make a similar detour we can only guess. Further east, however, from Shooter's Hill through Welling and Bexleyheath to Crayford and beyond, the long straight stretch of the modern highway undoubtedly follows the line of the Roman road that was laid out by the surveyors of Aulus Plautius in the first years of the occupation.

Watling Street north of the Thames must be of the same early origin, for it is aligned on the Westminster crossing as the northern continuation of the same road, disregarding Londinium and its bridge because they did not yet exist. The Roman road is closely followed by the modern Edgware Road, Maida Vale and the subsequent straight run of the A5 to Brockley Hill. Here the ancient road, still followed by the A5, swung from a north-westerly to a north-easterly direction, before resuming its north-westerly course to Verulamium. Attempts to find archaeological evidence for a continuation of Roman Watling Street south of Marble Arch via Park Lane to the Westminster crossing have so far failed. On the other side of the river there has been little more success in proving that the two Watling Streets met at the Westminster crossing. Various gravel surfaces have been found in this part of north Lambeth, and there are also comments by early antiquaries about the existence of a Roman road in the area west of Stane Street. Unfortunately these scraps of evidence are not only unsatisfactory individually, but also tend to be contradictory. I discussed this problem in some detail in 1969,[2] but was unable to arrive at a satisfactory conclusion. What is new since then is the proven existence of a Roman road heading from London Bridge in the direction of the Westminster crossing, which can no longer be considered merely hypothetical. The alignment of Watling Street north of the river therefore makes no sense unless at an early date it continued to the crossing and linked there with Watling Street south of the river. A significant circumstance, which may explain the unsatisfactory evidence for the link, is that this was at a very early date indeed, before the existence of London Bridge and Londinium. In an area where gravels abound and are not only used for road metalling but are artificially laid down for other reasons as well—to make floors and yard surfaces or merely to level the ground—a small section of a road may be distinguishable only if it continued in use long enough to be re-metalled a number of times, so that it presents a layered appearance with one surface above another, as was the case with the road from London Bridge in the direction of the Westminster crossing (**10**). This indicates that the road, and by implication the Westminster crossing itself, continued in use for at least a period of years after the building of London Bridge about 50. As soon as the bridge was built, however, it drew all the main routes to itself, and traffic from Verulamium to Richborough would now have passed through Londinium. The linking roads in the West End and north Lambeth therefore could have passed out of use after a very short existence, perhaps leaving behind a layer of gravel metalling only a few inches thick, which we shall be lucky to find and recognise in an area where there has been so much subsequent disturbance. Our best hope lies in places where the road crossed marshy ground and had to be supported on foundations of timber rafts underpinned by vertical posts, as was the case with the road in Borough High Street. Similar structures may yet be found in long-neglected Westminster, where they would almost certainly be needed in the marshes bordering Thorney Island.

It might be expected that Stane Street, the road to Chichester, would be of later origin than Watling Street, and its northern stretch from Ewell is aligned directly on London Bridge, and therefore is unlikely to be earlier than 50. It is this stretch that has always aroused admiration because of its exact alignment on the east gate of Chichester, and it therefore presumably marks the beginning of the lay-out of the road, which for impelling topographical reasons actually followed a course well to the east of this alignment south of Ewell.[3] The true Chichester alignment is followed by the modern highway along Kennington Park Road and most of Clapham Road. Between this stretch and London Bridge, however, the modern road makes a detour to the west along the significantly named Newington Causeway. There is little doubt that it follows the course of the Roman road, which would have curved to the west to avoid boggy ground at the western end of New Kent Road. The Roman origin of Newington Causeway is supported by observations of gravel metalling beneath the modern roadway at the Elephant and Castle and 300 yards (275m) further north.[4] It would have met Watling Street somewhere just south of St George's Church, almost opposite Borough Station, and from this point the two roads continued as one, curving west of the straight alignment to London Bridge to make the fullest use of the higher sandy levels of the three eyots. The existence of a channel east of the road in this area may explain why a more direct approach was impracticable.[5]

Two lesser roads from Londinium to the south coast branched from Stane Street and Watling Street respectively, and have been diligently traced through the Weald by I. D. Margary.[6] They are manifestly later than the primary roads from which they depart and were presumably constructed mainly on account of the Wealden iron industry, though some corn supplies may have come to Londinium from the South Downs. One left Stane Street for the Brighton area probably at Kennington Park, approximately on the line of Brixton Road, Brixton Hill, Streatham High Road and London Road, though the modern roads have in places wandered from the Roman alignment. The other left Watling Street just east of Asylum Road, Peckham, and passed through Nunhead, Brockley Rise, Beckenham and West Wickham, with its destination the Lewes area of Sussex. It has not left a legacy of major highways, and for that reason has been more easily traced by archaeological and topographical methods.

North of the Thames the most important exit from Londinium was to the west by way of Newgate Street, for this gave access to two major Roman highways, both of which were probably in existence before the building of London Bridge gave birth to Londinium—Watling Street North, the road to Verulamium and the north-west, and the road to Silchester and the west. This is the only road that led directly and permanently from the main east–west street of the Roman city.

The immediate route where it left Newgate is uncertain, for the Fleet with its valley had to be negotiated, and we do not know the position of the Roman bridge. Since cremation burials have been found under Holborn Viaduct on both sides of Farringdon Street, however, it seems likely that it was very near the site of the Viaduct. Further west there is no doubt that it continued on or near the line of New Oxford Street, though the latter is a modern road that is not the direct descendant of the Roman highway. Here also the position is approximately indicated by evidence for burials—the fragmentary inscription from the tomb of G. Pomponius Valens from Barter Street, north of the modern road, and a lead cist with coins of Vespasian from the north end of Endell Street to the south of it. Further west it continued on the line of Oxford Street to meet Watling Street at Marble Arch. There is evidence suggesting that it did not always coincide exactly with the modern road and that its precise position was not immutable. During excavations at Marble Arch in 1961–2, Francis Celoria and John Ashdown observed traces of a cambered gravel surface 20ft (6m) south of the southern kerb-line of Oxford Street, at a depth of about five feet, running parallel with the modern road for nearly 200ft (60m). This, however, was only a few inches in thickness and overlay pottery sherds of the late second century or later, so that it must represent the position of the Silchester road for a comparatively short period only. The alternative possibility is that this was merely the forecourt of an inn, built to the south of the road near its junction with Watling Street.

The Silchester road continued to the west approximately on the line of Bayswater Road to Notting Hill, where there was a change of alignment to take the most direct route to Staines by skirting the northern curve of the Thames at Brentford. Its course is closely followed by Holland Park Avenue, the northern part of Goldhawk Road, Stamford Brook Street and Bath Road. West of this point the line is lost through railway development, but it is picked up again by the modern highway in Kew Bridge Road, Brentford High Street and London Road. Here also the modern road gives only an approximation of the Roman line. The gravel road surface of the Roman road was found overlying a cambered foundation of brick-earth, with its drainage ditch on the south side, to the rear of 230–232 Brentford High Street in 1974, and again behind 240–246 in 1978, all well to the north of the present road. In the third century there seems to have been a shift to the south, nearer the modern road, for features of that date were found cutting through the earlier road surface.[7]

An alternative route to the west must have left Londinium at Ludgate and crossed the Fleet where Ludgate Circus now is, continuing via Fleet Street and the Strand, which is called Akeman Street in a charter of about 1000,[8] and must surely be on the line of a Roman road. The name means Bath Road, indicating that in Anglo-Saxon times it was regarded as a major highway to the west. In Fleet Street the road must lie to the north of the stone building with the tessellated floor found beneath the eastern end of St Bride's Church,[9] and south of the group of cremation burials found at the bottom of Shoe Lane.[10] It is probable that what Stow described as a 'pavement of hard stone' supported on timber piles, which he saw 4ft (1.2m) below the sixteenth-century surface, on the north side of Fleet Street between Chancery Lane and St Dunstan's Church, was the Roman road.[11] Further west, this may have continued in a series of short alignments on or near the line of Kensington Road, Kensington High Street, Hammersmith Road, King Street and Chiswick High Road, where it would have joined the main Silchester road.[12] It seems likely that this alternative road developed from local trackways at a somewhat later date than the main road to the west.

Within the Roman city the link between Ermine Street, the road to the north, and the street-plan is uncertain. The new north–south street that was laid out on the east side of the great forum, when the centre of the city was replanned in the late first century, would have met it directly at Bishopsgate, if it continued in a straight line north of the basilica, and could then have provided a direct route to the riverside along the line of the present Philpot Lane and Botolph Lane. Patterned mosaic floors that must have belonged to substantial Roman houses of a later date, however, were found on or very near this projected line in St Helen's Place and Crosby Square.[13] Since their exact position was not recorded, they do not rule out the possibility that the street continued to Bishopsgate, but if it did the mosaics must have been immediately adjacent to it, presumably in the front rooms of houses that faced upon it. Unfortunately, the mosaic floors on the west side of Bishopsgate Street also can only be approximately plotted, but the drawing of one found in Old Broad Street in 1854, and published by Roach Smith, shows quite clearly that the Roman floor was on the same alignment as the old Excise Office, which was aligned on Bishopsgate Street.[14] There seems no reason why a late Roman house should have been built on this alignment unless Ermine Street continued on the same course within the city, presumably to meet an east–west street immediately north of the basilica. Indeed, before the replanning of the centre of Londinium it must have done so, in order to meet an earlier east–west street further south. At no time after Boudica can it have had a direct line of approach to the bridge, as it did in the Middle Ages and later by way of Gracechurch Street, for important buildings in the centre of Londinium always blocked its way. Since the convenience of such a thoroughfare would not readily have been abandoned, it seems likely that Ermine Street was not laid out until after the initial planning of Londinium, which probably established the area where Gracechurch Street now runs as a central market-place from the beginning.

Ermine Street, to which access was subsequently given by Bishopsgate, is clearly followed by the line of modern Bishopsgate Street, for Roman walls, probably of a mausoleum, have been found parallel with the modern street on its eastern side, nearly 500 yards (457m) beyond the city gate,[15] and further south Roman burials have been found on both sides of the modern street. The curved line of Shoreditch High Street may wander from it, but further north the long straight line of Kingsland Road and High Street, Stoke Newington Road and High Street, and Stamford Hill probably follows it closely. In Edmonton, however, Fore Street probably curves to the east of it, and the precise course of

Ermine Street through Edmonton and Enfield is obscure, while attempts to locate it conclusively by excavation have so far been unsuccessful.

The road to Camulodunum (Colchester), which was later accommodated by Aldgate, like Ermine Street presents problems in its relationship with the Roman street-plan. This must surely have been a primary road, constructed soon after the Thames bridge was built, to link it with what was then the capital and by far the most important centre in Britain. It might be expected that it would have led directly, if not from the bridge-head itself, at least from the main east–west street of Londinium, as did the road to Silchester, a place of much less importance. Yet a diagonal road continuing the line of the Colchester road from Aldgate to the main east–west street cannot be reconciled with the records of Roman buildings in Fenchurch Street, and it must be assumed that it had a much shorter run into the city to link with the street grid at a more northerly point. This would indicate fairly conclusively that the Aldgate road was not the primary road to Colchester, as has been suspected for other reasons (see pp38–9). On this hypothesis the original road would have left the main street further south, perhaps in the neighbourhood of Hart Street, and would have passed through the eastern cemetery more centrally near Haydon Street and Alie Street. So far no archaeological evidence has been found to substantiate the existence of this hypothetical earlier road, and there is no obvious reason for its abandonment in favour of a more northerly alignment.

Beyond Aldgate traces of gravel metalling have been found on natural clay 10ft (3m) below the present street level in Aldgate High Street, which presumably follows its line.[16] Its course eastward of Whitechapel High Street is quite unknown, however, until the approach to the Lea crossing at Old Ford is reached. Here it was located by Harvey Sheldon in excavations at Lefevre Road and Appian Road, immediately north of Roman Road, with its surviving surface less than 2ft (0.6m) below the modern ground level. There was evidence of an early date, probably soon after the conquest, when it was constructed as a three-lane highway with a raised central lane, in total about 65ft (20m) wide. Later the southern lane was raised several times and the width of the road was reduced to about 32ft (10m). Coin and pottery evidence indicated that it must have continued in use at least until the late fourth century.[17] The alignment was in the direction of Aldgate and the City, crossing and diverging from the line of the modern road called Roman Road. To the north-east it would have met the river Lea between Iceland Wharf and Bundock's Wharf, at a point where pieces of Roman herringbone-patterned tiling, believed to have been part of the ford, have been dredged from the river.[18] Further east the line of the road seems to be followed in part by the modern Romford Road, where an ancient gravel road with side-ditches was observed in an excavation beneath the modern road in front of the Passmore Edwards Museum.[19] It seems likely that the modern highway approximately follows the Roman line to the crossing of the river Roding at Ilford.

If London Bridge and Londinium did not exist before about 50, the road found

heading for them west of the Lea crossing cannot be earlier. Yet it is inconceivable
that there was no road from Camulodunum to Silchester and the west, with access
to the regular Thames crossing, before that date. There is in fact a probable route
to the west of Old Ford that by-passes Londinium, perhaps following pre-Roman
tracks. This is followed by Roman Road and further west Old Street, both
significantly named, and in Old Street ancient road surfaces with stratified Roman
coins were found in a sewer excavation of 1867.[20] It would presumably have met
the Silchester road at Bloomsbury Way, but the intervening connections are
uncertain.

   Nevertheless, the main Roman road recently studied at Old Ford was clearly
aligned on the city, and the northern by-pass could only have joined it further
west. The by-pass may therefore have been merely a secondary road of later date.
An alternative Roman road from Colchester to the west that would presumably
have crossed the Lea at a more northerly ford has been noted in Essex north-west
of Ingatestone, where a gravel road surface was found near College Wood, but its
course further west is quite unknown.[21] There is, however some evidence for the
existence of the northern ford in Hackney Marsh, where an ancient gravel road
was found apparently heading for it. The road ran in a north-easterly direction,
and would have reached the Lea where it curves alongside the railway sidings.[22]
Further east, a well-attested Roman road from Great Dunmow to London headed
for an unknown ford over the Roding somewhere between Chigwell and
Wanstead. These northern fords, nearly two miles (3.2km) north of the road from
Camulodunum to Londinium, may originally have been established as the
crossing-places of the earlier road from Camulodunum to the west, but continued
in use to accommodate lesser roads when this was supplanted.

Roadside villages

The neighbours of Londinium were the nearest posting-stations of the road
network, which were an essential part of the official organisation of
communications. Here fresh horses were available for the imperial post, and inns
that provided refreshment and services for other travellers normally developed in
the same places. In the case of early military roads they were often originally
fortlets under army control, but usually soon lost their military character. Such
centres tended also to provide markets for local produce and sometimes attracted
a resident population sufficient for them to be defined by archaeologists as 'small
towns', though in ordinary terminology they would be described as villages. The
distance between posting-stations was normally 11–13 miles (17–21km), but their
precise position was often determined by geographical considerations or
historical circumstances, in particular early military occupation of a populous area
or strategic site. A range between 8 and 18 miles (13–29km) seems to have been
acceptable. On the roads from Londinium are several known centres of Romano-
British occupation that almost certainly originated as posting-stations, but no
doubt took on other functions as well. Ewell on Stane Street, 12 miles (19.3km)
from Londinium, was one of these. Here buildings and occupation deposits have

been found extending on both sides of the road for nearly $\frac{3}{4}$ mile (1.2km), and there is no doubt that a substantial population had been attracted to the site, a place where the road left the London Clay and reached the natural springs on the northern side of the chalk Downs. On Watling Street south of the Thames, the corresponding posting-station with accompanying occupation was almost certainly at Crayford, $13\frac{1}{2}$ miles (21.5km) from Londinium, where Roman buildings were found in the nineteenth century. On Watling Street north of the Thames, the posting-station mid-way to Verulamium was on Brockley Hill, 13 miles (21km) from the Roman city, and here the presence of suitable clays led to the development of an industrial centre for pottery production which dominated all other activities. On Ermine Street, the main road to the north, the first posting-station was presumably at Enfield, where evidence of considerable occupation, from the first to the fourth centuries, has been found $9\frac{1}{2}$ miles (15km) from Londinium.[23] Even on minor roads staging facilities of some kind were probably provided at similar intervals, and in favourable circumstances these could attract considerable roadside settlement, as for example at Little London (Chigwell), on the road to Great Dunmow and 12 miles (19.5km) from Londinium. A small roadside settlement 10 miles (16km) from London Bridge on the minor road to Lewes[24] was probably also a staging post for travellers. Such minor roadside stations were probably never or seldom used by the official post and cannot therefore be described as posting-stations; nevertheless it seems likely that they originated from official initiative like the roads themselves.

The posting-stations on the main east–west roads through Londinium raise interesting problems. One was undoubtedly at Staines, where the road to Silchester crossed the Thames near the mouth of the Colne. Here there is undoubted evidence of an early military presence, provided by the cheek-piece of a cavalry helmet of about the mid-first century, and an early ditch of military type with a square-cut gully at the bottom lay to the south of the roadside ditch. There was also an early civilian settlement, which was destroyed in 60 and subsequently rebuilt. Early fine pottery, notably lead-glazed ware, seems to have been made locally. The site was clearly determined by its strategic importance, and occupation here may well antedate London Bridge and Londinium, though not of course the Westminster crossing and whatever military occupation protected it. Staines is just over 18 miles (30km) from Londinium, an extreme range for the first posting-station, though it would have been more conveniently placed for the hypothetical station in west London, which would have been at least two miles nearer. If Watling Street, north and south, and a Silchester–Colchester road really antedate Londinium and London Bridge, an early posting-station at their junction becomes a logical necessity, but it has as yet no support from archaeological evidence. This problem is complicated by the possibility, even probability, that an earlier Silchester road did not intersect Watling Street at Marble Arch. After the establishment of Londinium, of course, any west London posting-station became redundant, but the importance of the traffic between Londinium and Silchester demanded an intermediate station half-way to Staines, and it was presumably this that caused the development of another roadside village at Brentford, 9¼ miles (15km) from both Londinium and Staines. It was conveniently placed near the ford over the Brent and near the point where the Silchester road approaches the Thames most closely; it was also a convenient centre for an area where there had been agricultural activity and a farming population from pre-Roman times, and all these factors no doubt contributed to its success in developing; but there can be little doubt that its initial establishment was due entirely to the Roman need for a half-way house on the long stretch of road between Londinium and Staines.

The road from Londinium to Chelmsford and Essex through Aldgate provides a greater problem, for here there is no evidence for any roadside occupation that is likely to mark the position of the first posting-stage out of Londinium. It ought to be at Romford, 12 miles (19.5km) from Aldgate, but no trace of Roman occupation has been found there. There is an unpublished record of a Roman building near the road at Ilford.[25] This, however, is barely 7 miles (11.25km) from Aldgate, probably too short a distance for a posting-station. The only site of substantial occupation known on this road between Chelmsford (*Caesaromagus*) and Londinium is in fact at Old Ford on the Lea crossing, less than 3 miles (4.8km) from Aldgate. Whatever the reason for this development, which seems to be mainly of late Roman date, it can have had little to do with catering for the needs of long-distance travellers, much less the official messengers who were the government's first concern in establishing staging-posts. A possible answer to the problem may be that the direct road from Londinium to Caesaromagus and Camulodunum was not used by the imperial post and posting-stations were therefore not set up on it, though this is surprising, particularly in the early period when Camulodunum was still the capital and Londinium was only gradually taking over its functions. If alternative routes were preferred for this purpose it is hard to see why the direct road to Aldgate was built at all.

We have documentary evidence for a number of the routes to London with their posting-stations in the Antonine Itinerary, an official road-book probably compiled in the early third century, which has come down to us in copies ranging in date from the seventh to the twelfth centuries. It gives the names of places on various routes in the empire and the distances between them in Roman miles. Seven of these routes begin or end at Londinium, and an eighth passes through it. From these we know that the first posting-station on Watling Street in Kent, believed to be at Crayford, was called *Noviomagus*, 'new place' or 'new market'; the first on Watling Street north, located on Brockley Hill, was called *Sulloniacis*; and the one between Londinium and Silchester, obviously at Staines, had the appropriate name *Pontibus*, 'at the bridges'. Rivet suggests that this and other plural forms for a single river-crossing meant that there were a series of stages or spans of the bridge.[26] The possibility of a second bridge over the Colne might however be borne in mind, though this would pre-suppose a branch road on the north side of the Thames, for which we have no evidence. There is also in the Antonine Itinerary a mysterious *Durolitum*, probably meaning 'fort at the ford', on the route between Chelmsford and London. This ought to be the missing posting-station on the road to Camulodunum, and the distance given would place it at Gidea Park on the eastern fringes of Romford, more than a mile from the river Rom and any possible ford. Moreover here, as nearer the stream in Romford, evidence for Roman occupation is lacking. Warwick Rodwell has suggested that *Iter IX*, the route in the Itinerary from which the name is taken, did not follow the direct road from Chelmsford to London, and that the ford in question was in the Roding valley, either near Passingford Bridge, which fits the distances better but where little is known of the local archaeology, or further to the south-east in Chigwell (Little London) where we know there was extensive Roman occupation and almost certainly a staging-post on the minor road to Great Dunmow.[27] Unfortunately we have as yet no evidence that either site had a direct link with Chelmsford. If, however, Chigwell was at the junction of two roads, it would explain the extensive development of Roman settlement there.

The town zone of Londinium

As might have been expected in a document containing lists and figures that have been re-copied many times, the Antonine Itinerary contains many errors and discrepancies, that provide endless material for argument to scholars who attempt to relate these terse lists to modern maps and known archaeological facts. When, however, there appears to be a *consistent* error it may not be a mistake at all, but may simply require re-interpretation. On this basis Rodwell has put forward an ingenious and attractive theory which, if correct, defines the limits of a town zone of Londinium fairly closely in several directions.[28] This was presumably land that came under the city's direct control and jurisdiction, containing its cemeteries and land allocated to its citizens for industrial and other purposes, probably including market-gardening. In the Antonine Itinerary there is almost consistently a short-fall in the distances given between towns, indicating that measurements were taken, not from town-centre to town-centre, but from their outer perimeters. Rodwell has demonstrated that the short-fall increases with the importance of the town. In the case of minor towns the point taken for measurement was at least $\frac{1}{4}$ mile (0.4km) beyond the settlement area, so that it also lay beyond the cemeteries and peripheral buildings. In the case of civitas-capitals the average distance beyond the city gates from which measurement was taken varied greatly, but averaged $1\frac{1}{2}$ miles (2.4km). In the case of the coloniae at Colchester and York the short-falls ranged from just over $\frac{1}{2}$ mile to just over 2 miles (0.8–3.2km), with an average of just under $1\frac{1}{2}$ miles (about 2.1km). The situation for the coloniae at Lincoln and Gloucester is more obscure, but there are indications of a short-fall at Lincoln of $1\frac{3}{4}$ miles (2.8km) and one of $3\frac{1}{2}$ miles (5.6km) to be divided between the colonia of Glevum (Gloucester) and the large civitas capital of Corinium. For London the short-falls are significantly greater, averaging $2\frac{1}{2}$ miles (4km).[29] As Rodwell points out, this implies a town zone for Londinium larger than that of any other city in Roman Britain, including the four coloniae, and no doubt reflects its status as capital of the province, which at the beginning of the third

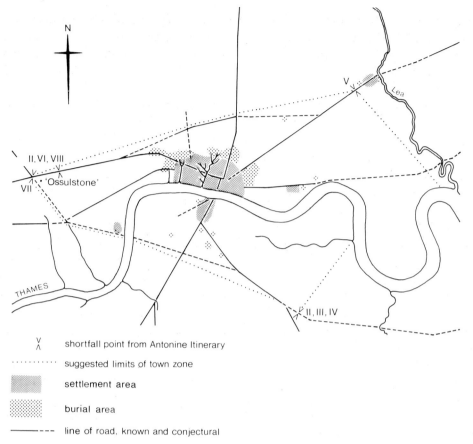

Fig. 21   Possible town zone of Londinium, based on shortfall points from the Antonine
Itinerary, as suggested by Warwick Rodwell. *After W. J. Rodwell*

century was still undivided. It must also imply that the civic status of Londinium,
as would be expected for other reasons, cannot have been less than that of a
colonia.

Rodwell makes an interesting attempt to define the limits of London's
town zone, suggesting that in the north the boundary was the early road from
Colchester to Silchester that is believed to underlie Old Street and may follow a
pre-Roman track. Further west this route is continued by the main Silchester road
along Oxford Street, and this would presumably have marked the northern
boundary to its western limit, which is indicated by the shortfall on Iter VII of the
itinerary as being in the neighbourhood of Marble Arch—a likely point, since it
was here that the road to Verulamium departed from the Silchester road, and it is
the junction of the hypothetical early roads from Kent to Verulamium via the
Westminster crossing, and from Camulodunum to Calleva (Silchester). Near this
point also once stood the mysterious 'Ossulstone', which later gave its name to the
Hundred containing London. It may have been a Roman milestone, for the outer
limit of the city's and would be a likely place to set one up, especially at a road

junction. On the other hand, the short-fall of Itinera II, VI and VIII lies more than $\frac{1}{2}$ mile (800m) further east, just east of the Tyburn stream, which might equally well have provided a landmark and natural boundary. It is unfortunate that we have no data from the Itinerary for Stane Street, which could have confirmed the position of the boundary of the town zone on the south side of the Thames. This should, however, enclose the Roman burials south of Great Dover Street, if these formed part of an extra-mural cemetery of Londinium. On Watling Street further east we have a short-fall point from Itinera II, III and IV, just east of the junction of Watling Street and the road from Lewes, which met at the crossing of the stream of the Peck. This would have provided a natural boundary some $2\frac{1}{2}$ miles (4km) from London Bridge, and seems likely enough for the eastern limit of the town zone.

North of the Thames the eastern boundary should be marked by the shortfall of Iter V, a point which lies just on the City side of the settlement of Old Ford, more than $2\frac{1}{2}$ miles (4km) from Aldgate and about $\frac{1}{2}$ mile (0.8km) short of the ford. This would suggest that the settlement lay outside the jurisdiction of Londinium and that the boundary of the town zone was well to the west of the natural barrier of the Lea; it would indicate that burials found there did not form part of an outlying cemetery of Londinium, but were the remains of the local population. Most of these burials, however, were late inhumations, and in the area investigated west of the ford the settlement seems to have been of little importance until the late third century. The boundary indicated by the Antonine Itinerary is of earlier date, and it is conceivable that it was later advanced to the river bank. Indeed, the Lea is such an obvious natural boundary that there must have been good administrative reasons for setting the territorial limit of Londinium a little way back from it. These were presumably connected with the control of the ford itself and possibly the use of the Lea for river-traffic. Changes of circumstances or the administrative changes of the early fourth century may have made these reasons no longer valid, so that the boundary could be advanced the short distance to its natural limit. There are reasons to believe that the late roadside village had close links with Londinium. One of its functions was presumably to minister to the needs of travellers, and the activities of a local smith probably served this market. A striking feature of the excavation, however, was the great quantity of cattle bones found, probably representing at least 150 individuals, with many showing unmistakable evidence of butchering.[30] Roman Britons were not great meat-eaters and it is unlikely that all this beef was required for local consumption by the small village community. It is possible, therefore, that Old Ford served as the Smithfield Market of fourth-century Londinium, a place where cattle were collected from the Essex farms and sold either on the hoof or as butcher's meat. The great quantity of lost coins of the fourth century found in excavations also suggests marketing activity. This may seem a long way from the city for an abbatoir, if not for a cattle market, but Sheldon has drawn attention to an anti-plague edict of Edward III 'that no animals be slaughtered nearer to the city eastward than Stratford'.[31]

The town zone of Londinium, if Warwick Rodwell's theory is correct, was an irregular wedge-shape, wide to the east on both sides of the Thames, and narrowing to a point in the west. Lack of symmetry in the allocation of land to towns in Roman Britain seems to have been the rule rather than the exception, as far as can be judged from the limited evidence, but even so Londinium is an extreme case. The shape was largely determined by pre-Roman lines of communication which had been replaced by Roman roads before the city came into existence. In a sense, however, it also reflects geographical reality, for the natural hinterland of London is to the east in Kent and Essex, and it is significant that these two kingdoms of the Saxon Heptarchy were most involved with the resuscitation of the city in the seventh century. Ptolemy, the geographer, describes Londinium as a city of the Cantii (Cantiaci) of Kent, an attribution that can have had no political or administrative meaning when he wrote in the second century, or even earlier, for Londinium was never a *civitas*-capital under the Romans and had not existed in pre-Roman Britain. The two other 'cities' he mentions in the same sentence as belonging to the Cantii, however, are *Rutupiae* (Richborough) and *Durovernum* (Canterbury), and it is likely that he had in mind the traditional route into Britain through Kent, a route that must have been taken by many Cantiaci before and after the birth of Londinium, as Trinovantes took the corresponding route to the west on the north side of the Thames. After the building of London Bridge both led to Londinium, and a very considerable part of the native element in the city must have originated in these two tribes, and no doubt still had family and trading connections with them. In the case of the Trinovantes these tribal links were probably broken by the Boudican revolt and its aftermath, and it may have taken a long time to re-establish them. The Kentish influence may therefore have predominated in the latter part of the first and early second centuries.

The limits proposed by Rodwell have the merit of containing all the major burial areas, north and south of the Thames, that are sufficiently near to Londinium to have been used by its population. This is as it should be, for cemeteries would have been under the control of the city, and were in fact one of the principal reasons why a town zone was needed. Within the suggested boundary indications of residential occupation outside the city itself are sparse, with the notable exception of Southwark, where a suburb, that in part at least was industrial, developed at an early date around the southern end of London Bridge and along the roads that led from it. The acceptance of the idea that the town zone of Londinium extended south of the Thames would finally settle the question of the status of Roman Southwark. If it lies within the town's outer boundary it can only have been part of Londinium and must have been under the direct control of its magistrates and senate (*ordo*). If would presumably have formed a distinct

26   Pottery wine-flagon, 50–75, with incised graffito, 'LONDINI AD FANVM ISIDIS', '*At London, to* (*at* or *by*) *the Temple of Isis*', found in Tooley Street, Southwark. Height 10in (25.5cm). *Museum of London*

ward, one of several in the city, called a *vicus*, not to be confused with the independent small towns that had the same title. The wards must have had a definite role in local government, but as constituent parts of a larger body. If Southwark was simply part of Londinium, it would explain the graffito on the famous 'Isis' flagon (**26**), reconciling the address '*Londini*', '*at* Londinium' with the possible location of an early temple of Isis in Southwark where the flagon was found.

Within the hypothetical town zone, apart from the major suburb in Southwark and the late Roman village at Old Ford on the border, there is, as might be expected, evidence of occupation at Westminster, just north of the old river-crossing. Roman building material found in the precincts of Westminster Abbey and what are said to have been the remains of a hypocaust pila actually under the nave of the Abbey church testify to the presence of a substantial Roman house, but there are no indications of its date or purpose.[32] Its position near the Westminster crossing may, however, be significant. It is conceivable either that occupation established before the building of London Bridge continued into much later Roman times, or that the Westminster crossing itself continued in use for some purposes with which the occupants were concerned. The limestone sarcophagus of one Valerius Amandinus inscribed to his memory by his sons,[33] found on the north side of the church, and the funerary sculpture of a child, found when building the Science Block of Westminster School, suggests that a well-to-do family was in residence and was burying its dead locally in some style at quite a late date. Since the sarcophagus was apparently re-used for burial in the Middle Ages, however, there is a possibility that it was brought from elsewhere.

More doubtful traces of a Roman structure are said to have been found when the present church of St Martin-in-the-Fields was built in 1722. There is said to have been an arch in Roman brick with a cement floor, and with several ducts side by side along its wall. If this was in fact Roman, it is likely to have been part of a heating system, and would suggest the presence of a comfortable house. Here also a burial was found, with a glass vessel in a stone coffin.[34]

The 'Roman bath' in Strand Lane, south of the Strand, is unlikely to be of Roman date, though there is a superficial resemblance to Roman brickwork due to the thickness of the bricks, which is about the same as that of Roman building-tiles ($1\frac{3}{4}$in; 4.4cm). They are, however, only 5in (12.7cm) wide, the width of bricks made in the last five hundred years for a different technique of one-handed brick-laying. Since the bath is on the site of a seventeenth-century building in the grounds of Arundel House, it is safer to attribute it to a whim of Thomas Howard, second Earl of Arundel and Surrey, the first great collector of classical antiquities in this country, who may have required a 'Roman bath' or *nymphaeum* as a suitable setting for some of his antique sculptures, and accordingly commissioned these special bricks to give the effect of the Roman brickwork he had seen in Italy.

Further east a Roman stone building with a pavement of coarse red and yellow tesserae was found by W. F. Grimes beneath St Bride's Church in Fleet Street, where the apse and sanctuary of the eleventh-century church had been built above it.[35] North of this, on the main Silchester road, a piece of Roman mosaic with a geometric pattern in black, red and white was found in the seventeenth century near the church of St Andrew Holborn, which is itself the successor of a Saxon wooden church, called 'the old wooden church of St Andrew' in a Westminster charter of 959.[36] The Roman buildings in Fleet Street and Holborn have two things in common: both are in close proximity to a group of Roman burials and to a Saxon church. In both cases a group of cremation burials was found immediately north of the church, and in the excavation at St Bride's several very early inhumation burials were found orientated with heads to the west. Professor Grimes considered that these were probably Christian Saxon burials, although a late Roman date could not be ruled out.[37] There is therefore no proven continuity of the cemetery. Nevertheless the neighbouring cremation burials range from the first century to at least the end of the third and probably into the fourth century.[38] It seems certain, therefore, that this was a recognised cemetery area when the Roman building was constructed, so it is unlikely to have been a dwelling, and was more probably a mausoleum, which could have been Christian. If so, its survival into the late Saxon period, perhaps with recognisable Christian symbolism still visible upon it, may have been the reason for the establishment of a church on this spot.[39] It is conceivable that the human remains found buried deep in the sanctuary before the building of its apse came from this Roman family tomb.[40] It is tempting to interpret the mosaic near St Andrew Holborn in the same way, though here we have much less information than at St Bride's. Nevertheless there is the same combination of pagan cremation burials, Roman extra-mural building and early church within a very small area. Certainly in default of other evidence it would be very rash to assume that either building indicates some sort of suburban development on the west side of the Fleet. Isolated extra-mural stone buildings by the roadside west of Bishopsgate and south of Aldgate High Street may also be tombs rather than dwellings or shops.

An area within the town zone where some occupation may be indicated is on the riverside at Stepney. A minor road almost certainly left the city at or near the site of the mediaeval Postern Gate, though perhaps originally further south, and led on the line of the Highway (formerly Ratcliffe Highway) towards the point just south of Stepney (East) railway station where firm gravels skirt the Thames at its northern curve. A small scatter of Roman pottery found here, however, may indicate only daytime activity on the riverside, such as boat-building or marketing fish, served also by the road. A little further west in Shadwell there was a watch-tower and accompanying small military establishment just south of the roadway, from the late third century. Burials along this road are more likely to be those of residents in Londinium than of local inhabitants.

A second-century pottery flagon, recently found in Welbeck Street, is said to have come from a well, and may indicate occupation on the Silchester road near the Tyburn crossing, just within the suggested western boundary of the town zone.[41]

The city lands of Londinium, if Rodwell is right, consisted of some 8000 acres

(3000ha), and contained one major extra-mural suburb in Southwark, covering an area of perhaps 60 acres (24ha) with some straggling roadside development beyond. Except in Westminster there is very little other certain evidence of residential occupation outside the city. There are, however, numerous groups of burials near most of the roads, some at a little distance from the city of Londinium itself, with that at Old Ford, if it is to be included in the town zone, an extreme case at $2\frac{3}{4}$ miles (4.5km). In this case the cemetery probably served the late settlement there, and it is reasonable to assume that the groups of burials south of the Southwark suburb were mainly those of its inhabitants. Known cemeteries must have been kept inviolate, but a considerable tract of countryside remained and was almost certainly used by people who lived in the city and its southern suburb. A series of ditches found south-east of the occupied area of Southwark suggests that there was a division of this area into agricultural plots,[42] and a similar use might be expected elsewhere. The various hoes, mattocks, rake-teeth and ploughshares found with the many craft-tools in the Walbrook indicate that some at least of the inhabitants of Londinium were concerned with work on the land. Later analogies, classical references to similar practices on the outskirts of towns[43] and common-sense suggest that their principal concern was market-gardening for the production of perishable food which it would be difficult or uneconomic to transport long distances. A pruning saw in the Walbrook series indicates that orchards also were probably planted. It is probable that some of the apples, plums, cherries, damsons, mulberries, raspberries, blackberries, peas, lentils and cucumbers, the seeds of which were found in a second-century pit in St Thomas Street, were locally grown. Figs and grapes from the same context are more problematical, and olives must have been imported.[44]

Beyond the town zone

It is probable that market-gardening and agriculture based on Londinium extended far beyond the restricted territory that was under the direct administration of the city, in areas suitable for that purpose and easily reached for daily work by its inhabitants, including of course those from its southern suburb. Commuting from town to country is a common custom in small towns in modern Italy, and was probably also practised in Roman Britain. Areas a little further afield that were obviously being used for agricultural purposes and had a small resident population but apparently no major buildings of any consequence, as in Putney, may have been worked by local farm labourers on behalf of a landlord who lived in Londinium, though we can only guess at the form of land tenure. Within the town zone itself land would presumably have been held in some form of tenancy allocated by the city authorities.

There is a remarkable absence of evidence for farm-houses of the more elaborate type, that would justify the title of 'villa', within a good many miles of Londinium. These had substantial walls, heating systems, bath-houses, and in later Roman times often acquired mosaic floors. They have therefore a good chance of being noticed even in a builders' excavation, but nevertheless it is possible that some have been lost entirely without record in the development of Greater London. The known villas nearly all lie to the south and south-east at Beddington, Keston, Orpington, Foots Gray and Fordcroft, from $9\frac{1}{2}$ to $12\frac{1}{2}$ miles (15–20km) from London Bridge as the crow flies, but much further by road, for all are away from the main roads to Londinium.[45] Extending the range to 17 miles (27km) would include also the group of prosperous villas in the Darenth valley and two others in Surrey south of Ewell. Londinium was probably the main market for the produce of all of these, and their owners may also have had close links with its ruling class. This in fact may be the real Kentish connection underlying Ptolemy's attribution of Londinium to the Cantii. It is conceivable that some owners of these villas may have been members of the *ordo* (senate) of the city and may have held local office there. If, as is suspected, the villas developed from pre-Roman farms, and their original owners were of British origin, they would have provided a convenient native land-owning element for the Roman administration to recruit into the *ordo* of Londinium when its first municipal administration was established, to give it some semblance of a normal Romano-British town.

There is no evidence of a comparable development of villas on the north side of the Thames within a similar distance of London, though it is clear that land suitable for agricultural purposes—mostly on brick-earth and gravel—was occupied and farmed both in west London and Essex, and no doubt also provided food for the city. Rural homes away from the roads may have been of a humbler character, as a result of a different form of land tenure, though as Harvey Sheldon has pointed out, our views may be distorted through lack of evidence, if buildings were mainly of wood in an area where there was no suitable building stone, or if built of stone were later robbed for the same reason. Nevertheless, a prosperous Romanised farm-house might be expected to have tessellated floors, not necessarily patterned, and to be provided with a bath-house, of which some evidence should survive in the form of broken flue-tiles and tiles from hypocaust pilae, even if the stone of its walls was removed for re-use. A few discoveries of this kind might change the whole picture.

Villas throughout southern Essex are sparse, even allowing for the fact that a considerable part of the land is on clay, which would have been thickly wooded and not readily available for agriculture. There were, however, two substantial Roman buildings not far beyond the supposed town zone of the city, and very much nearer than any of the villas south of the river. Unfortunately we know little about either of them. One was in Leyton, just north-east of the northern ford over the Lea on Hackney Marsh, by which it must have been approached from Londinium, a distance of little more than $4\frac{1}{2}$ miles (c 7.5km) in a direct line, though somewhat further by road. The other was a little further away at about 6 miles (9.5km), in Wanstead Park, where a mosaic floor was found in the eighteenth century.[46] This building, or building complex, may have extended over a considerable area, for tesserae and other traces of building material were found in the 1960s some distance to the east near the lake. It is possible, however, that these were not in situ, but had been re-deposited during the landscaping of the park. The proximity of these buildings to the Roman city suggests that they might possibly have been the country residences of high officials based in the capital rather than normal villas, for it would not be surprising if the south-western territory of the Trinovantes had been taken over as an imperial estate following the events of 60–1. Further afield, at a distance of more than 13 miles (21km) in a direct line, there was a Roman building with a hypocaust at Abridge, but this was very near the road to Dunmow, just north of the roadside settlement at Little London, and may have been a *mansio* belonging to that settlement, though it may equally well have been a farm-house.[47] Still further from Londinium there was a villa-type building remote from the main roads north of Havering, and there were Roman buildings near the Thames where it approaches the estuary at Grays Thurrock, Chadwell St Mary and East Tilbury. The latter group may have been farms, which could have supplied Londinium with their produce by water, but may also have been concerned with the production of salt in the estuary.

On the western side of Londinium there are only two known buildings that could conceivably have been small villas, at Ruislip and Wembley.[48] These had walls of flint or stone and were on or near isolated stretches of gravel suitable for cultivation. They were also well supplied with water from neighbouring streams, the Pinn and the Brent respectively. No comparable buildings have yet been found further south on the more extensive gravels north and west of Brentford, which were undoubtedly being cultivated. There is ample evidence of occupation in the Roman period, and drainage ditches suggest that fields were under cultivation. The recent discovery of a late Roman corn-drying or malting kiln at Sipson, just north of Heathrow airport, indicates that grain was included in the local crops.

The country immediately north of Londinium was on London Clay and was probably still thickly wooded. It was no doubt a useful source of timber, and may also have been suitable for raising pigs, which could be fed on acorns. It also provided material and fuel for pottery-making. Reference has already been made to the pottery industry that developed on Brockley Hill, where light-coloured earthenware was made in Mediterranean forms introduced by the Romans, such as flagons and mortaria. A pottery industry of quite a different kind flourished nearer Londinium in Highgate Wood (**27**). This was based on the native 'Belgic' tradition and produced grey wares with a brownish surface in forms of British or Gaulish origin, mostly beakers, jars and bowls. Pottery-making seems to have begun there about 50 and continued intermittently for just over a hundred years, though always on a fairly small scale. There is nothing to suggest that the site was permanently occupied, and the industry may well have been seasonal, with

27 Roman pottery kiln of the early second century, with stoke-hole in foreground, oven behind, as excavated in Highgate Wood. *B Brandham*

itinerant potters camping only for a few weeks at a time. It has been estimated that the total amount of kiln debris and wasters found in Highgate Wood, extending over more than a century, could have resulted from about 25 weeks' work.[49] There is no doubt that Highgate pottery was intended for the London market, but it represents only a tiny proportion of similar wares and forms made in the London area, probably by the same potters, and identified in material excavated in the City and Southwark. There were undoubtedly many more local sites of pottery production in the wooded clay-lands to the north of Londinium, and some of these may yet be found. There were also small groups of pottery kilns near the estuary at West Tilbury, Grays and Mucking, whose products were probably sold in Londinium as well as in local markets. Another centre of pottery production from the late first to the mid-second centuries was in the Upchurch Marshes south of the Thames, where grey wares mainly following a native tradition were made.[50] Tiles also were required for building in Londinium, and recently evidence for an important centre of this manufacture has been found in Canons Park, Edgware, just west of Watling Street.

An important industry of the Thames estuary and Essex coast was the production of salt by the evaporation of sea-water. The method was to trap sea-water in clay-lined pits near the tidal limit and to allow it to evaporate between tides to produce strong brine. This was then dried out in large containers supported over fires by fire-bars on clay pedestals. The result of this work was an accumulation of burnt clay, which in time produced 'red hills'. Evidence of salt-production has been found on the marshes near Cooling, North Kent, and on the opposite side of the estuary on Canvey Island. This must have been an important commodity in the internal trading of Londinium, for it was needed everywhere, and the only way it could reach most of the inland towns was by the road system centering on London Bridge. There is a possibility that the industry was also carried on nearer Londinium at Tilbury, perhaps based on the various villas in that area, for Romano-British 'hut-circles' found in the fore-shore there at about OD level seem to be more than 1ft 6in (0.45m) below the average level of high water in the Thames during the earlier Roman period (about 0.5m above OD), as indicated by recent evidence from Southwark. It has therefore been suggested that these were structures connected with an inter-tidal salt industry.[51]

In addition to farming and industry, an important aspect of human life for which evidence may be found in the Romano-British countryside is religion. Small shrines might be set up by the roads, for the convenience of the traveller who wished to ensure a safe and successful journey by an appropriate offering or vow of a future gift to a deity. There must have been something of the sort at Old Ford, for example, until it was destroyed, presumably by Christians in the fourth century. This had a large stone figure of a god, probably Mercury, the patron of travellers, which was eventually broken and thrown unceremoniously into a ditch. There may have been another on Watling Street where the Roman road bridged a stream at St Thomas Watering, and natural springs continued to flow centuries later. Here in 1690 a Roman building of stone and tile was found in which two marble heads had been placed, perhaps as offerings to the local water-goddess.[52]

There were also large religious establishments, sometimes at the roadside, as at Springhead (*Vagniacis*) between Crayford and Rochester, where a whole temple complex has been found, but often well away from the main roads, as at Harlow in Essex. The existence of an important temple on high ground in Greenwich Park north of Watling Street has long been suspected. It has been known since 1902 that there was a major Roman building on the site; in fact a portion of its tessellated floor has since been kept visible. Its nature, however, was uncertain until recently, although the great quantity of coins found on the site (more than 400) and the discovery there of fragmentary and uninformative pieces of inscription and sculpture strongly suggested it might be a temple. A small-scale exploratory excavation was carried out by H. Sheldon and B. Yule in 1978–9, however, and this demonstrated that there was a square or rectangular building with a raised tessellated floor on the site, the successor to an earlier building with a similar ground plan. Gullies that were probably post-pits were found just outside the walls and parallel with them, and there was an outlying gully a little further away. From the lie of the land the entrance must have been on the east side.[53] These features are consistent with the plan of a normal square Romano-Celtic temple, of which the robber-trenches found in 1978-9 would have represented the outer walls; those of the cella (sanctuary) were not in the area covered by the recent excavation, but the floor found in 1902–3 may have belonged to it. The vague records of the earlier finds suggest that there were separate rooms or a range of rooms at a lower level to the east of the building, possibly a font-annex like those at Springhead and Harlow. Such dating evidence as was found suggests a date of about 100 for the first structure and, more tentatively, a date after the middle of the third century for the second. The position high on a hill but apparently close to a natural spring is a likely one for a temple, and it is possible that the waters were considered to have curative properties.

It can hardly be denied that at present we have only the sketchiest idea of the nature of life and occupation in the Greater London area and beyond during the Roman period. This is due partly to the difficulty of investigation in an area that is now occupied intensively, and partly to the unsatisfactory nature of many of our records. Yet there must have been a close relationship between the Roman city and its hinterland, and we need to know much more about the latter in order fully to understand Londinium itself. Unfortunately small-scale excavations in an area that was mostly rural in Roman times produce little conclusive evidence of what was going on there. Large-scale rescue observation supplemented by as much excavation as possible over a big area, aimed at recovering a whole ancient landscape, seems to offer the best hope. Such opportunities occur when large clearances are made, as in gravel-quarrying, and it is essential that the archaeological potential of all such sites should be recognised from the outset.

7

Londinium in the
Antonine and Severan Periods

Crisis and decline in the later second century

Those who were familiar with the old museum collections of Roman London, consisting mainly of objects rescued from City building sites, were always puzzled by the overwhelming preponderance of material dating from the later first and early second centuries. Later Roman material was certainly present, but in comparatively small quantities. The facile but unconvincing explanation was that the later Roman levels, being higher, had been removed during the intensive building operations in the City in the later Middle Ages. (The same explanation was offered to explain the even greater scarcity of Anglo-Saxon material, but that is another story.) It was unconvincing because the inhabitants of cities have always dug holes—mainly to make wells and cess-pits and to dispose of refuse—and most of the antiquities now in museum collections were not left lying about on the contemporary ground surface when they were broken or no longer required, but were disposed of tidily in these holes, often at a considerable depth below the ground.

The limited amount of excavation that was then possible might have suggested that on some central sites in the City an actual break in occupation occurred in the latter part of the second century. In Gutter Lane, for example, just north of Cheapside, Professor Grimes found in 1946 a succession of hut-floors from the third quarter of the first century to about 180, above which were several feet of sterile soil through which mediaeval pits had been dug.[1]

A similar stratigraphical sequence has since been found on a number of sites in Southwark. At Toppings Wharf, near the southern end of the bridge, a succession of clay and timber buildings came to an end in the mid-second century and was followed by a deposition of dark earth that was not water-laid. On another Southwark site near the river in Montague Close, the end of early Roman occupation was marked by a layer of collapsed clay walling containing pottery of mid to late second century date, and this was overlaid by dark earth containing fourth-century pottery. Elsewhere on the site there were stone foundations of late Roman date. Six hundred yards (550m) further south on the site of 201–211

Borough High Street, beside the road leading to the bridge, occupation with buildings of timber and clay continued until at least the mid-second century. There was then no evidence of activity until stone foundations were laid and a well dug in the late third or early fourth century. Only on one site in Southwark, 1–7 St Thomas Street, did the earlier occupation continue until about the end of the second century, but here also there were no indications of activity through most of the third century. By the fourth century, however, the site was occupied by a complex of large stone buildings.[2] The abandonment of a barge in a small tributary of the Thames on the site of New Guy's House, just south of London Bridge Station, may also have been a result of the decline in Southwark in the later second century. Layers of silt which accumulated around and over the barge contained pottery up to about the end of the second century, when occupation seems to have come to an end on the neighbouring site of 1–7 St Thomas Street, but the vessel was evidently derelict before that date, and must have been abandoned some years earlier, perhaps because of a decline in the internal trade that required river transport. As yet only a small portion at one end of the boat has been examined, however, and the rest still lies buried some 16ft (4.9m) beneath the paths and gardens of Guy's Hospital.[3] It is therefore possible that the barge was simply abandoned because of old age or irreparable damage, and it may be coincidental that this happened at a time when we have abundant evidence for a general decline in activity.

Confirmation that a similar break in occupation to that of Southwark occurred on three sites in the Roman city itself has been given by recent excavations. All lay to the west of the Walbrook, and we have as yet no certain evidence that there was a similar break in the eastern half of the city. This, however, is entirely due to the chance that no opportunity for controlled excavation on a large scale has yet arisen on any inland site east of the stream. On the GPO site north of Newgate Street there was immediate rebuilding of the clay and timber houses and industrial work-shops after the Hadrianic fire of about 125. These were the last of the sequence, however; they were demolished and the site was levelled before the end of the second century. As in several of the Southwark sites a deposit of the mysterious dark earth overlay them, and the only evidence of later Roman occupation was a well that was dug through the dark earth and underlying Roman levels from a higher surface that had subsequently been destroyed. There were also numerous stake-holes that penetrated the earlier Roman levels through the dark earth, probably from a still higher and later surface of the Anglo-Saxon period. In Milk Street, a sequence of buildings ended by the Hadrianic fire was immediately followed first by post-fire structures of an obviously temporary nature, and then by a more substantial timber building with wattle and daub walls, covered with painted wall-plaster on the interior, and with a patterned mosaic floor(**28**). Contemporary gravel metalling adjacent to it to the north was presumably the surface of its courtyard. Dating evidence is not yet fully assessed, but the building is at present considered to have passed out of use about 170.[4] Immediately overlying the mosaic floor and gravel courtyard, which were on

different levels, was a featureless deposit of dark earth (**29**). At Watling Court, south of Cheapside, two substantial timber-framed buildings, one with lower walls of flint and ragstone, were built in the late first century, and a smaller house was subsequently added between them. Fragments of mosaic floors survived in two of them. All three houses were destroyed in the Hadrianic fire and were replaced by buildings of poorer quality, which were themselves destroyed by fire, probably in late Antonine times. No late Roman activity could be detected, and the late Roman to Middle Saxon periods were represented only by a thick layer of the ubiquitous dark earth.[5]

As might be expected, the dark earth levels have been the subject of much debate. When first seen in Southwark more than 30 years ago, they were considered to be flood silt, but examination by soil specialists of these levels in the recent Southwark excavations has established that they were not water-laid.[6] Flood deposits of such thickness on some of the relatively high sites in the City (eg north of Newgate Street), where dark earth has been found, would in any case have been most unlikely. Because of the obvious importance of this phenomenon, the dark-earth deposit at Milk Street was investigated very carefully to ascertain whether there were any changes of colour or texture, or any concentrations of small stones that might indicate decayed wooden structures or broken-up floor surfaces, or whether there were distribution patterns of finds of a particular date or degree of abrasion. In fact, however, no such variations or distinctive patterns could be found, and the distribution of finds seemed to be completely random, perhaps because the soil was regularly turned over in cultivation, which could erode structures and disperse their material. Soil samples are also being tested for particle size, amount of humus and types of pollen. Finds have consisted mainly of later Roman pottery sherds, much abraded, with very occasional fragments that are probably Saxon, and the darkness seems to be due mainly to particles of carbon. Soil specialists have as yet been reluctant to commit themselves to an interpretation, and are not happy about the suggestion that the deposit is the result of agricultural or gardening activities. Nevertheless, it is difficult to imagine any other explanation, and it would seem that we must envisage large areas within·the city walls and in its suburb south of the river, formerly intensively occupied, as being given over in late Roman times to activities that we would consider more appropriate to the countryside than to a city. Whether the dark soil was brought in at one time or was the result of a gradual accumulation of street-sweepings and other refuse, as Sheldon suggests, is still uncertain, as also are the dates of its deposition, which may vary from site to site. What does seem to be well established as a common factor is that the phase of intensive occupation in each case came to an end during the second half of the second century. This raises other difficult problems. What happened to all these people, and what are the implications for the state of Londinium at the time?

28 Mosaic floor of house in Milk Street built soon after the Hadrianic fire of c 125–30, and apparently abandoned about 170, after which it was overlaid with dark earth (seen in back section). *Museum of London*

Harvey Sheldon was the first to grasp this particular nettle. In an article written in 1975,[7] he pointed out that evidence from the roadside settlements and farms in the London area often suggests a similar break in continuity during this period, and that the two known potteries near Londinium, at Brockley Hill and Highgate, may have ceased production as early as 160, as if either the potters themselves or their London market had vanished.

He also suggested a possible connection between these indications of crisis in the latter part of the second century and the disastrous fires at Verulamium about 155 and at Chelmsford about 200. Chelmsford (*Caesaromagus*) does not seem to have recovered for nearly a century, and at Verulamium Insula XIV was apparently left unoccupied until late in the third century, though other insulae seem to have been rebuilt in the latter part of the second century. Staines also had its late Antonine fire, some time towards the end of the second century. In Londinium itself no evidence of widespread fire in this period, in any way comparable with the Hadrianic fire, has yet been found. There was certainly an Antonine fire at Watling Court, but this must be assumed to be local until evidence is found on many more sites. Nevertheless, Marsh has noted a considerable quantity of burnt samian pottery of this date in the London

29   Deposit of dark earth overlying remains of Roman house of mid-second century, Milk Street, photographed after removal of post-Roman features (see pp141–3). *Museum of London*

collection, mostly from later dumping in the Walbrook valley to raise the ground level. At Watling Court, the Antonine burnt level was succeeded by the dark earth deposits, so it is possible that the fire was simply a means of disposing of a building no longer required. Local fires for the same purpose may well have occurred elsewhere. In a more recent excavation at Well Court, south of Cheapside, a site nearer the main east–west thoroughfare of the Roman city, the destruction of an Antonine building by fire was however followed by the laying of a concrete (*opus signinum*) floor of poor quality, so that in this more central position occupation certainly continued after the fire, probably into the early third century.[8]

Sheldon was taken to task by the late John Morris for suggesting that the century 150–250 was a period of decline, mainly on the grounds that archaeologists have difficulty in dating throughout this period because of the curious scarcity in Britain of coins minted between 180 and 253, and the less certain dating of late samian; they were therefore forced to rely on coarse pottery which had been dated to the Antonine period by the coins normally found with it, but could, he suggested, equally well be of any date in the first half of the third century, so that the supposed gap in occupation was illusory.[9] The difficulty of dating in this period is true enough, though somewhat exaggerated by Morris. He failed to take account, however, of the evidence, produced by site after site, of an actual break in the sequence of occupation, sometimes eventually followed by a later Roman occupation of a very different kind. The difficulty lies in giving a precise, rather than an approximate, date to this break, and thereby identifying the historical circumstances in which it occurred.

The reigns of Antoninus Pius and Marcus Aurelius were not a particularly happy or stable period for Britain. There was trouble with the Brigantes of the north early in the reign of Antoninus, resulting in a temporary withdrawal from the new frontier recently established in Scotland. Initial success, marked by the issue of coins in 155 showing a dejected Britannia, was followed by more trouble in the north, and a possible uprising in North Wales as well, for there were fires at Wroxeter and Worcester, and some forts in Wales were rebuilt or re-occupied in the reign of Marcus Aurelius. The army in Britain seems to have had a shortage of manpower about this time, and was reinforced by cavalry from the Danube in 175. In 180, just after the death of Aurelius, there was a disastrous incursion of tribesmen across the northern frontier, and the reign of Commodus began with another series of campaigns, for which victory was claimed in the coinage of 184–5. Following all this there was mutiny in the army itself, which went so far as to attempt to set up its own emperor, a legionary legate named Priscus, foreshadowing the events a few years later, when the governor of Britain, D. Clodius Albinus, in the scramble for power that followed the assassination of Commodus in 192, made a serious bid for the empire with the backing of the legions in Britain.[10]

What effect all these military and political troubles had on London and south-eastern Britain can only be guessed. It might be expected that, with the forces of imperial authority over-stretched and pre-occupied elsewhere, there would have been some breakdown in law and order. It is also possible, as Sheppard Frere has suggested, that the Saxon pirates and raiders who were to be the scourge of the south-east in the next century, had taken advantage of the situation and were already giving trouble in the reigns of Marcus Aurelius and Commodus. There is a sharp increase in this period of coin hoards, which usually indicate insecurity, in East Anglia, Kent and along the south coast, the area that was subsequently to be provided with special protection against Saxon depredations.[11]

It is clear, however, that disturbances and warlike incursions of any kind short of a wholesale massacre cannot account by themselves for the apparent disappearance from Londinium of a large proportion of its inhabitants. Fear of raids, in fact, is more likely to have kept them huddled together, seeking the safety of numbers, than to have dispersed them. People leave a city, reluctantly and therefore gradually, because they can no longer make a living there, but economic recession is unlikely to have caused a general exodus in a single generation, unless much better opportunities could be found elsewhere. This seems unlikely, and there is no obvious reason in the known troubles of the period why craftsmen should not have continued to ply their trades in Londinium. If fewer of them did so, it may simply mean that there were now fewer people in the city, and by implication in the neighbourhood and beyond.

In order to put the evacuation of parts of Londinium into any historical context, it is necessary to know precisely when it began. Fortunately we have good evidence of this, based on coin finds rather than the less certainly dated pottery, from the centre of the Roman city. In the valley of the Walbrook there is abundant evidence of human activity during the first hundred years of the city's existence. There seem to have been few buildings, and those were probably not more substantial than huts and booths, but there was an abundant loss of coins, personal ornaments and tools, most of which found their way into the stream itself or into flood deposits which from time to time covered its banks. Throughout London's history, until the final covering of the Walbrook in the fifteenth century, there was always a tendency of the stream to silt up and overflow, due partly to the gradual rise of the level of the Thames and partly to the infiltration of refuse. It therefore required regular attention by clearing the channel and maintaining its banks. If this was neglected for long the valley flooded and became a quagmire, so that the stream itself could not be approached closely except at its regular crossing-places. This seems to have happened very soon after the middle of the second century. Coins of issues in a continuous sequence up to and including the 'Britannia' coins of 155 were dropped into the stream in considerable quantities, but with that issue the coin-loss ends abruptly. The end of the sequence is clearly connected with the collapse of the banks and the resulting flooding, for one of the latest coins found in the stream-bed on the Bucklersbury House site, Walbrook, a coin of Marcus Aurelius as Caesar, dated 153–4, was found above a fallen timber of the revetment.[12] The issue of 155 was not by any means the latest to arrive in quantity in Londinium, and later issues of

Antoninus Pius, Marcus Aurelius and Commodus dated from 159 to 183 constituted 18 per cent of the coin finds from a recent riverside excavation at New Fresh Wharf. There is little doubt that the abandonment of the Walbrook valley took place very soon after the middle of the second century. The immediate cause may have been natural—perhaps a small rise in the relative level of the Thames that made the Walbrook silting catastrophic. It is possible also that a contributory factor may have been dumping near the mouth of the stream as preliminary work for the construction of a new waterfront. Significantly, however, no immediate attempt was made to remedy the situation by raising the banks, and a large area in the centre of the city that had previously been much frequented, though probably not densely inhabited, was now abandoned for many years.[13] It seems eventually to have been reclaimed piecemeal by dumping on the marsh, and more substantial later Roman buildings, with walls partly at least of stone and sometimes with fine mosaic floors, began to appear beside the stream. This reclamation seems to have taken place during the third century, some of it probably before the middle of the century.

The evidence from the Walbrook valley, therefore, conforms well with that from Southwark except that, as might be expected, the later phase of large buildings and apparent prosperity begins earlier in the centre of Londinium than in its southern suburb. The period of abandonment, however, seems to begin at about the same time, except on a site in St Thomas Street that continued to be occupied until late in the second century. Harvey Sheldon writes: 'It is difficult to assign the abandonment of these structures (the earlier clay and timber buildings) to a period much later than the middle years of the second century', but adds cautiously that associated pottery is limited and it might eventually prove to be of later Antonine or even Severan date.[14] A full assessment of the dating evidence from the recent excavations in the western part of the City will throw more light on this, but in the meantime it seems reasonable to assume that Londinium suffered a grave decline in its population not later than the third quarter of the second century. Sheldon has suggested that the Plague of Galen, a pestilence brought to western Europe by troops from the east about 166, may have contributed to this depopulation. Certainly an epidemic is a likely explanation, particularly if, as Sheldon's subsequent researches seem to show, there is widespread evidence for a decline in occupation beyond the London region.[15] London itself, as the principal gateway to Britain, in subsequent periods was especially prone to receive and transmit plague from overseas with its other imports, and it would be surprising if this never happened in Roman times. Certainly the cultural break in continuity, as reflected by archaeology, is not unlike that of the fourteenth century, in which the Black Death brought established occupation and industry to an end in many places, and a new pattern of a very different nature eventually emerged. We need not be too concerned by the failure of historians to mention all the troubles of a remote province, and it may be significant that one of the difficulties of the army in Britain at this period was apparently lack of manpower.

Certainly the basic cause of Antonine decline in London seems to have been depopulation and, as Sheldon has shown, this was not merely a local phenomenon. Its origins were probably more complex than a single epidemic; in fact, the evidence from the Walbrook suggests a failure to maintain occupation of its valley somewhat earlier than the historic date of the arrival of the Plague of Galen in the west. Other imported diseases, not necessarily epidemic, may have taken their toll, and there may have been a decline in birth-rate due to little-understood physiological, psychological or social causes, such as sometimes followed the cultural changes imposed in various parts of the world in the nineteenth century. A decline in the native population, however, can have had only an indirect and therefore gradual effect on cosmopolitan Londinium, by reducing its trade and supply of labour. We need much more information, and particularly more precise dating of the abandonment of individual sites, before any proper assessment of causes can be made. A statistical study by Sheldon of sites that were deserted about this time in south-east Britain indicates that the peak period for this, following the estimates of the excavators, was the early third century.[16] Londinium, therefore, with its crisis apparently in the third quarter of the second century, seems to have been well in advance of south-east Britain in general. If this apparent chronological difference is real, and not due merely to the varying approaches of archaeologists to a difficult problem of dating, it would give some support to the suggestion that a principal cause of the decline in population was an imported disease, which had its most immediate impact at the point of entry.

It would be quite wrong to give the impression that Londinium at this period was an abandoned ghost town, left to gradual decay and the inroads of nature. All the evidence indicates that the authorities, both local and governmental, remained in full control. Houses and workshops that were no longer required seem to have been demolished deliberately in Milk Street and on the GPO site in Newgate Street, and were overlaid by dark earth, which must initially have been brought from elsewhere and deposited at the cost of considerable labour, whether it was subsequently gradually augmented or not.

The large public baths on Huggin Hill and the smaller bath-house north of Cheapside were both deliberately demolished, probably by about the end of the second century, evidently because their maintenance for the shrunken population of the western half of the city was no longer justified.[17] In neither case was the site redeveloped after clearance, but the survival of derelict and abandoned buildings was evidently not tolerated.

The new riverfront

The importance still attached to Londinium by the Roman authorities is demonstrated, moreover, by their construction of two of its most impressive public works at about this time. One of these was a new and massive timber waterfront, which has been located and examined in three places—near the eastern extremity of the Roman city on the site of the Custom House, just west of the Tower of London; at New Fresh Wharf, just downstream of the Roman bridge; and at Seal House, Upper Thames Street, just upstream of the bridge. In each case the associated pottery suggests a date in the latter part of the second century, as do the coins from New Fresh Wharf. This would also agree with a tentative date from tree-ring analysis of the timbers, which suggests by comparison with the dated West German pattern of tree-growth that the trees from which they were made were felled in the latter part of the second century. Similar results were obtained both from the Custom House and from New Fresh Wharf.[18] Unfortunately Carbon 14 dating of timber from New Fresh Wharf, averaged from several samples, has produced a date about a century later—AD295 ± 35 years. The series of dates from samples taken, however, is self-contradictory, showing an earlier date for the outer (and therefore younger) part of the timber, and a much later date for the inner (and older) wood. It would seem therefore that something has gone wrong, probably through pollution of the

30 Samian pottery imported from Central and East Gaul in the late second to early third century, found associated with the Antonine/Severan waterfront at New Fresh Wharf (p151). *Museum of London*

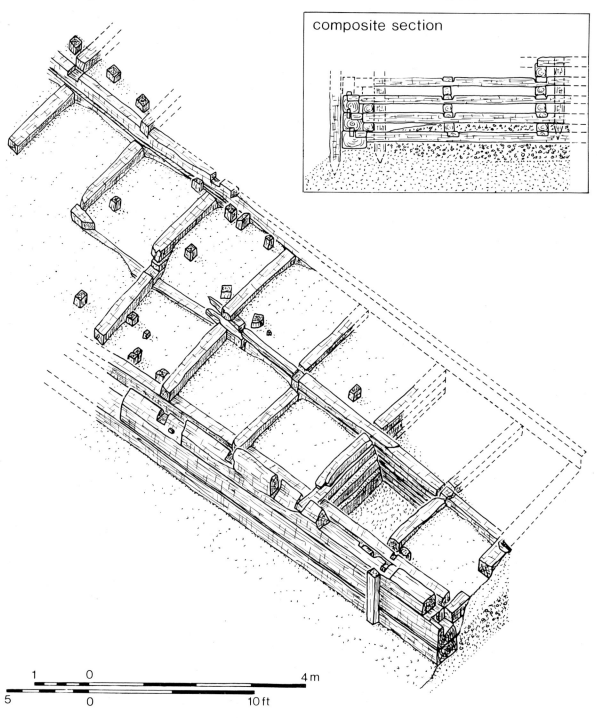

Fig. 22   Antonine/Severan wharf excavated on the site of the Old Custom House, 1973. *Axonometric drawing after T. Tatton-Brown*

timber by later organic material. There is no doubt that the pottery associated with the quay excavated at New Fresh Wharf is predominantly of the late second and early third centuries, and much of it was imported. Quantities of complete but cracked or otherwise damaged pottery had been dumped there, sometimes in groups from a single source, as if a crate-load had suffered damage in transit. The imports included beakers and mortaria (mixing-bowls) from the Middle Rhine; samian vessels, mostly from Lezoux in Central Gaul, with a smaller quantity from East Gaul (**30**); and a load of colour-coated beakers, also from Lezoux. The new waterfront stood much further out into the river than its predecessor, and most of this dumping probably occurred at the time of construction. The coins lost on this site also are nearly all what one would expect to find in circulation in the late second and early third centuries—15 earlier bronze coins (Vespasian to Hadrian), 15 Antonine bronze coins (Antoninus Pius to Commodus), a silver denarius of Septimius Severus (dated 197) and a forged denarius of Elagabalus (copying an issue of 219). By contrast there were only two late Roman coins of the period covered by the C14 date—a period of inflation when debased coins were produced and circulated in huge quantities. Both of these, like some of the earlier coins, had found their way into post-Roman river deposits.

It is clear that the recession or decline that emptied Southwark and many areas in the western part of the city, and probably caused the abandonment of the Walbrook valley, did not suspend the activities of the port of Londinium for very long, if it did so at all. Some customers evidently still remained and some London merchants were still continuing their activities. More surprisingly, a public authority was able to find the resources and labour necessary to carry out the immense task of reconstructing London's waterfront. We do not know why this was necessary. An earlier waterfront, built in the later first century, lies north of Lower Thames Street, near the new building line of the widened street, about 100ft (30m) north of its successor. This was equally massive and its main structure seemed perfectly sound when recently excavated, so that there was no obvious reason for replacing it. An immense amount of dumping must have been necessary to extend the waterfront to its new line, but it is unlikely that this was done on one occasion, and it is probable that an intermediate early second-century waterfront lies under Thames Street (see p91–2).

The Antonine or Severan waterfront at the Custom House consisted of a front wall of massive timber beams laid horizontally, with a multiple-box framework of horizontal jointed beams behind (fig 22). It survived to a height of 5ft (1.5m) or so in places, and had presumably been covered with a plank platform at a higher level. The interior of the box framework had gradually filled with silt, but there had been no attempt to pack it deliberately, and it had obviously been built out into the water. There were vertical piles driven into the river-bed within the box-structure, presumably the foundations of warehouses that stood on the wharf floor. The construction in the eastern part of the site was different, with a series of massive east–west beams at the front apparently originally tied in at the top with lesser beams running north–south that were probably laid on vertical posts with tenons, but these had been displaced by later robbing. Here there were indications of deliberate packing with old building material. A triple row of vertical posts with planking between them had stood in front of the main quay wall in this area, probably to serve as a protective fender.

The Antonine/Severan riverfront at New Fresh Wharf was similar in construction to the eastern part of the Custom House wharf, and both closely resembled the Roman riverside quay at Xanten on the Rhine. A foundation of ground piles with sawn flat tops had first been driven into the foreshore and a dump of material from demolished buildings was laid around them to consolidate them or to provide a working platform. Beams running at right angles to the front wall were laid on some of the ground piles and cradled the massive sill-beam in large notches cut in their upper surfaces. Other massive squared beams, only slightly narrower than the sill-beam, were laid on it horizontally to form the front wall of the quay, and were braced back to various arrangements of piles by horizontal beams laid north–south and jointed to the east–west wall-timbers (**31**).[19]

31   Antonine/Severan waterfront at New Fresh Wharf, showing inner structure, with superimposed timber baulks of front wall (A) and mortised tie-back timbers (B) (view to sw). *Museum of London*

A Roman quay of similar but lighter construction was located just upstream of the bridge at Seal House, Upper Thames Street, in 1974. Its position more than 30ft (10m) south of the southern frontage of Thames Street indicates that it is of later Roman date, and is likely to be of the same period. This was evidently for down-river traffic, and in marked contrast with the river-front at New Fresh Wharf very little pottery was found associated with it. It seems likely that the quay at New Fresh Wharf and its predecessor specialised in ceramic imports, and this part of the water-front was probably the destination of the ill-fated ship with a cargo of samian pottery that came to grief at Pudding Pan Rock off Whitstable. The earlier quay to the north is very near the suspected samian warehouse of the early second century on the site of Regis House (see p107).

The provision of a new waterfront built out into the river, and probably extending from above the bridge to the Custom House site—a distance of at least 600 yards (550m)—must have required the felling of a great number of trees, and the services of a considerable number of skilled carpenters supported by many more labourers, even if the work were carried out gradually over a period of years. Yet it all seems to have taken place within the time when shortage of labour must have been a major problem, if the theory of the depopulation of south-eastern Britain is correct. It is likely, therefore, that resources were drawn from a large area, and perhaps skilled direction from outside the province, in view of the continental parallels, though similar techniques had been used in Londinium for terracing and a waterfront at an earlier date. The work is likely to have been beyond the capability of the local senate at this particular time, and was presumably undertaken as the result of a decision at a high level in the provincial administration. The reason for it is not obvious. If the old waterfront needed repair, this could have been undertaken piecemeal by substituting new timbers for old in the same position, a much easier task than building a completely new line of wharfs further out into the river. It has been suggested that a temporary drop in the river-level during the Antonine period made it necessary to move the riverfront forward into deeper water, so that shipping could continue to be accommodated beside the wharfs. Professor Grimes's Walbrook section can hardly be reconciled with a general fall in the river-level, however, for this would have transformed the stream into a torrent cutting a deep bed, with no tendency to silt or flood. If the river in front of the old waterfront was now found to be too shallow, it is more likely to have been due either to the dumping of refuse on the river-bottom or to the introduction of ships taking a deeper draught. The process of advancing the waterfront of the City of London continued in spite of the rising river-level in mediaeval and post-mediaeval times, when another reason was the need to create more riverside space for handling cargoes. This is unlikely to have been a consideration in Antonine or Severan London, but the new waterfront testifies to the continuing importance of the port of Londinium to the Roman rulers of Britain, whatever crisis or decline was being suffered by its population. It is also clear that there were still merchants who were eager to make use of the new facilities.

The City wall

If the provision of a very substantial new waterfront is surprising at a time when the population of Londinium seems to have dropped dramatically, it is little short of amazing that this should have been accompanied, apparently within a fairly short space of time, by the greatest public work ever undertaken by the Romans in London. The building of a massive wall just over 2 miles (3km) long round the entire city on its landward side is a task that is often underestimated by those who see only its few visible surviving fragments. Surprisingly, at a period when the urban working population seems to have abandoned whole districts in the western part of the city, it was to enclose rather more than had been occupied by the great expansion of the late first century. In the neighbourhood of Bishopsgate the city boundary was extended a little to the north to enclose an area that had until recently been part of the northern cemetery. On the western side the former industrial suburbs and burial grounds north of St Paul's were enclosed, and the western line of the wall lay beyond the cemetery around Warwick Square. The reason for placing the wall, and by implication extending the city limits, so far to the west was no doubt due to the need to have the defensive line near the edge of the relatively flat ground, overlooking the steep drop to the valley of the Fleet. Altogether some 330 acres (130ha) were enclosed, making Londinium, with its shrunken population, in area easily the largest city in Britain and fairly highly placed among Continental Roman cities—much larger than Turin and Vienne, about the same size as Milan and Lyons, but much smaller than Autun and Nîmes.

Curiously no riverside wall was built at this time to make a complete circuit round the city, probably because it would have cut off the fine new quays and gravely inconvenienced the activities of the port. The ends of the wall at Blackfriars and the Tower must have been provided with special fortifications to prevent attackers on land from clambering round the wall, although no evidence of these has yet been found. For the river-front itself, however, the Thames seems to have been considered sufficient defence. This is less surprising when it is remembered that after the collapse of the later Roman riverside wall which subsequently completed the circuit (see Chapter 9), the landward wall alone defended London adequately through all the vicissitudes of the Middle Ages.

The nearest good building-stone was the ragstone quarried in the neighbourhood of Maidstone in Kent, and this could be brought all the way by barge, down the Medway and up the Thames to be unloaded on the wharves of Londinium. Some saving of material could be achieved by making use of two of the existing ragstone walls of the fort, and the city wall was laid out accordingly, running from the site of the Tower of London in the south-east via the roads to Colchester and the north, where gate-houses were built at Aldgate and Bishopsgate, to the north-east corner of the fort. The north and west walls of the fort now became part of the city wall, and the new wall began again at the south-west corner of the fort, with which it was joined, and ran in a south-westerly direction to a point just north of Newgate Street, where it turned south and ran to the river, accommodating the Silchester road and the road along Fleet Street and

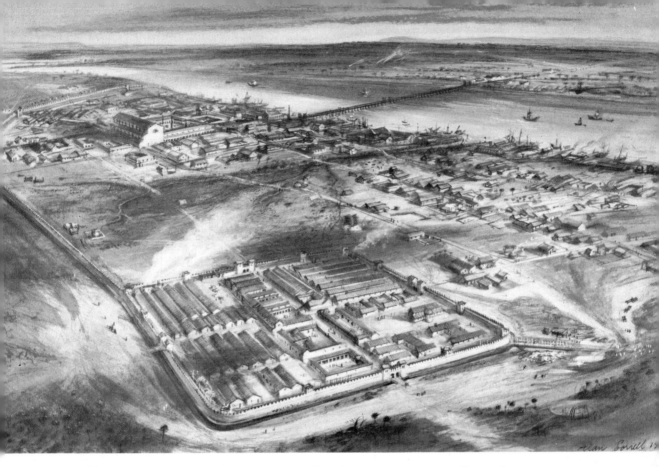

32 Building the Roman city wall. Reconstruction by Alan Sorrell showing wall complete to NE corner of fort and foundations being laid from SW corner (view to SE). *Author*

the Strand by gate-houses at Newgate and Ludgate respectively (see map, fig 28, p174, **32**).

The new wall was 9ft (2.7m) thick at ground level, where it was faced with a sandstone plinth, and 8ft (2.4m) thick above this. The foundations, laid in a trench, were usually of clay and flints, with a layer of ragstone above as a bedding for the wall (**33**). On the interior, at ground level opposite to the external plinth, was a triple course of flat tiles forming a facing only. Squared ragstone blocks were laid like bricks in four or five regular courses above the plinth and facing-tiles to form the outer and inner faces, and the space between was filled with random lumps of ragstone, around which lime mortar was poured. The lumps of ragstone and mortar set into an intensely hard rubble concrete, and the section above could be commenced (**34**). First a level working-surface was made by laying a triple course of tiles right across the wall from front to back. Then, leaving a slight off-set or ledge on the inner face of the course of tiles, the same process was repeated at a higher level. Six courses of squared ragstone blocks were laid to form the inner and outer faces, and again the interior was filled with ragstone rubble concrete. This time, and subsequently, only two courses of flat tiles were laid across the wall as a levelling course, and the process was again repeated, each

33 Roman city wall, Crosswall; external face showing top of foundations, sandstone plinth and courses of squared ragstone blocks above. *Museum of London*

time with a reduction in thickness of a few inches by means of an off-set on the inner face of the tile course. In places a fourth tile course has been recorded surviving at a height of about $14\frac{1}{2}$ft (4.4m) above the plinth. Above this course the city wall seems to be an entirely mediaeval rebuild, with no trace of Roman work. This may therefore be the actual Roman parapet walk on which the defenders would have stood, protected by a crenellated breastwork or parapet in front of them (fig 23). Coping-stones which almost certainly come from this crenellation indicate that the breastwork would have been just over 2ft (0.6m) thick. If the top of the fourth tile-course is in fact the parapet walk, the total height of the city wall would be about 21ft (6.4m) from ground level to the top of the crenellations, allowing a height of about $6\frac{1}{2}$ft (2m) for the parapet. This is closely comparable with the height of the Roman city wall at Canterbury, which appears to have survived in one place to the top of its crenellated parapet, just over 21ft (6.5m) above its foundation.

Access to the parapet walk was by small rectangular towers projecting from the inner face of the wall, each evidently containing a wooden stairway. Only four of these are known, three on the eastern side of the city, from the Tower to Cooper's

Row, and one on the western side south of Newgate, found when extending the Central Criminal Court (**35**); but they must obviously have been placed at fairly frequent intervals along the entire length of the wall, and no doubt others will eventually be found. Within the fort, of course, there were already corner and intermediate turrets serving the same purpose.

Other essential building was the provision of at least four gate-houses to give access for pre-existing roads at Ludgate, Newgate, Bishopsgate, Aldgate and possibly in the neighbourhood of the mediaeval Tower Postern. Aldersgate, though a Roman gate, seems to have been inserted into the wall at a later date, and initially the west gate of the fort probably provided all the access needed in this part of the wall; although its use by civilians must have caused problems if the fort continued to serve its original purpose as a barracks. Like the north gate of the fort (Cripplegate), the west gate would have given access only to minor roads, probably mainly used by the military occupants. The only gate-house of the city wall we know much about is Newgate, the Roman ground-plan of which was reconstructed from observations made between 1875 and 1909.[20] This was like an enlarged copy of the west gate of the fort, with a double entrance flanked by rectangular guard-rooms which projected respectively 7 and 14ft (2.13 and 4.26m) in front of the wall and similar (but reciprocal) distances behind (fig 24).

34 Roman city wall, Cooper's Row; internal face showing facing course of tiles at ground-level, four courses of ragstone blocks, bonding-course of tiles with off-set and (above) core of ragstone rubble concrete with facing removed. *Museum of London*

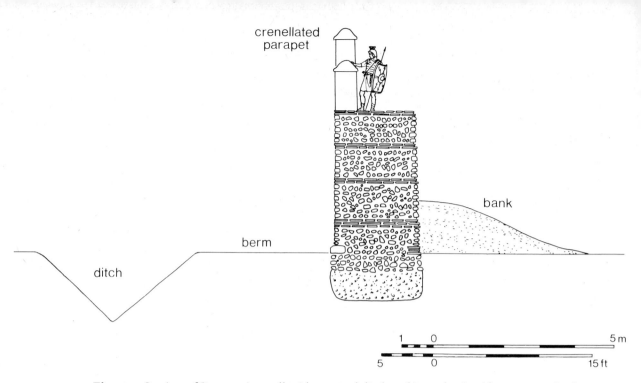

crenellated
parapet

bank

berm

ditch

1 0   5 m

5   0   15 ft

Fig. 23 Section of Roman city wall with external ditch and inner bank. *After reconstruction by J. Maloney*

At Aldgate the width seems to allow only for a single arched entrance, suggesting that traffic on this road was not very great when the wall was built. Only the flint-and-clay foundation of the north-east corner of the north tower of the first Aldgate was seen, but this was sufficient to show that there was an external buttress on the corner and that the projection of the tower from the wall was about 9ft (2.74m).[21] There is little doubt that both gates and internal towers were crenellated like the wall itself, for large coping stones with lateral projections have been found re-used as building material, and these are of about the same width as the coping-stones of the wall parapet, but evidently came from a more complex structure with off-set walls.

Outside the city wall an additional defence was a V-shaped ditch about 12–16ft (3–5m) wide and $4\frac{1}{2}$–$6\frac{1}{2}$ft (1.35–2m) deep, lying 9–15ft (2.7–4.5m) in front of the wall. This was probably dug before the wall itself was built, for the earth from it and from the foundation trench of the wall was piled against the inner face of the wall soon after it had been built, forming a bank 6–7ft (about 2m) high and spreading 13ft (4m) or more from the base of the wall.[22] Its purpose was presumably to give added strength to the base of the wall, and perhaps also to protect the inner face from stone-robbers and from casual mischief.

Most of our dating evidence comes from the internal bank and the deposits on which it was laid. Inevitably it gives us only a terminal date *after* which the bank was constructed. When however this evidence is collected from site after site, always with similar results, it becomes convincing. There are now about half-a-dozen sites where a considerable amount of pottery has been excavated in recent

35 Internal turret of Roman city wall, found when extending Central Criminal Court, Old Bailey; view from above to south, along line of wall. *Museum of London*

years from the bank or from deposits immediately preceding it, and none has yet produced a single piece that could be firmly dated as later than the late second century. The most recent is the excavation by John Maloney at Duke's Place, where the bank contained pottery of about 180.[23] The only problem is that this is a period when pottery is difficult to date closely, because of the scarcity of related coin evidence in the very late second and early third centuries. We have, however, two pieces of good coin evidence for the date of London's Roman wall. When the north and south walls of the fort were incorporated in the new city wall, it was necessary to build a reinforcing wall against their inner faces, in order to bring them to the standard thickness of the new wall, which was nearly double that of the fort wall. In a deposit cut by the reinforcing wall and therefore antedating it, Professor Grimes found a worn coin of Commodus of 183–4.[24] As the coin had evidently been in circulation for some time, the thickening cannot have been added to the wall before the closing years of the second century, and might equally well have been built at least ten years later. It has been argued that the thickening of the fort walls was a finishing touch, that could have been added some time after the enclosure of the city by its new wall. The thinner fort walls, however, were an obvious weakness, and there is a very strong probability that the whole process was completed as quickly as possible. There is, moreover, no indication of the sort of haste to meet an emergency that might have led to skimping of material or labour.

The coin of Commodus therefore indicates that the completion of the wall was certainly not earlier than 190, and might well be as late as 210. Our other coin evidence demonstrates that it cannot have been much later. John Maloney observed at Duke's Place that the angle of the lumps of masonry in the core of the wall showed that it had been built from east to west; and in view of the greater vulnerability of the eastern side of the city than the north, which was protected by the marshes of the upper Walbrook, and the west, which was protected by the river Fleet, it was logical to commence the work at the Tower of London and finish it with the stretch of wall between Newgate and Blackfriars. It is from this part of the wall, presumably the latest, that we have evidence giving an approximate date when the work must already have been completed. In the internal turret at the Old Bailey, rubbish began to accumulate in a dark corner beneath the stairway, obviously when the turret was in general use, but probably after the first pride in the new fortification had abated. When this process had gone on for some time, a coin-forger threw a handful of coins and two coin-moulds for casting imitation silver denarii into the unswept corner. Since the coins consisted of a genuine silver denarius of some value as well as three old bronze coins that were still acceptable currency, his reason for doing so was presumably the need to dispose of incriminating evidence in a hurry. The find throws an interesting light on the spare-time activities of the garrison of the city wall. Its principal value, however, is the evidence it provides to date the accumulation of refuse on the gravel floor of the turret. This was piled only in the north-west corner of the turret, and undoubtedly found its way there while the

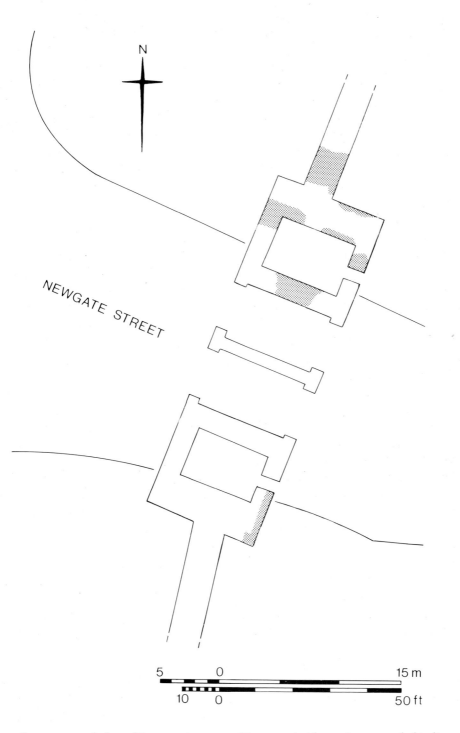

Fig. 24 Reconstructed plan of Roman city gate at Newgate (with portions recorded indicated by shading). *After P. Norman and W. Reader*

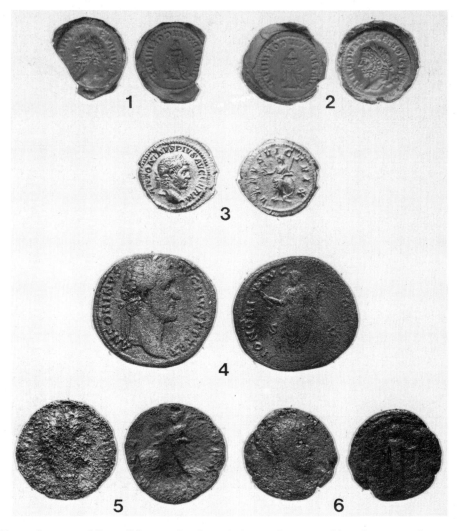

36   Forger's scattered 'hoard' from refuse layer in internal turret, Old Bailey; (1) and (2) terra-cotta double moulds of *denarii* of Septimius Severus (1) and Geta (2), both with same reverse of Caracalla; (3) unworn silver *denarius* of Caracalla; (4) and (5) *sestertius* and *as* of Antoninus Pius; (6) *as* of Commodus. *Museum of London*

stairway still existed. There is no question of later dumping when the turret was in ruins, as seems to be the case with evidence of a somewhat similar nature from a wall-turret at Verulamium. The refuse deposit in the London turret contained pottery attributed to the early third century with the coins and moulds thrown in by the forger. The bronze coins, which were perhaps intended for melting down and casting in the moulds, comprised two of Antoninus Pius, dated 145–61, and one of Commodus, 180–92. The silver coin, possibly the model for another mould, was a denarius of Caracalla dated 213–17, in almost mint condition. The two moulds were double, and were taken from three denarii which similarly

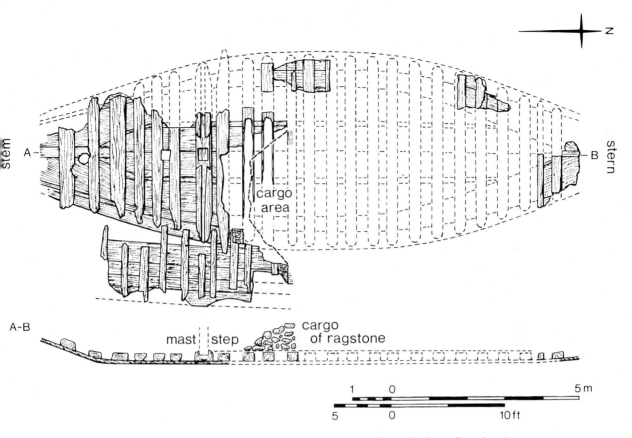

Fig. 25 Plan and section of remains of Roman barge, with collapsed side, as found in the river-bed at Blackfriars in 1962. *After P. R. V. Marsden*

showed practically no signs of wear. One had an obverse of Geta (210–12) and the other an obverse of Septimius Severus (201–10). Both had the same reverse of Caracalla, dated 215 (**36**). No traces of metal-working were found, and the actual forging must have been carried on elsewhere.[25] Subsequent dumped deposits in the turret contained pottery attributed to the mid-third century. It seems likely that the forger was at work not later than about 220–5, and that the turret was then by no means new. We have therefore on coin evidence a bracket of about 30 years, between 190 and 220, within which the city wall should have been completed, with the less conclusive pottery evidence favouring a date in the earlier part of the bracket centering on 200.

This is in the middle of London's recession, when whole areas in the western part of the city, the Walbrook valley, and most of the suburb in Southwark appear to have been derelict. Yet the building of the wall made great demands on skilled supervision and labour and on supplies. The whole operation seems to have been carried out smoothly and remarkably consistently, with hardly any variation in construction beyond an occasional minor error, as when the builders working in Duke's Place left an offset at a tile course on the *external* face. Every contingency arising from changes of level and the presence of streams was met by adjustments that must have been planned in advance. The tributaries of the Walbrook and other streams were accommodated with brick culverts so that the flow of water could pass unimpeded through the wall, and a considerable fall in ground-level at Duke's Place was not allowed to affect the horizontal courses of the wall; instead the sandstone plinth was continued at the same level across the hollow, more than 3ft (1m) above the ground.

The logistics of the operation are as impressive as the engineering. At least 85,000 tons (86,000 tonnes) of ragstone had to be quarried in the Maidstone region and brought to Londinium by barge down the Medway and up the Thames. The remains of a Roman sailing-barge with some of its cargo of ragstone still on board was found in 1962 near Blackfriars Bridge, and such dating evidence as we have suggests that it might well have been bringing stone for building the western side of the city wall when it was wrecked near the mouth of the Fleet (fig 25). The vessel itself had probably been built earlier in the second century, for a worn copper coin (*as*) of 88–9 had been placed for luck in the mast-step before the mast was fitted, in accordance with a custom that still survives. The coin itself was not new at the time, and had obviously been selected for its reverse, which represented Fortuna, the goddess of good luck, holding a ship's rudder. The wreck seems to have broken up on the river-bed during the third century, for a pottery fragment of the late third century had been washed with river gravel into the bottom of the boat before the side collapsed above it.[26] It has been estimated that the capacity of the barge was about 900 cu ft (25m^3) and, if it is typical of the barge fleet, not less than 1300 barge-loads of ragstone would have been required for building the city wall.

Skilled work was also needed, presumably at the quarries, for shaping more than a million squared blocks of ragstone for facing the wall. More skill was required, probably in the same part of Kent, to grind into shape well over 4000 chamfered blocks of sandstone for the plinth. A similar number of coping-stones with curved upper surfaces, of limestone probably from the Cotswolds, were required for the battlements of gates and turrets as well as the parapet.[27] These all needed transport to Londinium, and the massive coping-stones required cranes for handling and placing in position.

The whole task was one that would probably have exceeded local capability at any period, and if south-east Britain really was depopulated at the time when it was undertaken, resources must have been drawn from the whole province and perhaps beyond it. The decision to build the wall must have been taken at the highest level, and within the chronological limits prescribed by the archaeological evidence there were only two personalities powerful enough to give the order and ensure that it was carried out—Clodius Albinus, governor of Britain and usurping emperor, and his eventual conqueror, Septimius Severus, who finally emerged as undisputed victor in the civil wars that followed the assassination of Commodus in 192.

In determining which of the two is more likely to have been responsible, it is necessary to consider the purpose of undertaking such a great operation at that

37 Limestone block, sculptured with head of Mars wearing Corinthian helmet, attributed to screen of gods (see fig. 27), second to third century, found re-used as building material in the fourth century riverside wall near Blackfriars (see pp 168–9). *Museum of London*

particular time. City walls serve as a defence against an enemy, actual or potential; as a means of controlling and protecting the citizens in their dealings with the world beyond the city, particularly for customs control and law enforcement; and perhaps may also help to foster civic pride and self-consciousness, particularly if rival cities are furnished with walls. In the late second and early third centuries the last two functions can be dismissed out-of-hand as reasons for building the wall of Londinium; its purpose was undoubtedly for military defence. Very few towns in the north-western provinces, apart from the Augustan colonies of Provence, had walls at this date. In Britain most town walls are now considered to have been built in the late third century, but with few exceptions they had been preceded by ditch and rampart defences constructed in the late second century.[28] Unlike city walls these required little skilled labour and virtually no transport; they were therefore well within the capabilities of the local communities they were intended to protect, and there is no reason why they should not have been constructed simultaneously in response to a single decision of policy. Masonry-built walls were a very different proposition, and the town walls of Roman

Britain seem to have been built over a very considerable period of time, probably at least half a century. Londinium was not provided with a circumvallation by earthwork in the late second century; but about the same period a very considerable investment of highly skilled labour was made to defend it with a massive masonry wall. There are, however, no indications of hasty work to meet a sudden emergency, and it must have taken many months to complete. Like the contemporary earthwork defences of other towns, it was constructed against a threat that had not yet materialised, and the most likely period for this was in the years of preparation for the final showdown between Clodius Albinus and his rival Septimius Severus. Severus recognised Albinus as Caesar in 193, in order to postpone their inevitable conflict while he dealt with his other rivals in Italy and the east. After his defeat and execution of Niger in Syria, however, he declared Albinus a public enemy in 195. Albinus, hailed as Augustus by his troops, took most of the army in Britain across to Gaul in the following year and was finally defeated with difficulty at Lugdunum early in 197. It is hardly credible that Albinus did not foresee in 193 his eventual need to fight on the Continent, in

38 Limestone block, sculptured with bust of Mars (left), and purse and shoulder of Mercury (right) attributed to monumental arch (see fig. 26), late second to third century; found re-used as building material in the fourth-century river-side wall near Blackfriars (see pp168–9). *Museum of London*

which case he had three years to make his preparations. In the light of recent troubles, he must have foreseen the consequences of removing most of the army from Britain, and the loss of a province would have been an inauspicious beginning to his principate. The fortification of the towns, and above all the most important strategic centre at Londinium, would have seemed a logical insurance against this, since with Londinium as its base and the network of communications mainly intact, a Roman army could have reconquered Britain without much difficulty, even if it had been completely over-run by invading barbarians.

It has been argued that if the wall had been built by Albinus it would have been knocked down by Severus; but the latter was far too good a general not to recognise the strategic value of a strongly defended Londinium, and after the death of Albinus it was indisputably under his control, with the rest of the Roman world. He had no reason at all to undertake the not inconsiderable task of destroying such a strongly-built structure, and had pressing matters awaiting his attention in Britain that would in any case have left little time for such pettiness. Conversely, he had no particular motive for building it if it had not already existed. When he came to Britain in 208, his strategy was to deal with the troublesome northern tribes in their own territory, and he had the troops necessary to do so. Severus could only have been concerned with a springboard in the south for reconquest if alarming reports of the state of Britain had reached him at an earlier date, soon after the death of Albinus. If they had, he might have sent orders for the fortification of Londinium in advance of his own arrival, but it is unlikely that anything so well-built and carefully planned could have been achieved in the state of chaos that would have been his only reason for ordering it.

Monumental embellishments

The new quays and city wall were great public works with an obviously practical purpose, and the only surprise is that they should have been successfully accomplished at a time when other archaeological evidence suggests that Londinium had declined both in population and in prosperity. More astonishing is the discovery of an important group of monumental sculptures that can probably be attributed to this same period. When the fourth-century riverside wall was found in 1975 just to the east of Blackfriar's, it contained 52 massive blocks of limestone re-used as building material. Most of these had ornaments or portions of figures sculpted in relief (**37**, **38**), and 45 of them had come from two large and richly decorated monuments. In a brilliant comparative and architectural study Tom Blagg has reconstructed these as an arch at least 26ft (8m) high and 25ft wide (7.57m at the front and 7.46m at the back), and a screen more than 20ft wide (6.2m as reconstructed) with one end at least free-standing (figs 26, 27). Both were ornamented with figures of deities; the arch with at least four full-length figures including Minerva and Hercules, with a series of busts including Mercury and (probably) Mars on the frieze, and with medallions containing busts, one of a Season or Abundance, in the spandrels. Blagg has suggested that the deities on the frieze may be the divinities of the Days of the Week, in which case a diademed goddess on the right would be Venus. The screen had at least six full-length reliefs of deities, each standing in a separate arched niche, which were arranged in pairs. Portions of five reliefs were found, representing Vulcan, Minerva, Mercury (probably), Diana and Mars (37). There is also a Wind-God from the top of the panel at the free-standing end. Tom Blagg's carefully measured comments, arising from his detailed comparative studies, are worth quoting *verbatim*. He suggested 'that the London Arch is not earlier than late Antonine, or, more probably, Severan in date', and more tentatively 'that the

Fig. 26 Reconstruction of monumental arch from carved slabs re-used as building material in the late Roman riverside wall. *After reconstruction by T. Blagg*

Fig. 27 Reconstruction of screen of gods from carved slabs re-used as building material in the late Roman riverside wall. Vulcan, Minerva, Mercury (?), Diana and Mars are represented on the front, with an unidentified female figure on the back. *After reconstruction by T. Blagg*

work was carried out by Romano-British masons'. He was unable to date the screen of gods more closely than to say 'that it probably belongs to the second or third centuries', but suggested a stylistic affinity with sculptures from the area 'lying north-east of a line between Metz and Strasbourg, and including the middle reaches of the Rhine and the Moselle'.[29]

The arch was obviously not a triumphal arch, which would have glorified human achievement, but is likely to have been a monumental entrance to a precinct devoted to religious or recreational activities—quite possibly both. It is significant that massive sculptured blocks have been found only in the western part of the riverside wall—not only in the portion at the extreme west excavated by Charles Hill and others in 1975–6, but also in a stretch of wall observed during sewer excavations at the foot of Lambeth Hill in 1841, some 220 yeards (200m) to the east. Roach Smith recorded that the lower part of the wall here contained huge stones, 'sculptured and ornamented with mouldings, denoting their use in the friezes or entablatures of edifices, at some period antecedent to the construction of the wall'. There were also 'fragments of sculptured marble, which had also decorated buildings, and part of the foliage or trellis work of an altar or tomb', likewise re-used as building materials.[30] Significantly, the few sculptured stones from the recent excavation that did not belong to the arch or screen of gods included three that undoubtedly came from temples or shrines. One was a relief with a unique group of four mother-goddesses, instead of the usual three, and the others were two altars, each with a third-century inscription relating to the rebuilding of a temple, one probably of Jupiter, the other almost certainly of Isis (see pp176–81). It is reasonable to assume therefore, that a large area south of St Paul's Cathedral, in the south-western corner of the walled city, was occupied during the third century by a precinct of public buildings, including temples, which was probably entered by the monumental arch. It is an area of which we know little from other archaeological evidence, though the scarcity of domestic refuse has been noted, and an elaborate system of terracing has been observed in the neighbourhood of Lambeth Hill. In 1981, massive foundations of an east–west and a north–south wall, consisting of large limestone blocks on oak piles and rammed chalk, were found on the lower terrace at Peter's Hill, Upper Thames Street, evidently part of a public building that could have been a temple. Quite possibly the precinct contained places of entertainment as well as temples, for in the Roman world they were often closely associated—as, for example, in the so-called Triangular Forum at Pompeii, which contained three temples, including one of Isis, a theatre, a smaller concert theatre (*odeon*), a gladiatorial school and a gymnasium. Blagg has cited architectural parallels of the late second century at Champlieu (Aisne), where a decorated arched entrance gave access to a complex of temple, theatre and baths. Something of this sort probably stood in the south-west corner of Londinium.

Apart from the stylistic dating of the arch, there are several good reasons for suggesting that this contribution to the amenities of Londinium is more likely to have been of the Severan period than any other within the possible date range. Public works that were a luxury rather than a necessity would have been undertaken only at a period of relative stability, and the earlier Antonine governors of Britain, including Albinus, had more pressing matters demanding their attention. Moreover, interest in the project at a very high level was required to achieve the standards demonstrated by the architectural fragments, particularly if sculptors from another province were recruited to assist with the work, as the stylistic affinities of the screen of gods seem to suggest.

In 208, Septimius Severus with his wife, Julia Domna, and two sons, Caracalla and Geta, arrived in Britain. The whole family spent the rest of the year and the early months of 209 in the south, almost certainly in Londinium, presumably living in the Cannon Street palace. In the summer Severus departed for the north, taking Caracalla with him, leaving the young Geta, on whom he had bestowed the title of Augustus, behind in the south in charge of the administration, with Julia as his adviser. She remained there while Severus was campaigning in Caledonia, but rejoined her husband when he went into winter quarters on Hadrian's Wall. Any improvements in Londinium at this time are likely to have been directly due to the presence of the imperial family. Apart from its waterfront and splendid new city wall, Londinium must have appeared run-down and neglected, with large areas derelict within the western wall. The Huggin Hill baths and other buildings that were no longer needed had probably already been demolished, perhaps to provide material for dumping when the waterfront was advanced, and the western part of the city must have seemed a particularly depressing waste-land. It would have been surprising if Julia, an energetic and forceful lady, had not determined to do something about it during her months of residence. Skilled builders in masonry may have been in short supply, since their services were in demand for rebuilding the northern defences, but sculptors and monumental masons could have been made available for the embellishment of Londinium at the command of the empress. Her particular interest was religion, so that the decision to build a new temple precinct would have been in character, as would the favouring of an oriental cult. Julia herself was Syrian, but the Severan dynasty seems to have had a special attachment to the related Egyptian cults of Isis and Serapis. It is possible that the worship of Isis had lingered on in Londinium since its early days in Southwark 140 years earlier, but it is more likely that it was reintroduced by the Severan court.

In our present state of knowledge, which is patchy in the extreme, the 70 years or so between about 150 and 220 present us with a curious paradox—a period of decline and abandonment in many parts of Londinium, including practically the whole of Southwark, immediately followed by major public works of an enduring character. It can hardly be questioned that the population of Londinium went through a crisis of some kind a few years after the middle of the second century, as a result of which their number was drastically reduced and whole districts were abandoned, presumably with a considerable reduction, if not abandonment, of the industrial and commercial activities with which those districts had been concerned. It is equally clear, however, that the Roman authorities in Britain never lost sight of the strategic importance of Londinium as a port and centre of the road network, and went to great lengths to re-establish it and maintain it. An enormous investment was made in what appears to have been a decaying city, and there is no doubt that a succession of Roman rulers saw Londinium as the key to effective control of Britain. Yet, paradoxically again, the administrative and political importance of the city was considerably reduced by its latest benefactor. Septimius Severus took measures to prevent the rise of a second Albinus by dividing Britain into two separate provinces, Britannia Superior, the south and west, of which Londinium presumably continued to be the capital, and Britannia Inferior, the north-east and extreme north, with a new capital at York (*Eburacum*), where he proceeded to build a palace, and where he himself died early in 211.

It is possible that the reduction in status suffered by the London palace at this time is reflected by substantial alterations that were made to it at an unknown date after the early second century. The great state rooms north of the central courtyard were demolished during the Roman period, and replaced by a later Roman structure with a hypocaust and with lower floors of rammed chalk containing flint pebbles burnt cherry-red. Probably at the same time the pool in the courtyard was filled in, partly with debris from the demolition. The more utilitarian south and east wings of the palace, however, do not appear to have been demolished and rebuilt.[31]

8

Londinium
in the Third Century

When Julia Domna and the two rival emperors, her sons Caracalla and Geta, left Britain in 211, Londinium had all the external appearance of grandeur—its great new wall that had extended the city's boundary to the west and at one point in the north, enclosing cemetery areas that had formerly lain beyond it; an impressive line of wharfs recently built out into the river, extending from the eastern end of the city to the bridge and beyond it; and a district of temples and probably places of entertainment at its western end, containing new monuments as impressive as any that had been seen in Britain. All these, however, had been imposed by the will of powerful rulers, and it is difficult to judge to what extent this external renaissance was accompanied by a recovery of the vitality of the city itself and its people from the crisis of depopulation 50 years earlier.

The first half of the third century has always presented problems to students of Roman Britain, because coins are the ultimate basis of archaeological dating, and those issued in this period rarely passed into general circulation in Britain, so that they are not usually found on archaeological sites. This phenomenon itself is obviously significant, but no explanation yet offered either by historians or numismatists seems completely satisfactory. Fewer coins may have been paid to the army, in spite of a recent pay increase, because of possible reductions in the garrisons, and as a result of the introduction by Severus of a system of deductions at source; but civil sites closely connected with government such as Londinium are unlikely to have received all their cash-flow through military channels. The hoarding of better coins because of the rapid debasement of the currency certainly took place, but new coins were invariably more debased than their predecessors and should have passed into circulation until overtaken by the next noticeable wave of debasement, a period long enough, one would have thought, for a somewhat greater number of new coin-losses than the finds suggest. Moreover the bronze coins of this period are no more common than the increasingly debased silver as site finds in London. Roach Smith lists in his series of more than 1700 coins from the Thames, for example, 22 silver coins and only 16 bronze of the period 217–53.[1] It is generally agreed that the main coinage in circulation in Britain in the first half of the third century was the dwindling stock of second century bronze, and this would have been quite insufficient for a large population vigorously engaged in retail trade, such as we seem to have had in London in the late first century. It may be suspected that the inhabitants of Londinium in the third century were far fewer in number and that their activities and way of life were very different. Wealth, as we shall see, was not lacking, but it seems to have been concentrated in fewer hands. Perhaps this is what happened to the coins also, for it would be wrong to leave the impression that hardly any coins fresh from the mint reached Londinium in the first half of the third century. Nearly all those we know, however, come from a single hoard found in Lime Street in 1882. As many as 800 have been recorded, consisting of both silver denarii and antoniniani (double-denarii of reduced weight), and ranging in date from Commodus (183) to Trajan Decius (249–51). They were found by labourers in an urn of black pottery, at a depth of 17–18ft (5–5.5m) and, as usually happens on such occasions, were at once dispersed. Nearly 600 passed into the hands of four antiquaries, who allowed John Evans to publish their coins;[2] and a further 210 were secured by another collector, from whom they were eventually purchased by Guildhall Museum.[3] How many more there were we shall never know, but it would be surprising if there were less than 1000 coins in the hoard, and it may well have been very much larger. This may be an instance of the retention in a hoard of relatively good coins with some silver content into a period of utter debasement, for only nine years after the closing date of the hoard the silver disappeared almost entirely and the antoninianus became virtually a copper coin. It is possible, therefore, that the hoard was not abandoned until the 260s, though in that case it is a little odd that the owner did not continue to add the coins of Aemilian and Valerian in the period 252–60, when some silver content still remained.

Third-century inscriptions and sculptures

It is clear that there was wealth in Londinium in the third century, for a very considerable proportion of the sculptures and inscriptions found in the city belong to this period, even omitting those from the monumental arch and screen of gods, which are probably Severan. Several inscriptions and works of art are definitely post-Severan and cannot be attributed to any stimulus arising from the presence of the imperial family. If the patronage of Julia Domna and her sons had attracted sculptors to Londinium, there is reason to believe that these continued to receive commissions after the departure of the court, and even developed a somewhat idiosyncratic local school of sculpture.

There is, for example, a head of oolitic limestone, 12$\frac{1}{2}$in (31.7cm) high, considerable larger than lifesize, that was found incorporated as building material in the late Roman bastion of the city wall in Camomile Street. It represents a middle-aged or elderly man with deeply furrowed forehead and cheeks, and with the short hair and beard that are characteristic of about the middle of the third century (**39**). The size seems to indicate that it is an imperial portrait, and Professor

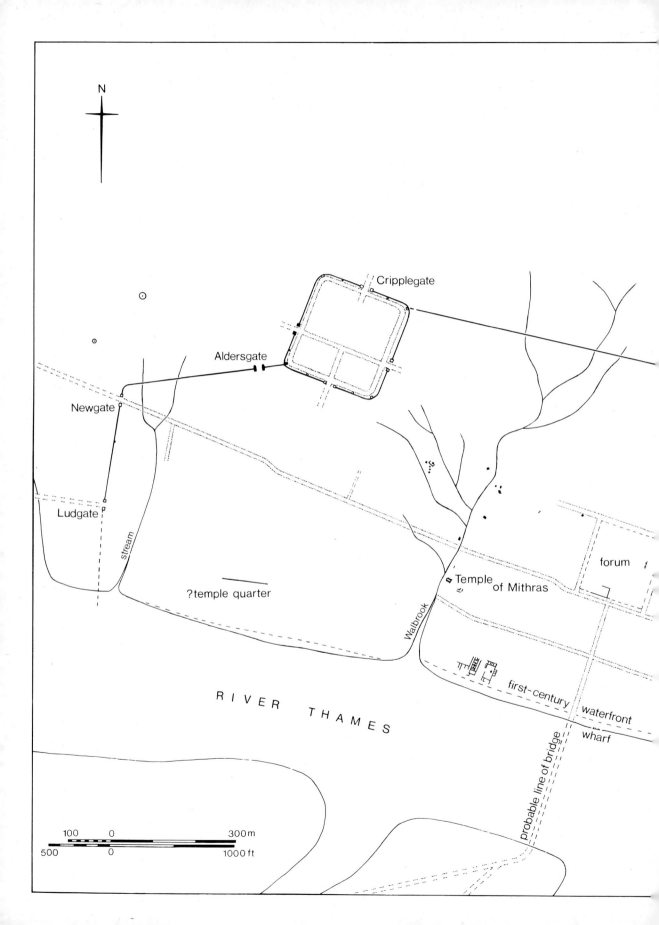

N

Cripplegate

Aldersgate

Newgate

Ludgate

stream

?temple quarter

Walbrook

Temple of Mithras

forum

first-century waterfront

wharf

probable line of bridge

R I V E R   T H A M E S

100   0   300 m

500   0   1000 ft

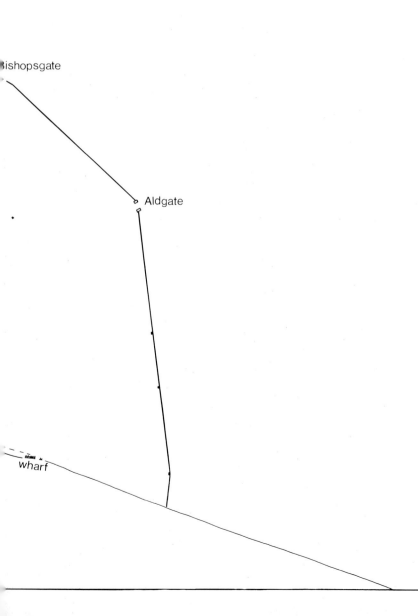

Fig. 28 Map: features of Londinium in the third century. *C. Unwin*

Bishopsgate

Aldgate

wharf

buildings
line of town wall
burial
burial group
probable line of road
possible line of road

Toynbee has suggested that it might be Philip I or Trajan Decius.[4] The other sculptures from the bastion come from the Roman cemetery, however, so that this rather fine but battered head could be from the funerary monument of an individual who died in Londinium. If so, the size suggests that he was an important official, considered worthy of an imposing and expensive memorial.

Much lower in the ranks of officialdom was Celsus, the *spectulator*, a member of the military staff of the governor of Britannia Superior, who had been seconded from *Legio II Augusta Antoniniana* for executive duties in the administration of justice. His tombstone, which was commissioned by his brother *speculatores* in London, had a portrait in relief of Celsus, but unfortunately little has survived its apparent re-use as building material in Playhouse Yard, significantly near the line of the city wall, though no bastion is known there.[5] The title *Antoniniana* ('Caracalla's Own') was not given to the legion before 213,[6] so the tombstone of Celsus was evidently set up after that date.

Another military tombstone that is almost certainly of the third century was found in the eastern cemetery in Goodman's Fields. This was commissioned in memory of Flavius Agricola, a serving soldier of *Legio VI Victrix*, by his wife Albia Faustina.[7] Since soldiers were not allowed to marry during their period of service before 197, Agricola must have died in London after that date, possibly in transit, but more probably while stationed in the capital on staff duties of some kind.

For the same reason, the larger and more elaborate sculptured stele in memory of the centurion Vivius Marcianus of *Legio II Augusta* should be later than 197. This was commissioned by his wife Januaria Martina, and has a full-length portrait in relief of Marcianus, holding his centurion's staff in one hand and what appears to be a scroll in the other.[8] This again probably indicates that he was a staff officer with administrative duties.

On neither of these tombstones is the legion given the title *Antoniniana*. Its absence might indicate a date between 197 and 213, or later in the third century when the memory of Caracalla was no longer honoured; inscriptions at Caerleon dated to 244 and to about 255–60 do not include the title,[9] and its comparative rarity in inscriptions suggests that it may have been dropped after the death of Caracalla in 217. The only clue to dating is the doubtful criterion of the quality of lettering—better in the small memorial tablet of Flavius Agricola, which could be of the early third century, than in the large sculptured tombstone of Marcianus, which might be somewhat later.

Two other third-century inscriptions are of even greater interest. These were found in 1975 re-used as building material in the later Roman riverside wall near its western end, together with the massive sculptured blocks of the monumental arch and screen of gods discussed in the last chapter. There is little doubt that they came from the same religious complex that seems to have occupied the south-western corner of the city. Both are altars with inscriptions relating to the rebuilding of temples which, in the conventional phrase used for such restoration, 'had fallen down through old age'. They are considerably damaged, but have been skilfully read by Mark Hassall.[10] One, which is incomplete, records the rebuilding of a temple dedicated either to Jupiter (the most likely reading), to Mithras, to the Great Mother (Cybele), or to Isis. The one letter, M, that remains of this part of the inscription, could be fitted into the standard dedicatory formula for any of these deities. The restoration was done by one Aquilinus, described as a 'freedman of the Emperor' (*libertus Augusti*), together with three others, named Mercator, Audax and Graecus. Imperial freedmen often held high posts in government service, and Aquilinus was evidently such a man. The other three were probably junior colleagues in the imperial bureaucracy, which made considerable use of skilled and educated slaves, who could hope to receive their freedom as they advanced in the service.

The other altar is more complete (**40**), but broken in half and difficult to read in places. It records the rebuilding of a temple, almost certainly of Isis, by M. Martiannius Pulcher, described as pro-praetor (governor) under two joint-emperors. Uncertainty about one letter in an abbreviation makes it possible that

39 Portrait-head of elderly man, larger than life-size (height about 13¼in, 33.6cm). ? mid-third century, from fill of bastion in Camomile Street. *Museum of London*

Pulcher was an acting-governor of equestrian rank or a deputy-governor, rather than the governor of Upper Britain, who would have been of senatorial rank. Whatever his exact status, Martiannius Pulcher is a new name in the list of rulers of Britain, and this is the first piece of actual epigraphic evidence associating the governorship with Londinium. It is considered that the style of lettering is too late for the very brief joint rule of Caracalla and Geta, so that the two emperors reigning together must be either Trebonianus Gallus and Valerian (251–3) or Valerian and Gallienus (253–9). The only doubt about the name of the deity arises from damage to the D in the word ISIDIS ('of Isis') and a rather wide space between this letter and the preceding I, into which another letter could be fitted. Similar irregularities occur elsewhere in the inscription, however, and no alternative reading has been proposed. I have suggested in the last chapter that Isis was the deity most likely to be favoured by the Severan dynasty, which was probably responsible for the architectural embellishments of the precinct where the temple stood (p171). If, however, the temple itself had been built by the orders of Julia Domna in 208–9, it had fallen down 'through old age' in less than 50 years, whereas the monumental arch and screen of gods were presumably still standing when the riverside wall was built more than a century later. It is possible, however, that monumental masons capable of building with massive sculptured blocks were available, but that ordinary builders in stone and rubble concrete were not, in view of the work that was required of them in the north of Britain, not only in repairing the defences, but also for building at York, which Severus made into a second capital, with its own palace. New temples required for Londinium may therefore have been jerry-built by inexperienced builders, or even constructed of wood, side by side with the enduring monumental structures. There is also the possibility of local subsidence on a terraced slope. It seems less likely that a pre-Severan temple of Isis had survived in the precinct when these embellishments were added, or that arch, screen of gods, terracing and massive building on Peter's Hill were all constructed when the temple was rebuilt in the mid-third century. Public works on such a scale suggest the initiative of a higher authority than Martiannus Pulcher, and we have no evidence of any imperial visit at this date.

Mark Hassall has made the interesting suggestion that the two inscriptions might possibly refer to the same temple, since Isis is one of the four possible deities for the dedication of the first. In that case the governor (or acting-governor) would have given the order for the reconstruction, which would have been carried out under the supervision of the imperial freedman and his colleagues. Mark Hassall made it clear, however, that he regarded this possibility as less likely than the alternative; that two separate temples, one dedicated to Isis and the other

40 Limestone altar commemorating rebuilding of temple, probably of Isis, by M. Martiannius Pulcher, governor or acting-governor of the province under two joint-emperors, probably 251–3 or 253–9 (see above). Height 1.22m. Found re-used as building material in fourth-century riverside wall near Blackfriars. *Museum of London*

most probably to Jupiter, were rebuilt, not necessarily at the same time. One important circumstance is common to both, however; in each case the initiative for rebuilding came from government officials, not from the city council or from wealthy private citizens.

There is in fact a suggestion of the close connection of all the third century monuments that we have considered with the bureaucracy of provincial government. This may also be true of another, one of the most mysterious sculptures found in London, though the interpretation on which the suggestion is based has not been universally accepted. This sculpture was found built into the riverside wall and was probably from a shrine in or near the precinct from which came the altar-inscriptions, monumental arch and screen of gods. Uniquely, it represents four mother-goddesses instead of the usual three (**41**), and it seems likely that the interloper in an otherwise conventional triad is the more naturalistic second figure from the left, who is distinguished from the others by her less formal posture, her head-covering and the fact that she is nursing a baby.[11] She could be intended to represent not merely a Nursing-Mother goddess (Dea Nutrix), whose cult was common in Gaul and has Mediterranean affinities, but also a deified empress, whose normal veil had been replaced by the shorter head-covering that was familiar in the Rhineland. Relatively few empresses were deified after their deaths, and only one who found a dynasty, however short-lived, is likely to have been represented as a Nursing-Mother. There was in any case no point in an elaborate political compliment unless it gratified the reigning emperor. This limits the possibilities to Faustina II, mother of Commodus, deified in 175–6; Julia Domna, deified by Elagabalus, who claimed to be her grandson, about 220; and Julia Maesa, deified by her own grandson, Severus Alexander, after death in 225. The first can probably be ruled out, for such a compliment must have been inspired by a recent deification, and Faustina was deified a year or two before her son's accession, in the reign of Marcus Aurelius, her widower, for whom this particular symbolism would have been inappropriate. Facially the figure represented is quite unlike Julia Domna, who had neat features and a small chin, and with its rather heavy jowl is less unlike the coin portraits of Julia Maesa; but recognisable portraiture cannot be expected from a provincial sculptor who was working without a model. There would be no mystery if we had an inscription, but another curious feature is that the large panel for this at the base has been left completely blank. It seems most unlikely that a work of this quality had a painted inscription, so it must be assumed that it was never finished, but went to a shrine where it was presumably kept for more than a century, without explanatory dedication or donor's name. If the former had some political significance, it may have become expedient to suppress it before the inscription was added. This explanation raises difficulties, however, if the emperor concerned was Severus Alexander, since he was not murdered until 235, about ten years after his grandmother's death. It must also be said that this interpretation is not acceptable to Professor Jocelyn Toynbee, our greatest authority on Romano-British art, who would prefer to explain the fourth goddess as a sculptor's error.

41 Limestone relief of four mother-goddesses, holding (l-r) fruit, a child, a dog and a basket of fruit. Width 1.20m. Found re-used as building material in the fourth-century riverside wall near Blackfriars. *Museum of London*

She suggests that the sculptor was commissioned to put a standing figure of the donor at the extreme right, but instead put in a fourth seated goddess. In that case the donor must have been female, and was presumably a wealthy private citizen. A political compliment, on the other hand, is more likely to have come from a high official who could ensure that news of it reached the emperor and hope thereby to gain some advantage. This interpretation, therefore, would place the relief of the four goddesses in the group of officially sponsored monuments of the early and mid-third century described above.

Without this monument, there are sufficient to suggest that patronage for sculpture and architecture in third-century London came mainly from

officialdom, directly or indirectly, rather than from independent merchants and entrepreneurs. It is significant that the five inscriptions that can confidently be attributed to the third century relate either to officials in the imperial service or to legionary soldiers, whose principal function in Londinium would have been staff-work for the governor—as is explicitly stated in one instance. Duties of a humbler and more directly military nature, as guards and escorts, are likely to have been allocated to auxiliaries. It may also be noted that all these monuments were probably set up between 200 and 260, a period for which other datable artifacts and deposits are difficult to identify because of the lack of coin evidence.

A period of recovery and change

Other evidence of activity in the first half of the third century is not completely lacking, however, and more will probably be found as a result of further refinements in the dating of pottery, on which archaeologists are almost completely dependent for this period. Chris Green has already attributed a number of pottery sherds in Lower Thames Street to the early or mid-third century.[12]

A re-assessment of the pottery evidence from the Temple of Mithras in Walbrook by Joanna Bird has led to a revision of its date of building from the late second century to the 240s—a revision fully accepted by Professor Grimes. Occupation of the Walbrook valley had therefore recommenced before the middle of the third century, though it was now of a very different character. Dumping on the marshy ground to reclaim it by raising the level was followed by the construction of substantial buildings with walls of ragstone and tile, very different from the flimsier wooden structures that had been abandoned about 160. A number of the new buildings had finely patterned mosaic floors, such as the one found north of Bucklersbury in 1869 and others found on the site of the Bank of England in 1805 and 1933–4. Unfortunately mosaics of this kind cannot yet be dated stylistically, and we have no archaeological evidence for their date. The Walbrook temple was probably an appendage of a similar stone-built house that lay to the east of it and was dated on pottery evidence as not earlier than the Antonine period.[13] Presumably the reclaimer of this particular portion of the Walbrook valley would have built his own house before building a Mithraeum behind it, so it can probably be attributed to a date before the middle of the third century. A house with a rather inferior mosaic near a tributary of the Walbrook in Ironmonger Lane was built over a pit attributed to the first half of the third century, and was itself probably of the later third century.[14] One result of the reclamation seems to have been the enclosure of the banks of the Walbrook as private property, so that the earlier practice of dropping coins and other small objects into the stream was not generally resumed. The temple of Mithras stood in an open area, but it was the repository of secrets, and it is unlikely that the

42 Remains of Mithraeum, a basilican temple with western apse, built on east bank of Walbrook about 240; as excavated in 1954 (view to E). *Museum of London*

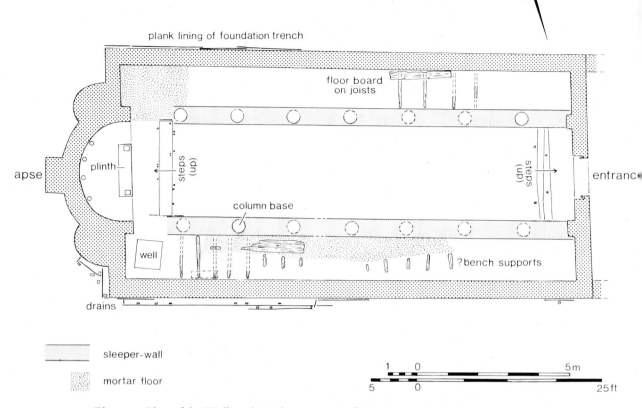

N

plank lining of foundation trench

floor board
on joists

apse

plinth

steps
(up)

steps
(up)

entranc

column base

well

?bench supports

drains

sleeper-wall

mortar floor

1   0   5m

5   0   25ft

Fig. 29 Plan of the Walbrook Mithraeum in its first phase (mid–third century); a basilican temple with nave separated from aisles by sleeper walls bearing columns, and with a raised sanctuary within a western apse. *After W. F. Grimes*

uninitiated were allowed to have ready access to it. It was probably enclosed so that the only approach was through the house to the east (fig 29).

Who were the builders and occupiers of these houses? A few years ago we would have said without hesitation that they were wealthy merchants, but this now seems less likely in third-century Londinium. The mercantile element no doubt remained, but was probably less prominent than the bureaucracy.

In this connection it is worth considering a small problem raised by the Mithraeum. After it was built a number of cult sculptures of Italian marble were installed, and there is no doubt that these were carved in Italy. They include a marble head of Mithras (**43**), that was almost certainly fitted to the principal cult image, a group representing Mithras slaying the bull, which would have stood in the sanctuary within the western apse. Professor Toynbee has commented that its general style, and particularly the way in which the hair is worked, point to a date between 180 and 200.[15] There is also the figure of a Genius, which she suggests could have come from the hand of an Italian carver of the mid-second century.[16] There is a very classical head of Minerva, which she assigns to 'the hellenizing

43 Head of Mithras in Italian marble, attributed to about 180–200; found in two pieces carefully buried in the Walbrook Mithraeum (see p211–12). Height 14½in (37cm). *Museum of London*

44 Marble votive medallion relating to a Danubian cult of twin rider-gods associated with a mother-goddess (the central figure). Diameter 4⅜in (11.1cm). Found in the Walbrook Mithraeum (p187). *Museum of London*

45 Marble relief of Mithras sacrificing the bull, enclosed in zodiac circle; found in Walbrook in 1889, almost certainly in the Mithraeum. Dedicated by Ulpius Silvanus, veteran of *Legio II Augusta*. Height 17½in (44.5cm). *Museum of London*

phase of Roman artistic taste during the central decades of the second century'.[17] There is a river-god, which she dates on grounds of technique and style to the second quarter or middle of the second century.[18] Finally, there is a very fine head of the Egyptian god, Serapis, which should not be earlier than the last quarter of the second century.[19] We have, therefore, a group of imported marble sculptures ranging in date, in Professor Toynbee's expert opinion, at least from the middle of the second century almost to its end. Since dating from style and technique is not an exact science, it was just possible, when we thought the temple had been built in the last decade of the second century, to suggest that most of these Italian marbles were commissioned and imported at the time of building. If it was built fifty years later, as we now believe, that is impossible, and the full implications of Professor Toynbee's date-range must be considered. The latest of the sculptures was probably fifty years old and the earliest a century old when they were installed. It is a collection of several generations that could hardly have been assembled by a nouveau-riche. Moreover, the head of Mithras, at least, must have been brought from another Mithraeum, which had presumably also been owned by the builders of the London temple. Mithraism was equally popular among soldiers, officials and merchants, and it now seems most likely that the Walbrook Mithraeum was built by a Roman official from a well-established family, who had come to Britain in the course of his career and had brought his religion and his heirlooms with him. It is noteworthy that in the art from this temple there are indications of influences from Central Europe that are more easily explained by the posting of an official than by trading connections. Finds include a marble votive plaque (**44**) relating to a characteristically Danubian cult of twin rider-gods with a mother-goddess,[20] and a silver strainer at present parallelled only by another from Stráže in Slovakia, that was almost certainly derived from the neighbouring Roman province of Pannonia.[21] Professor Toynbee has also recognised possible Danubian influence in a marble relief of the bull-sacrifice found in Walbrook in 1889, almost certainly in the Mithraeum (**45**). The Mithraic scene is enclosed by a zodiac circle, known in only two other examples, one from Stockstadt in Germany and the other from Siscia in Pannonia.[22]

Recovery in Southwark did not generally begin before the middle of the third century, though on a site in St Thomas Street, in the north-eastern part of the suburb, a building with a plain tessellated floor and flint walls seems to have been constructed in the early third century.[23] As in the city, the nature of the later occupation was very different from that of the earlier, and was much less dense. The new stone-based buildings were very much larger, and as only portions of them have been recorded, it is impossible to be sure of their nature and purpose. Harvey Sheldon has suggested that most of the structures observed may belong to as few as three large complexes, one near and on the site of the Cathedral, one in Southwark Street and one near St Thomas Street. There were also robbed walls probably of a late Roman stone building at 201–11 Borough High Street, near the southern end of the settlement, and a stone building with hypocaust pilae, built in the late third century, at its eastern side near the river. Elsewhere on sites earlier occupied by buildings the late Roman levels, where they survive, consist mainly of the dark soil that may indicate agricultural or horticultural activities.[24] It has been suggested that the late Roman buildings in Southwark were public, but it would be surprising if administrative buildings were placed outside the city walls, particularly as there was plenty of room within them in the western part of the city. It is quite possible that an inn or temple would have been built in Southwark, but it is just as likely that these sites would have been used for large residences for the rich and important, analogous to those built in the Walbrook valley, which also probably extended over a considerable area.

A group of broken sculptures dumped in a late Roman well under the cathedral most probably came from the adjacent building complex, and gives some clue to its nature.[25] A most unusual limestone figure of a hunter-god must have come from a shrine or temple (**46**), as must an altar dedicated by one Cassianus, from which unfortunately the name of the god has been broken away. A figure of a Genius, the personification of the spirit of a locality or group of people, also presumably came from a shrine, public or domestic, and a date in the first half of the third century is suggested by the treatment of drapery and cornucopiae. The oldest of the sculptures is a fragment of a statuette in marble from the Greek islands, representing a muscular left leg adjacent to a dolphin, and the figure was evidently that of a sea-god, Neptune or Oceanus. Very classical in style and possibly a small copy of a major larger sculpture, it has been attributed by Professor Toynbee to the first or second century. A small work of art of this kind might have been dedicated as a votive offering at a temple, but might equally well have been used as a household ornament, particularly in a bath suite. So far the finds from the well might suggest that the adjacent buildings belonged to a temple complex, but this view cannot easily be reconciled with the fact that they were accompanied by two others that are obviously funerary. One is part of the tombstone of somebody whose name included the letters TIC or TIO, and who died at the age of 33 or 34, (or, much less probably, 83 or 84), dedicated by a woman named Matrona, a word meaning of course 'Mother', but occasionally found as a personal name throughout the Roman world, and particularly in North Africa. The other is the upper portion of a unique ash-chest in an unidentified stone similar to that of the Genius. It represents the draped figure of a woman reclining on a couch, holding a bunch of grapes in her left hand, and some other edible object—a fruit or cake—in her right (**47**). This object is not exactly a lid, for it has no back, and seems to be intended to be slid into position as the cover for a niche. It seems likely that it was intended to be visible, and the probable context would be a *columbarium*, a sepulchral chamber in which the ashes of the dead were placed in niches in the walls. This suggests a large mausoleum, and if it stood in the neighbourhood of the cathedral it was remote from other Southwark burials, which have mostly been found a considerable distance to the south, south of Long Lane, or to the south-west, west of Southwark Bridge Road. A mausoleum would be unlikely in a temple complex, but it might well be associated with a rich family residence, as at Lullingstone, where the villa can also provide examples of a

46 Limestone figure of hunter-god holding bow, with quiver on back, accompanied by stag (?) and dog (p188). Height 2ft 5in (73.5cm). Found in late Roman well under Southwark Cathedral. *Museum of London*

small private temple near the house and chapels, both pagan and Christian, that are actually within it. The finds from Southwark Cathedral, if found in a more remote place would certainly have been attributed to a substantial villa, and it seems likely that a comparable household was established just to the west of the southern end of the bridge in the later third century. We have no means of judging, however, whether it was concerned with the villa-like activity of horticulture, which was almost certainly going on in the neighbourhood, or whether it was simply the residence of an important bureaucrat of Londinium who preferred to commute across London Bridge. A combination of both functions is by no means unlikely.

We can perhaps make certain tentative deductions from the Cathedral finds about the nature of the owner. Like the builder of the Mithraeum he was no parvenu, and brought at least one valuable heirloom with him—the marble figurine of the sea-god. The figure of the hunter-god he may well have commissioned himself, and its size suggests it occupied an important place in his

47   Cover of funerary ash-chest, representing deceased woman on couch, holding grapes (see p188). Found in late Roman well under Southark Cathedral. Length 15in (38cm). *Museum of London*

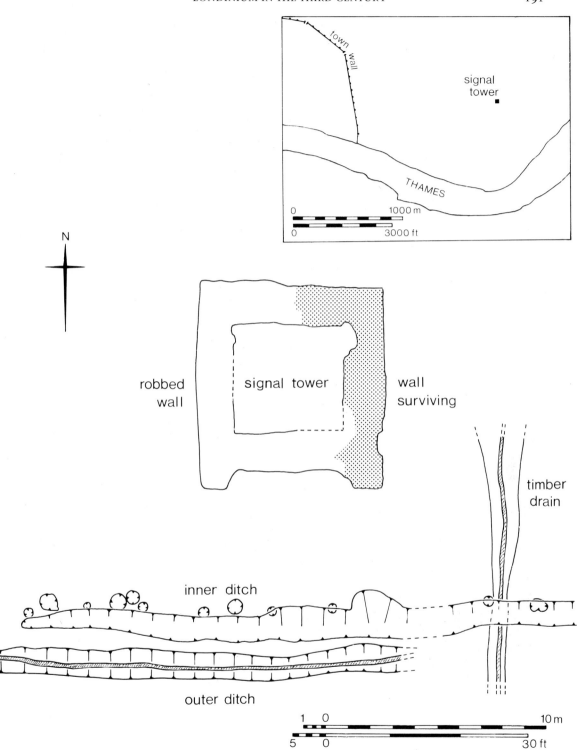

Fig. 30 Plan of signal tower at Shadwell, excavated by Tony Johnson in 1974 (see pp192–4).
After T. Johnson

household worship. It might not be too fanciful to suggest that the choice of cult could indicate a taste for the field sports that were a principal relaxation of the officer class. The ash-chest has no known parallel, and was presumably specially commissioned by someone who was familiar either with the couch monuments of the first–third century near Rome, or more probably with the sarcophagus lids with reclining figures of the later second–third century, which were of Asiatic origin, but were imported into Italy and sometimes copied there.[26] Familiarity with a Mediterranean fashion would be more likely in a high-ranking member of the military or official class, who would have moved from province to province in the course of his career, than in a wealthy merchant or Romano-British landowner, whose horizon would be narrower. If the owner of the Cathedral complex of Roman buildings belonged to the official class, this does not necessarily preclude him from a share in whatever horticultural activity was going on in Southwark, either in retirement or as a profitable side-line while in office in Londinium. It may be suspected that the 'dark earth' deposits in the western part of the Roman city itself owed their origin to similar activities by a similar class of person.

Among the possibilities cited to explain the appearance of large buildings in Southwark in the late third century is that there was an influx of wealthy Gauls into Britain, driven from their homelands by the barbarian invasions of that period.[27] It is difficult to see, however, how refugees, whose principal wealth had been the lands that were devastated, could possibly have transferred much capital to another province. They might certainly have introduced new ideas and fashions, but none of the strange features of the art from the well under Southwark Cathedral can be paralleled in Gaul.[28] Moreover the appearance of large stone buildings in Southwark, at some uncertain date in the later third century, seems to be merely a continuation of a process which apparently began in the Walbrook valley somewhat earlier than the invasions of Gaul.

The Signal Tower at Shadwell

Britain had its own troubles with Teutonic barbarians in the third century, and the lower Thames valley was as accessible to Saxon raiders from the Continent as it was to merchants. The fort at Reculver on the north Kent coast was built either about 220, or more probably soon after 225, and its prime purpose must have been to protect the Thames estuary. It is larger than was needed for the auxiliary cohort (*Cohors I Baetasiorum*) that was stationed there, and probably also contained naval personnel. Other measures were no doubt taken, and later in the third century there is evidence for a signalling system which presumably gave early warning of the arrival of raiders. This seems the only possible explanation of an interesting site excavated by Tony Johnson in 1974 in London's derelict dockland, about $\frac{3}{4}$ mile (1.2km) east of the Tower of London. Its principal feature was a building 26ft (8m) square, with walls 6ft (2m) thick, built of chalk and mortar with a knapped flint facing. There were buttresses at both ends of the south wall. Most of the material of the walls had been removed by stone-robbers in the seventeenth

48 Partially robbed foundation of signal tower, Shadwell, with two ditches and post-holes of stockade to wouth (top), later third century (view from above to south). *T. Johnson*

century, but the east wall had been protected because it lay beneath an alley, and survived to a course of bonding tiles just above the Roman ground surface. The thickness of the walls indicates height, and the building can only have been a tower. It had been built on a gravel slope, but no terrace had been cut; instead the foundations had been levelled by digging deeper foundation trenches to the north. Initially a line of large posts had been set up about 18ft (5.5m) south of the tower, presumably for a stockade, but this was subsequently replaced by a double ditch running east–west, presumably as a defence on the river side. Neither extended across the whole area excavated, but they overlapped in front of the tower (fig. 30, **48**). Traces of clay floors, sill-beam constructions and burnt wattle and daub walls showed that there had been timber buildings to the east that were probably contemporary with the stone tower, and a bronze belt terminal of distinctive type provided evidence for military occupation. There had been some earlier settlements in the neighbourhood, but the tower with its accompanying structures dates from the later third century. It was placed where it could be seen from the eastern side of the city defences and where it overlooked the curve of the river at Limehouse.[29] If it was in fact a signal tower intended to keep a watch on the river, and it is difficult to imagine any other possible function, it must have been one of a series that probably extended to the estuary. The obvious place for the next one downstream would have been the neck of land overlooking the Isle of Dogs, with a view over Blackwall Point and down the river to Woolwich Reach.

It must be assumed that the measures taken to protect the lower Thames and Londinium were effective, for the new buildings in Southwark, which as far as we know had no defences, imply a general sense of security. In times of real danger, whatever their purpose, they would surely have been built within the city walls, where there must have been enough room in the late third century, at least to the west of the Walbrook, to accommodate all the late Roman building complexes in Southwark. There may have been certain disadvantages, such as inconvenience for attending to estates on the south bank, and the legal necessity of building family mausolea in cemeteries some distance from home beyond the walls, but these must have been outweighed by considerations of security if piratical raids had seemed likely. The destruction exemplified by the broken sculptures in the well almost certainly came much later, and may be attributable to Christian iconoclasm.

Trade in Londinium in the third century

In the earlier part of its history trade, both internal within Britain and external between Britain and the rest of the empire, had been the life-blood of Londinium. The city had also been the seat of Roman bureaucracy from the beginning, but it had been the traders, busy exploiting the needs and resources of the province, that had given the place its vitality. There is little evidence that this continued to be the case in the third century. There was certainly wealth that enabled a relatively small number of people to build large houses and to patronise the arts, but such evidence as we have suggests that its possessors were connected with government rather than trade.

There may well have been a general recession in all trading, if suspicions of a decline in population in the late second century are correct. The effects of this may have been worse in Londinium than in the civitas capitals, which were the market centres for their local tribes, among whom the essential minimal trading of an agricultural community must have continued. Londinium was concerned much more with long-distance trade in more specialised commodities, and above all with trade between Britain and the world outside. The third century was a period in which Britain was becoming much more self-sufficient, to the advantage of the native producers, but with disastrous effects on the importers. This is most easily demonstrated by the pottery trade, which has left indestructible evidence. Imports of fine wares and specialised pottery from Gaul and the Rhineland dwindled, and their place in the British market was gradually taken over by similar products from native kilns around Colchester, in Oxfordshire and in the Nene valley. The pottery trade was much less important than it sometimes appears to archaeologists, but it is symptomatic of what was happening generally. The British pewter industry was developing in the west of Britain, and could supply most of the needs of the two British provinces for metal table-ware, and Whitby jet was becoming popular for jewellery.

Political circumstances in the late third century increased the isolation of Britain, for the Roman empire came near to disintegration, with a succession of frontier wars and civil wars between rival emperors and would-be emperors. In the west the commander of the Rhine legions, Cassianius Postumus, made himself the ruler of Gaul, Spain and Britain in 259, and ruled well until his assassination nine years later, when he was followed by two short-lived usurpers, Marius and Victorinus, in whose reign Spain seceded from the Gallo-Roman Empire. Tetricus I then became ruler of what was left of it in 270, but more fortunate than his predecessors was able to abdicate and surrender three years later to Aurelian, who not only spared his life but gave him a government post. With all this going on, Britain must have been left pretty much to its own devices, and was probably content that this should be so. In spite of its Saxon raids, it must have seemed a haven of peace to many poor wretches in Gaul, particularly after the barbarian invasions of 253 and 276. It is doubtful whether the third-century Britons were prosperous, however, as is sometimes suggested. They may have exported more than they imported, but they would have been heavily taxed, for the cost of officials and defence had to come from somewhere. Moreover, the currency grew steadily more debased, to give emperors more spending-power, until it finally collapsed about 260 in a flood of small copper coins that were nominally double-denarii of silver. Prices no doubt soared as in any period of inflation, and it is not surprising that forgers attempted to redress the balance by making a similar token coinage themselves, the familiar 'radiate' copies, so-called from the emperor's radiate crown which had always been characteristic of the double-denarius. The Emperor Aurelian made the first of many subsequent attempts to stabilise the currency, by introducing a somewhat larger token coin that was nominally of even higher value, as governments today would issue a new bank-note to supersede earlier issues; but either there was a failure to distribute the new coins in Britain, or they were unacceptable because they were considered to be over-valued. Instead, forgers continued to supply the local coinage by striking more and more radiate copies, mostly of coins of the Gallic usurpers, and these became smaller and smaller as prices rose. A number from the same dies have been found in London, and were almost certainly made there, probably in the early 280s.

Londinium at this time can hardly have been favourable to commerce, but little evidence concerning the late third century port has yet been found. The excavations at New Fresh Wharf, 60 yards (55m) downstream from the mediaeval London Bridge and probably about the same distance from its Roman predecessor, at first appeared to demonstrate convincingly a decline in activity at the Roman wharf before this date. The site produced great quantities of imported pottery of the late second and early third centuries, probably broken in transit; this included samian ware (**30**), mostly from Central Gaul, but with some from East Gaul, and coarser ware such as flagons and mortaria from the Rhineland. Imported wares of the latter kind were presumably required to supply domestic needs in Britain in the interval between the demise of the Verulamium and Brockley Hill potteries and the full development of the new British industries. There was a little pottery of the late third century from New Fresh Wharf, including Oxfordshire wares, but in quantity it bears no comparison with the imported wares of the late second and early third centuries. [30] Coins from the site seemed to tell the same story; there were 17 of the period AD 138–222, the latest being a contemporary forgery of a denarius of 219; no coins were found of the period 222–259, not surprisingly, as they rarely occur as Romano-British site finds; remarkably, however, there was only a single coin, a radiate copy of reduced size, of the period 259–286, a time of high inflation when Britain was flooded with debased coinage. All this seemed to suggest that activity at the Antonine/Severan wharf on this site had greatly declined by the late third century. A recent (1983) reassessment of the stratigraphy and phasing by Michael Rhodes, however, has indicated that most of the silts excavated at New Fresh Wharf had been deposited when the Roman quay was constructed in the late second—early third century. A disturbance in the Saxon period had redistributed silt of this date from the quay over the greater part of the area excavated, so that most of the finds, including those that were residual in later deposits, had originally come from a single massive fill of silt within the quay. This was at first believed to be an accumulation after its construction, but now appears to have been deliberate packing when it was built—on this site at least presumably not earlier than the Severan period, a date conforming with the latest pronouncement of the dendrochronologists. By contrast, only a very small volume of purely late Roman silt was excavated at the southern edge of the area investigated. In these circumstances the statistics of finds are misleading, and there is no real indication of what was happening on this important wharf in the later third century. It is to be hoped that the excavation on the neighbouring site of Billingsgate will produce definite evidence of the history of the Roman water-front in this period and later.

A few pottery imports continued to reach the London area after the middle of the century, presumably through the port of Londinium. I am indebted to Mrs Joanna Bird for the information, in advance of her published report, that the latest group of samian pottery yet found in Britain, manufactured in East Gaul about AD 260, comes from the excavation around the signal tower at Shadwell. It is perhaps significant that this was a military site, and the pottery may therefore have reached Britain, not in the normal course of commerce which should have distributed it more widely, but in the baggage of an officer or military unit. Nevertheless, the quantity of late East Gaulish ware found at Shadwell, comprising some eighty decorated vessels, is excessive for a personal import, and the transportation of 'mess crockery' by the Roman army at this period seems rather unlikely.

Carausius and the London Mint

The isolation of Britain became practically complete when M. Aurelius Mausaeus Carausius crossed from Gaul to Britain and declared himself emperor late in 286 or early in 287. He was a man of humble origin, born near the Belgian coast, who had distinguished himself in service against the bands of brigands terrorising Gaul. As a result he was given command of the Channel fleet, with orders to suppress the raids of Saxon and Frankish pirates. He was remarkably successful, but was accused of diverting the pirates' booty to his own use, and even of ensuring a richer haul by waiting until the raiders were returning with their spoil before attacking them. It is sometimes suggested that this was a trumped-up charge, due to the jealousy of Maximian, but it seems more likely that Carausius had high ambitions from the beginning, and saw the acquisition of wealth as a necessary first step towards their fulfilment. His subsequent success points to careful preparation. As soon as he learnt that his arrest was imminent, he departed for Britain, where he apparently encountered no resistance from the governors of the two provinces and was immediately accepted by their three legions. They had no doubt been promised a handsome donative, which Carausius was presumably able to pay from his pirate loot.

In order to do so, he set up the first official mint in Londinium, a mint which was to continue to produce coins for nearly 40 years. This had the mint-mark ML, for *Moneta Londinii* (50, 1,2,), and issued coins of gold and silver of a high grade, as well as base metal coins of good size and weight, conforming with the reformed standard that Aurelian had established, but had not succeeded in imposing in the west. These sometimes had the value mark XXI, like the comparable coins of Aurelian, sometimes explained as meaning that each coin was worth twenty sestertii. The silver coins were similar in size to the old denarius, but their value must have been very high, and we do not know how it related to the nominal value of the base metal coins. The gold and silver were no doubt supplied from the bullion and plate captured from the pirates, and these coins were probably used mainly for donatives. Very few have survived the melting-pot, and most presumably perished in a demonetisation of the usurper's coinage, which almost certainly took place when Britain was recovered by the central empire. The base metal coins, however, passed into general circulation and often occur as site-finds. The introduction of these coins was probably accompanied by stern measures against forgers, and the production of the small radiate copies probably ceased.

London was not the only mint of Carausius in Britain, though it was the most prolific. There was also a mint which used the mark C or CL, claimed by various authorities on behalf of Camulodunum (Colchester), Calleva (Silchester), Colonia Lindum (Lincoln) or less plausibly Clausentum (Bitterne), with Camulodunum as the favourite candidate. There was also a mint that used the mark RSR, formerly identified with Rotomagus (Rouen), for Carausius was able to retain control of part of north Gaul when he crossed to Britain. It is now considered, however, that the letters are merely an abbreviation for the office concerned with the payment of military donatives (*Rationalis Summae Rei*), and that these coins were produced by a branch of the London mint.[31] Later in the reign of Carausius unmarked coins were produced from another mint which was probably Boulogne, where he continued to maintain a toe-hold on the Continent until just before his death in 293.

The portrait on his coins is that of a genial rogue, but the roguery was probably no worse than that of many other emperors who lacked the geniality. Carausius undoubtedly had qualities that made him popular; otherwise he could hardly have taken over Britain so easily, even with his ill-gotten wealth, and the flattering words on some of his coins, '*Exspectate veni*' ('Eagerly awaited one, come!') may not have been an entirely unwarranted boast of the hopes he raised. He certainly proved to be an effective ruler, and with the aid of his fleet was able to maintain his separate empire for his lifetime, though he was disappointed in failing to achieve recognition as a brother emperor by Diocletian and Maximian, who were now jointly ruling the central empire.

Londinium under Carausius

This situation of political and economic isolation cannot have been healthy for London, which has always owed much of its importance to its convenience as a link between Britain and the world beyond. In compensation the city probably had a resident emperor again, and for a much longer period than ever before. Needing both to rule Britain and to keep a watchful eye on the defences of the south-east, Carausius must have spent a great deal of time in Londinium. If there had been rivalry between the capitals of Upper and Lower Britain, circumstances now tilted the balance decisively against York, where no Carausian mint was ever established. The old palace of Londinium was still in use in the late third century, for a coin of about 270 was found in the ash filling of a hypocaust in the south wing, presumably deposited while the heating system was still functioning.[32] This would have been the obvious place for Carausius to have taken as his residence, but like many other rulers in similar circumstances he may have preferred accommodation in a more modern and comfortable building, using the palace only for official purposes. No doubt he could have taken his pick of the large houses that had been built in the Walbrook valley and elsewhere, or he could have built a new residence for himself.

Some building, or rather rebuilding, was going on about this time in the eastern part of the city, though it is not of course suggested that Carausius himself was responsible for it. It does, however, reflect a measure of confidence and prosperity that is more likely to have developed under his rule than in the chaotic period just before his arrival—the only alternative dating allowed by the archaeological evidence. A building with ragstone walls had been constructed partly on the site of Lloyd's building in Lime Street in the late first or early second century. This was demolished and a substantial new building was built to replace it, with ragstone walls, floors of red *tesserae* and concrete (*opus signinum*) and with a hypocaust for underfloor heating. After the demolition of the earlier building a small hole was made with a pointed stick in a dump of clay above the demolished wall. Into this were dropped 30 radiate forgeries, mostly of coins of the Tetrici, and nearly all of the reduced size that suggests a date of about 280 or later.[33] The hole was then covered with a piece of tile and the coins were abandoned. They lay within a corner of a room of the new building that was constructed above the demolished walls, and were well below its floor level. It seems likely that they were deposited as a foundation offering to bring good fortune to the new building, a common custom in Roman times as later; and if the coins were already an illegal currency and valueless that would not have diminished their effectiveness for the purpose, since all money is the same to the gods. Whether this interpretation is correct or not, the deposit was certainly made during the interval between the demolition of the early building and the construction of its successor, and so gives us a date of about 280+ for the latter. If the coins were cheerfully abandoned because they were already quite valueless, that would suggest a date after the establishment of the new coinage of Carausius about 287.

A hoard of nearly 600 similar small radiate copies was found in a gully or pit cut into gravel metalling, on the western side of a possible north–south road south of Newgate Street and north of Paternoster Row,[34] a part of the city that seems to have been largely derelict in the late third century. They were found in a corroded mass which was probably the contents of a purse. In this case the latest coin to be copied was one of the Emperor Tacitus, dated to 276. The copy could have been produced any time in the ten years after this date, and it seems likely that the hoard was hidden in the 280s. There were of course no banking facilities, so that any savings had to be hidden for security. The failure to recover this hoard may have been due to accident, such as the sudden death of the owner, or may have been due to the fact that it was no longer worth retrieving after currency reform and the introduction of a more stable coinage. In this hoard also there were several die-linked coins that were probably produced locally, though the whole assemblage was much more heterogeneous than the little 'hoard' from Lime Street, which consisted almost entirely of die-linked coins, which must have come straight from the workshop that produced them.

The rescue of Londinium

In 293 Carausius was murdered by his finance minister, Allectus, who declared himself emperor, perhaps to save himself, as his victim had done six years earlier. Allectus continued to use the London and C mints only, for Boulogne had by this time been lost. He issued no good silver and few gold coins, but introduced a new smaller denomination in base metal, marked with the letter Q, usually considered to stand for *quinarius*, before the mint letter. Allectus seems to have been a less effective ruler than Carausius, and certainly lacked the latter's military ability. In 296 there was a successful invasion by an army of the central empire, under the command of Constantius Chlorus, who had been appointed ruler of the outer western provinces with the rank of Caesar, by the two joint Augusti, Diocletian and Maximian. As such he was a junior partner in the empire, with the prospect of eventual succession to the senior rank of Augustus, on equal terms with Galerius who served in a similar capacity as Caesar in the east. Diocletian had recognised the need for some devolution of power in the unwieldy empire, and had taken Maximian as his partner as Augustus of the west, while he himself ruled the east. The appointment of the Caesars carried the devolution a stage further and also ensured the succession.

The invasion of Constantius was intended as a two-pronged attack, in which one division under his praetorian prefect, Asclepiodotus, was to land on the south coast, while the other, commanded by Constantius Chlorus himself, was to make for the Thames estuary and London. Advantage was taken of fog in the Channel to evade the fleet that Carausius had used so successfully to keep his enemies at bay. Asclepiodotus landed in or near the Solent, but the transports of Constantius were lost in the fog and had to turn back. Allectus seems to have been taken by surprise and was unable to marshal his full strength to meet Asclepiodotus, with the result that he was defeated and killed in a battle somewhere near Silchester. The survivors of the defeated army fled to Londinium, which was evidently still a repository of wealth, and proceeded to loot it. The city was saved, however, by the timely arrival in the Thames of Constantius' galleys, which had been successful in their second attempt. A splendid gold medallion, found at Arras, was struck at Trier to commemorate the arrival of Constantius at Londinium and the welcome he received from its grateful citizens (**49**). The obverse has the armoured bust of the Caesar, and the reverse shows him on horseback being welcomed at the city gate by a female figure personifying Londinium and labelled LON. Below, one of Constantius' war-galleys is shown on the Thames. He is described in the inscription as REDDITOR LVCIS AETERNAE, 'the restorer of eternal light'—the light of civilisation that came from Rome. To London, the creation of the Romans and always more Roman than British, this restoration and the ending of a long period of isolation must have been particularly welcome.

49 Gold medallion of Trier mint found at Arras, commemorating the rescue of Londinium and the recovery of Britain by Constantius Chlorus in 296. Reverse shows war-galley on the Thames and Constantius on horse-back welcomed by personifcation of Londinium, lavelled *LON*, at the gates of the city. Actual diameter, 1⅔in (4.3cm). *Museum of London neg.*

The County Hall ship

It is to this period at the very end of the third century that an important London find can be attributed. Excavation in 1910 on the site of County Hall, on the south shore of the Thames near Westminster Bridge, brought to light a substantial fragment of a Roman ship, consisting of part of its bottom and the lower portion of one side, which had collapsed and lay horizontally beside the bottom (fig 31).[35] The surviving remains were some 38ft (11.6m) long, but most of one end was missing, so that the original size can only be estimated approximately. The vessel was probably about 60–70ft (18–21m) long, with a beam of 15–16ft (4.6–4.9m), and was carvel-built with planks held together by draw-tongued joints in the Mediterranean tradition, although the timber was from a species of oak (either *Quercus robur* or *Q. petraea*) that grows in central and northern Europe and not in Mediterranean countries. It was not a flat-bottomed barge like the other two Roman vessels found in London (pp141 and 163–4), but had a rounded bottom and projecting keel, and is considered to have been a very small merchant-ship of about 60 tons. It is dated by coins of Tetricus and one of Carausius found under one of the ribs, and another coin of Carausius and one of Allectus found lying directly on the bottom of the ship. It cannot therefore have been sunk before 293, but there is no positive evidence to suggest that it survived into the fourth century, though that possibility cannot be ruled out. The single piece of pottery that is certainly associated with the ship is a sherd of a flanged bowl of coarse dark grey ware that could date from the end of the third or from the fourth century. This was found in stiff clay filling a hole beneath a rib in the bottom of the ship. Several large round stones, each weighing about three pounds, were also found in the bottom of the ship, one of them partly embedded in a strake (longitudinal timber). One of these stones, preserved in the Museum of London, is a septarian nodule from the London Clay. It was suggested in the original report of 1912 that these were warlike missiles and that the ship had been subject to attack during the

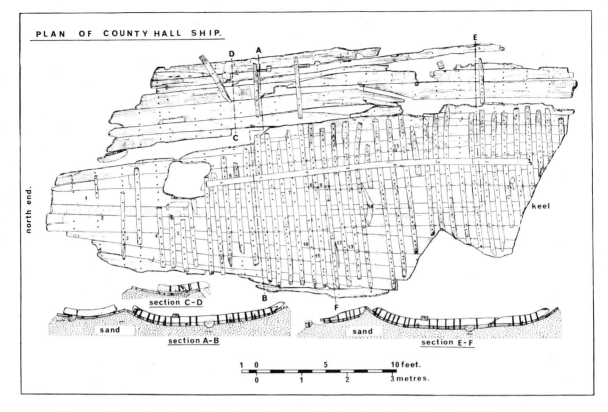

PLAN OF COUNTY HALL SHIP.

Fig. 31   Plan and sections of remains of Roman ship found on site of County Hall in 1910. *Original record by W. E. Riley re-drawn by P. R. V. Marsden*

invasion of Constantius Chlorus. The idea that the wreck was 'one of Allectus' vessels that endeavoured to escape in the fight of London, but was overtaken and destroyed by the fleet of Constantius in 296' was discounted by Wheeler and Marsden, in their subsequent accounts of the ship, and both rightly point out that this is a conjecture entirely unsupported by evidence. The attempt to link the destruction of the ship with a particular historical event would be condemned by most archaeologists today, and in any case the vessel was not a warship.

Yet the evidence of the stone partly embedded in the strake requires further consideration. It was suggested that it must have been thrown from a considerable height to have penetrated in this way, although when found the waterlogged timbers were soft and cheese-like. A heavy stone tossed from the neighbouring bank could have penetrated a timber in this state, if it were unprotected, but it can probably be assumed that a considerable layer of silt had accumulated above the wreck before the wood got into this condition, so that the impact would have been greatly reduced. When the ship was found it was covered by no less than 7 feet of silt, and this had been much compressed by subsequent dumping and building above it. It is therefore quite likely that the stone did in fact strike with very great force before the ship was sunk. If so, it was presumably propelled by light artillery, such as a stone-throwing catapult (*ballista* or *scorpio*). There were considerable other signs of damage, some of it followed by makeshift repairs. The centre portions of three ribs had been renewed, and there were several fractured boards over which a thin layer of clay had been laid; above this short lengths of thin oak boards had been wedged between the ribs. One hole had been repaired with the plug of clay containing the pottery sherd, and several large iron nails were found driven through the strakes to the ribs, probably to replace broken trenails. Another large hole, that is likely to have been the result of breaking the mast, was unrepaired and may have been the damage that finally sank the vessel. A portion of wood, probably from the mast, lay in the river-bed nearby. The worst damage of all, by which a substantial part of the ship was completely removed, must have taken place after the sinking, either fairly soon afterwards while the wood was still serviceable and worth salvaging, or centuries later by accidental destruction when it had become soft. There is evidence, therefore, for cumulative damage rather than a single act of destruction, and measures were at first taken to keep the vessel afloat—they could hardly have made it seaworthy. Was it perhaps a ship abandoned in the Thames and subsequently moored in a quiet place well away from the city, possibly in an inlet, where it was used for target practice or perhaps merely scuttled because it was not worth substantial repairs? A decline in commerce would have resulted in redundant ships, and these may have been many scattered about the lower Thames and its inlets, as they were in the great shipping slump of the 1920s. The patching-up received by the County Hall ship, before it was finally sunk, may have been merely the minimum necessary to keep it afloat after a disastrous accident, until it could be moved to a place where the wreck would inconvenience nobody—but this also is merely a conjecture unsupported by evidence, like the more romantic theory put forward by Messrs Riley and Gomme in 1912. Its only advantage over the latter is that it would explain the two phases of damage—the first followed by emergency repairs and the second resulting in a final destruction that seems to have been intentional.

The picture of third-century Londinium that emerges from our scraps of evidence, archaeological and historical, is by no means clear. It was obviously not by any means in a state of decay, but still a town of considerable importance and wealth. Nevertheless, its population was almost certainly shrunken, when compared with that of its heyday in the late first and early second centuries, and large areas within the walls in the western part of the city were probably unoccupied and perhaps used for horticulture. There were, however, quite a number of fine new residences in the central and eastern part of the city, and before the end of the century a few in Southwark. The temple precinct in the south-western part of the city was evidently well maintained after a period of some neglect, though the former site of the great Huggin Hill baths was left empty or occupied only in places by inferior buildings. The whole character of the city seems in fact to have changed, probably as a result of a decline in commerce and consequently of the activities of the port. Londinium had always been concerned with government, but with the decline of other activities this aspect of life became predominant. On the very small scale of a Romano-British town, the differences between the Londinium of the first century and of the third are like those between Sydney and Canberra, or Rio de Janeiro and Brasilia. At the end of the century, London was more important to the empire than to Britain.

9

Londinium
in the Fourth Century

Historical background

The restoration of Britain to the empire by Constantius Chlorus was soon followed by fundamental administrative changes. Diocletian had commenced a complete reform of the whole imperial system, by which the civil and military branches of government were separated. Londinium was not directly affected by the military reforms, except that the staff soldiers, who had been concerned with many aspects of government under the command of the provincial governor, would now have disappeared. The political status of the city was, however, drastically changed, both to its disadvantage and advantage. In accordance with Diocletian's policy of devolution to improve administrative efficiency, Britain was divided into four small provinces, Britannia Prima, Britannia Secunda, Maxima Caesariensis and Flavia Caesariensis. London was therefore now the capital city of an area only approximately half the size of the province it had administered in the third century and a quarter of the original undivided province of Britain, of which it had once been the capital. Diocletian's devolution of government, however, was accompanied by the organisation of a closely-knit chain of command. Administrative responsibility under the Augusti and Caesars was centralised in the hands of Praetorian Prefects, each of whom controlled a large part of the empire. Under the prefects were deputies (*vicarii*), who were each responsible for a group of small provinces called a diocese. Thus the four provinces of Britain formed a diocese, under the overall control of a *vicarius*, who was himself responsible to the Praetorian Prefect of the Gauls. There is little doubt that the headquarters of the *vicarius* were in Londinium, for the city's convenience for access both to Gaul and to all four provinces of Britain made it the obvious choice.

The boundaries between the four British provinces are quite unknown, but certain deductions have been made about their approximate whereabouts. Initially the governors of all the four provinces were of equestrian rank, but later in the fourth century Maxima Caesariensis had been promoted in status and had a senatorial governor. From this it has been deduced that Maxima contained

London, which was administratively the most important city as the seat of the *vicarius* of the diocese.[1]

There has been much debate about the significance of the names Maxima Caesariensis and Flavia Caesariensis, and it has been suggested that for a short time they formed a single province called Caesariensis, which was subsequently divided into two, one named Flavia after Flavius Constantius Chlorus, the western Caesar, and the other after Maximian, the western Augustus until his abdication in 305.[2] It was further suggested that the province was called Caesariensis after its capital Caesarea, and that Londinium was given this title in 296, following its loyal welcome to Constantius. Much later in the fourth century Londinium was certainly called Augusta, and the suggestion was made that it was promoted in title when Constantius received his own promotion to Augustus in 305.[3]

It is an ingenious theory, but there is no corroborative evidence from historians, and the London mint, which was now producing the large silver-washed bronze coins (*folles*) of a new reformed coinage, used the mint-mark LON for Londinium when it started producing them for Constantius and his colleagues soon after 296 (**50**, 5). It is true that in its next issues, covering the period to 306, the mint-mark is unaccountably omitted—as might have been the case if the name of the city had been officially changed or a change was under discussion, but no new mint-mark had yet been approved. This would perhaps be a rather more likely explanation than the alternative suggestion that the omission of the mint-name was some sort of punishment for London because of its close association with the usurpers Carausius and Allectus, or because Constantius' welcome there was less hearty than the Arras medallion suggests.[4] This is unconvincing, quite apart from the improbability of hostile feelings between London and Constantius Chlorus, for a punishment would surely have followed immediately, not after an issue of Diocletian's reformed coinage with the first syllable of Londinium in full. In a new issue of somewhat reduced size and weight, which commenced towards the end of 306, however, the mint-mark PLN appeared (for *Pecunia, Percussa* or *Prima officina Londinii*), and thereafter continued for the next fourteen years, with comparatively short-lived variants such as ML (*Moneta Londinii*), until 320, when the first three letters of the name appeared again in the mint-mark P LON, which continued until the London mint ceased to function about 324 (**50**, 8–9). It is quite clear from this that London was officially as well as popularly called Londinium from 306 to 324, and if there had ever been any idea of changing the name it had been abandoned. The name Augusta for London is not mentioned until after 367, and is used officially in the abbreviation AVG for the London mint only in its brief revival under Magnus Maximus in 383–8 (**50**, 10). There can surely be no connection between this late name for London and the promotion of Constantius Chlorus in 305. As we shall see, there is a good reason for the award of the honorific title much nearer the date when it first appears.

Constantius returned to Britain in 306, with the intention of putting the northern frontier in order and of campaigning in Scotland, like Severus a century

50 Roman coins of London mint, actual size:
1–2 Carausius, 288–293, mint-marks ML, ML XXI
3–4 Allectus, 293–6, mint-marks QL, ML
5 Diocletian, 297–8, mint-mark LON
6 Constantine I, 307–313, mint-mark PLN
7 Constantine I, ADVENTVS AVG type, 310–2, mint-mark PLN
8 Constantine I, 320–4, mint-mark P LON
9 Helena, 324–5, mint-mark P LON
10 Magnus Maximus, gold *solidus*, 383–8, mint-mark AVG OB

earlier. He was joined by Constantine, his son by his first marriage, who had been serving with Galerius, the Augustus of the east. Galerius, like Constantius, had been promoted when Diocletian and Maximian abdicated, and had been keeping Constantine virtually as a hostage. He reluctantly consented to Constantius' request that his son should assist him in Britain, and Constantine was able to join the expedition. His subsequent presence as a free agent in Britain was to change history. Constantius was already ailing when he came to Britain for the second time, but nevertheless won a great victory over the Picts before he died at York, like Severus before him. Constantine was at once proclaimed Augustus by the army in Britain, and this was the first step in his rise to the mastery of the Roman world, which was to result in the triumph of Christianity. Constantine's power-base in Britain did not give him enough strength to retain the title of Augustus, but he was a force to be reckoned with, and was therefore reluctantly recognised as Caesar by Galerius, who gave the title of Augustus of the west to Severus II, so restoring the tetrarchy of two Augusti and two Caesars that had been established by Diocletian. The system was disrupted, however, by the revolt of Maxentius, the son of the retired Maximianus, who himself resumed his rule. A period of dynastic strife and shifting alliances followed, during which Constantine struggled for recognition as Augustus. He entered briefly into an alliance with Maximian on this condition, but after the enforced abdication of the latter was reduced again to the rank of Caesar. His promotion, together with that of Maximinus, was finally conceded early in 309, so that there were four Augusti until the death of Galerius in 311.

It is either to this period or to the year of the short-lived alliance between Constantine and Maximian (May 307–May 308) that a dedicatory inscription to the god Mithras found in the London Mithraeum must belong. Only the right-hand end of the marble tablet has survived, with the first line ending GGGG, apparently preceded by a v. The letters AVGGGG were the standard abbreviation for the titles of *four* Augusti, and this was evidently a dedication on behalf of the reigning emperors recognised by Constantine, who exercised political control over Britain. In 307–8, these would have been Galerius, Maximian, Maxentius and Constantine himself. In 309–11, they would have been Galerius, Licinius, Maximinus and Constantine. The former date has been preferred by R. P. Wright,[5] however, because his reconstruction of the missing left-hand portion would allow space for the title of a Caesar also, who in 307–8 would have been Maximinus, while in 309–11 the title was not used.

Constantine made an alliance with Licinius and marched against Maxentius, who still held Italy with an army four times the size of his own. Nevertheless Constantine won great victories near Turin and Verona, and finally defeated and killed Maxentius in the battle of the Milvian Bridge at Rome. This was the battle which is said to have convinced Constantine that he was under the protection of the Christian God, because of a sign he had seen in the sky and a dream he had subsequently. It seems likely, however, that he had leanings towards Christianity from the beginning, under the influence of his mother Helena, although he was not actually baptised until just before his death. Early in 313 he met Licinius at Milan, and they issued jointly the famous Edict that gave freedom of worship to all. This did not end the persecution of Christians in the east, where Maximinus still ruled. He was, however, decisively defeated by Licinius a few months later, and the whole of the eastern empire fell into Licinius' hands. Constantine then ruled the west and Licinius the east for the next ten years, though not in amity. Battles were fought, in which Constantine had the advantage, and Licinius himself revived the persecution of the eastern Christians. His final defeat and execution in 324, however, left Constantine the undisputed master of the Roman world, and assured not only the triumph of the Christian Church, but also eventually its very close association with the Roman State.

John Casey has argued convincingly on numismatic evidence that Constantine revisited Britain on two occasions after his departure for Gaul in 306.[6] If so he would undoubtedly have stayed in London, and it is the mint of Londinium that provides the evidence for these visits. Alone among the 14 imperial mints that were striking coins in the period 307–13, Londinium produced an issue of bronze folles with a reverse representing Constantine on horseback, with a captive beneath his horse's feet, and the inscription ADVENTVS AVG ('the coming of the Emperor') (**50**, 7). These coins can be dated by their mint-mark to the years 310–2, and have usually been explained as a commemoration of Constantine's entry into Rome after the Battle of the Milvian Bridge on 28 October 312, or as possibly referring to 'Constantine's threatened or actual presence at Rome to fight Maxentius' before the battle was fought.[7] Casey points out, however, that in eight out of ten other examples of an *Adventus* coinage issued between 296 and 335, it is known that the emperor was either present in the mint-town itself or was in its neighbourhood when the issue was made. In the remaining two instances the circumstances are unknown, but nowhere is there positive evidence of such a coinage being produced to commemorate a distant event. Moreover, since Constantine seems to have made a very rapid swoop on Italy, it would be surprising if the mint-master of distant Londinium could have had the new issue ready before the end of 312, even if it was prepared as soon as the news arrived of Constantine's close proximity to Rome. Casey suggests, therefore, that the emperor actually came to Britain some time between July 310, when he is known to have been in Trier, and the summer of 312, and that the purpose of his visit may have been to withdraw some troops from Britain to take part in his Italian campaign or to replace others withdrawn from the Rhineland for that purpose. Casey points out that there is in fact a reference by the fifth-century historian Zosimus to the presence of troops raised in Britain in the army gathered together by Constantine for the attack on Maxentius.[8]

There is, however, also a later *Adventus* issue of similar type from the mint of Londinium, differing only by the omission of the captive beneath the horse's fore-feet. This is of lighter weight and can be attributed by the letters accompanying its mint-mark to the period 313–7. As with the earlier issue it is known only from the London mint, and a similar argument can therefore be advanced for a second imperial visit. This issue with the mint-mark PLN is attributed to 313–4, and with the mint-mark MLL (a variant of the ML mark of the London mint) to 314–5. Within this period, Constantine's movements elsewhere are well-attested except between April and October 314, so that the summer of that year would have been the only possible time for a visit to Britain. Possibly a campaign was necessary in the north, if Constantine had in fact withdrawn troops two years earlier. Casey points out that it must have been about this time that Constantine took the title *Britannicus Maximus*, which is first recorded in 315, and strongly suggests a military intervention more recent than Constantine's campaign with his father nine years earlier. Less convincing is the argument that the province Maxima Caesariensis was given the name at this time, to commemorate Constantine's new title of Maximus, for it makes the unlikely assumption that it had previously been named Galeria Caesariensis after the Caesar of the east (see n 2). Moreover the change would barely have taken place in time for the new name to have appeared in the Verona List, dated within the limits 312–4, and pushed to the latest extremity of its possible date by this hypothesis.

Support for at least one visit to Britain by Constantine after his establishment in power is given by Eusebius in his *Life of Constantine*, written immediately after the emperor's death.[9] Casey points out that the sequence of events described is: (1) the proclamation of Constantine, which Eusebius knew took place in the context of Constantius' funeral; (2) Constantine's attacks on barbarian peoples round the Rhine; (3) Constantine's expedition to Britain; (4) his examination of 'other parts of the whole' (i.e. his father's territory) to tend what needed help. The account of the Italian campaign then follows immediately. It seems clear that the crossing to Britain cannot be the original campaign of Constantius Chlorus, but came after Constantine's settlement of the Rhine frontier in late 306–7, and before his invasion of Italy in 312.

The personal involvement of Constantine with Britain in the early years of his reign may have given encouragement and confidence to the Christians there, who in any case had not suffered under Constantius Chlorus the awful persecutions that had taken place elsewhere in the empire. It is now considered unlikely that St Alban was martyred under Constantius, and much more likely that he was executed under the authority of Geta Caesar in 208–9. Augulus, a bishop martyred at Augusta in Britain, according to a later martyrology, probably also suffered in the early or mid third century, since it is inconceivable that he was martyred in the later fourth century, when London was called Augusta. If so, Christians were organised under a bishop based in London at a surprisingly early date; certainly they were able to emerge from the shadows as an established Church, with a bishop in each of the small provinces of Britain, immediately after the Edict of Milan. When a Council of the Church was called at Arles, only a year later in 314, it was attended by three British bishops, Restitutus, Bishop of London, Eborius, Bishop of York, and Adelfius, Bishop of Colonia 'Londinensium'—a name that is obviously corrupt, but probably stands for Colonia Lindumensium (Lincoln).

51 Marble head of Serapis, hand of Mithras, and figure of Mercury, as found carefully buried in the Walbrook Mithraeum, beside an inverted stone bowl possibly marking their position. *Museum of London*

It seems certain that the Christians were powerful in Britain quite early in the reign of Constantine—sufficiently so to initiate attacks on the places of worship of the Mithraists, who were their hated rivals. This special antagonism arose not only from the fact that Mithraism had been the strongest rival of Christianity, but also from the close similarity between certain rites in both religions. Baptism by water and a communion feast practised by the Mithraists seemed to the Christians a blasphemous parody. It may be suspected also that Mithraists had been prominent in encouraging earlier persecution of the Christians. The Mithraea at Carrawburgh and Rudchester on Hadrian's Wall were attacked and their sacred images were destroyed quite early in the fourth century, obviously on the orders of a senior officer, who may well have owed his office to the favour of the pro-Christian emperor. Similarly in Londinium, the Walbrook Mithraeum was attacked, and those images that had not been concealed by the Mithraists, such as the massive limestone relief of Cautopates, were broken up and removed. An initial abortive attack, in which the marble head of Mithras was broken by a blow on the neck, apparently with an edged weapon, seems to have alerted the congregation, so that the more precious marble sculptures were buried intact, together with the broken but repairable head (**51**). If the inscription relating to the four Augusti was destroyed in the Christian attack, as is probable, the event must have taken place after 307–8, but perhaps not so many years later, and certainly during the reign of Constantine I, at least 40–50 years before 377, the date of the earliest recorded destruction of a Mithraeum in Rome itself.

In the meantime the external dangers which were ultimately to overwhelm the Roman empire were always present. If Constantine visited Britain for a third time in 314, his main purpose is likely to have been to take military measures against the troublesome tribes north of Hadrian's Wall or against the Teutonic raiders from the other side of the North Sea—possibly both. This was also probably the reason for the subsequent visit of his son Constans, when ruler of the western empire. This event is known to have taken place very early in 343, though the purpose of the visit is unrecorded. Since crossing the Channel in mid-winter was then something of an ordeal, it seems likely that a serious emergency caused yet another emperor to set foot in London. Unfortunately there was now no mint of Londinium to record the event. Constans is said to have come with only about 100 men, so that his purpose was neither to quell a rebellion, as has sometimes been suggested, nor to take part himself in any campaign. His visit was somehow concerned with the *areani*, intelligence agents who operated beyond the frontier.[10] Evidently his purpose was reorganisation and preparation rather than immediate military action, and it is possible that some renegotiation of treaties was necessary with northern tribes beyond the frontier. There is a hint that Constans was also concerned with the Channel defensive system, and the 'Saxon Shore' fort of Pevensey was built about this time or soon after. It was probably as a result of this visit, also, that the command of the Count of the Saxon Shore was established.

The defences of Britain were, however, weakened by the rise of another usurper and the inevitable civil war that followed, draining troops as always from the defensive garrisons. Magnentius, a man of barbarian origin, according to one tradition the son of a Briton, and an able soldier who had risen to high command, revolted against Constans in Gaul in 350 and murdered him. He was strongly supported in Britain, with disastrous results, for Magnentius was finally defeated by Constantius in 353 and killed himself. Extensive reprisals followed in spite of a promise of amnesty, and a special investigator was sent to Britain to hunt down supporters of the usurper. Nobody was spared; even the *vicarius* of Britain was forced to commit suicide, and confiscation of property took place on a large scale. The effect on Londinium must have been devastating, for if the *vicarius* himself was involved, we may be quite sure that most of his subordinates were too. Many of those fine houses in the city and Southwark must have changed their owners, and some may even have been abandoned.

It may be significant that the Walbrook Mithraeum, which had continued in use as a pagan temple after the Christian raid some years earlier, on coin evidence seems to have been left to fall in ruins soon after the middle of the century. Its latest coin, which dates from 341–6, was found in building debris over the last but one of the building's nine successive floors. The house to the east, to which the Mithraeum probably belonged, may have shared the same fate but, if it did not, presumably had a new owner with no interest in the cult, although he took no steps to destroy the temple or to remove the last traces of paganism from it, but simply left it derelict. The abandonment of the temple may however be sufficiently explained by the more rigorous anti-pagan policy of Constantius, and need not be due to a change of ownership.

Better times for pagans in the west came temporarily when Julian, a philosophical pagan, was given command in the western provinces by Constantius with the rank of Caesar, and for the whole empire when the death of Constantius in 361 left him the master of the Roman world. During Julian's campaign on the Rhine frontier in 359, he took steps to remedy local food deficiencies by organising a fleet of 600 ships, 400 of them newly built, to transport corn from Britain to the lower Rhine. This may have resulted in some revival of the port of Londinium, which had always taken the lead in trade with the Rhineland, and could offer greater facilities than any port in East Anglia. We do not know how long this export trade continued, however, and any revival of London's port activities may have been too brief to affect the nature of the city as a whole.

Londinium, the key to Britain

Trouble with the Picts and Scots began again in 360, and Julian, who was himself fully occupied in Gaul, sent his commander, Lupicinus, to Britain. Lupicinus came in mid-winter to Boulogne, where he collected transports and embarked his troops. He sailed to Richborough and thence marched to Londinium, 'intending there to form his plans according to the situation of affairs and hasten quickly to take the field'.[11] Here the strategic importance of Londinium as the base that was essential for imperial control of the whole island is explicitly recognised. It was the nerve centre where intelligence from all parts could be gathered and assessed, and from which action could be initiated in whichever direction it was needed. This military conception of London as a base and potential springboard for rescue operations became predominant as the Roman empire fell more and more on the defensive, and it is thought that underlies all the additional measures take in the fourth century to defend the city. Nothing more is known of the campaign of Lupicinus, but he was evidently successful in imposing terms, and was able to return to Gaul in a few months.

Londinium performed the same role in a much graver crisis that arose a few years later. The barbarians were learning to act in unison, with deadly effect, and in 367 there had been successful attacks on Britain by Picts from Scotland, Scots from Ireland, and Attacotti from the western isles or Ireland, coinciding with attacks from the Germanic tribes north of the Rhine on the coast of Gaul and probably of Britain as well. Hadrian's Wall was overrun or by-passed; the *dux Britanniarum* was besieged or even captured, and the Count of the Saxon Shore was killed. There was widespread pillaging by the barbarian hordes, and matters were made worse by the low morale and lack of discipline in the Roman army in Britain. Many soldiers deserted or went absent without leave and roamed the country, no doubt looting on their own account, and there was a complete breakdown of law and order. The Emperor Valentinian sent an experienced general, Theodosius, with the military rank of *comes* ('Count'), to collect a large task force and regain control of Britain. Theodosius crossed to Richborough early in 368, and as soon as he was joined by the four regiments that were allocated to him, marched towards London. On his way he rounded up various predatory bands who were loaded with loot and were driving in chains the prisoners from whom they had taken it, with the intention of selling them as slaves. Theodosius freed these unfortunates, presumably captured in the Kentish villas, and restored their possessions, except for a small portion with which he rewarded his soldiers. He entered Londinium amid scenes of great jubilation and established his base there. It would appear that no barbarians had actually entered the city, but it had been 'overwhelmed by hardships' (*mersam difficultatibus*) as might be expected if its hinterland had been devastated and its lines of communication cut. Theodosius declared an amnesty for the deserters and recalled those who claimed to be on leave, so that gradually he was able to rebuild the army. He also re-created the administration, headed by a new *vicarius*, and appointed a new *dux Britanniarum*. The following year, 369, he was ready to take the initiative, and marched from Londinium. He succeeded in clearing the invaders from all parts of Britain, and carried out a thorough-going restoration of the cities and forts that had suffered damage.

It is in connection with these events that the name *Augusta* is first used for London. Ammianus tells us that in 368 Theodosius marched 'to Londinium, an old town which posterity has named Augusta'.[12] This states fairly explicitly that it was still called Londinium in 368, but had since been named Augusta. When Ammianus describes the events of 369, however, he says that Theodosius marched 'from Augusta, which was earlier called Londinium'.[13] It would be too much to claim, on the authority of this contemporary historian, that the city was re-named in 368–9, for Theodosius himself would certainly have had no authority to give it such an honorific title. It may, however, be suggested that the re-naming was associated in the mind of Ammianus with the events of that year. If Augusta was a title of honour awarded by the emperor, it must have been given in commemoration of a success in which the city had played a notable part. Within the limits of possibility imposed by the signatures of the London mint (ie between 324 and 383) there is no more appropriate occasion than the year in which Theodosius rebuilt the army in Britain under the protection of the walls of Londinium, and marched from that secure base to restore the diocese of Britain to the empire. One of its provinces was now named Valentia in honour of the joint-emperors Valentinian and Valens, and it would not be surprising if Londinium, which must have figured largely in Theodosius' reports, received the imperial title at the same time. It is usually considered that Valentia was a fifth province that was either recovered by Theodosius after being swamped by the enemy or was now created by reorganisation, and that it was either somewhere in the north or in Wales. Stephen Johnson has made an alternative suggestion that it was a name given to the whole group of four provinces.[14] If in fact it was a name for the diocese of Britain as a whole, it would have been a natural corollary to rename its principal town and the seat of its *vicarius* as Augusta. The *Notitia Dignitatum*, however, lists Valentia as a fifth province with a governor of consular rank.

It is self-evident that the name Londinium, probably pronounced *Lūndinium*, as it was spelt by Ammianus, continued in general use, for it survived into the post-Roman period as *Lūndene*, dropping the Latin ending, and with a change of gender as *Lundonia* in Bede's Latin. The name was never forgotten, whatever happened to the city in the Dark Age of the fifth and sixth centuries, and we still call the capital by the name given to it by the Romans in the first century. The only difference is that somewhere along the line the *i* changed to *o*, evidently at an early date since the *o* form occurs on the Saxon sceatta coinage of the eighth century and is used by Bede. Other early variants in the spelling of the second syllable are with *u* and *e*, and it is clear that with the dropping of the Latin ending the pronunciation of the vowel became as indeterminate as it is today.

The name Augusta was probably only used for official purposes, as in the signature of the London mint, abbreviated to AVG, when the mint was re-established for a short time by a new usurper, Magnus Maximus, in 383 (**50**, 10). Maximus, a native of Spain, had served in Britain under Count Theodosius, and at the time of his revolt held a high command there, probably as *dux Britanniarum*. The Emperor Gratian had become unpopular with the army, and the troops in Britain declared for Maximus, who was a vigorous and efficient leader with considerable potential as a ruler. His revolt had grave effects on the defences of Britain, however, since inevitably he required an army to fight his battles on the Continent, and this could only be obtained by depleting the garrisons of the north and of Wales, where many forts were abandoned, although Hadrian's Wall itself was still held. Maximus had, however, carried out a successful campaign against the Picts and Scots in the previous year, and had established friendly relations with some of the tribes beyond the northern frontier. Although over-stretched the defences still held, while Maximus dealt successfully with Gratian, who was killed, and became master of Gaul and Spain as well as Britain. When he invaded Italy, however, he was attacked and defeated by Theodosius, and was executed near Aquileia in 388.

The ancient enemies were soon causing trouble again, and in the last years of the fourth century a final Roman task force was sent to Britain, under the command of Stilicho, the great Vandal general of the young Emperor Honorius. Very little is known either about the reasons for the expedition—though these can be surmised from previous events—or its accomplishments. We cannot even be sure that Stilicho led it in person, though it was certainly under his orders. We can be fairly certain, however, that once again a Roman relief force marched along the old road from Richborough to Londinium, and Londinium itself, as we shall see,

has produced the one piece of archaeological evidence that can probably be attributed to this expedition. Stilicho's purpose was not to restore the lost garrisons or
even to strengthen those that remained, but deliver some discouraging blows
to the troublesom Picts, Scots and Saxons, and to rationalise Britain's defences, so
that they had a chance of surviving further withdrawals, which in fact took place
two years later in 401. Hope of retaining Britain in the empire had not yet been
abandoned, however, and while it remained Londinium was recognised as an
essential link in the imperial system of communications. In the defence of the
island itself it was strategically important as a nerve centre, particularly for the
Saxon Shore. Moreover, like all the walled cities, it increased in military
importance as the strength of the standing army was reduced. If raids on the open
country could not be prevented, fortified towns could provide both places of
refuge and bases from which counter-attacks to restore order could be made. In
south-eastern Britain the towns could be envisaged as a second line of defence
after the Shore forts, fulfilling a similar military function further inland, but only
if they were adequately garrisoned. It is doubtful whether this was the case for
long after Stilicho's expedition.

The riverside wall

Fore more than a century after it was built only the wall on the landward side of the
city seems to have been considered an adequate defence for Londinium. This is
less surprising when it is remembered that the same landward wall alone served
London as a formidable defence for half a millennium in the Middle Ages—a
fortification that was respected by William the Conqueror himself until the
citizens came to terms with him, and over which he was careful to maintain
control by building a castle at each end. It is clear that the river itself and the
fortified bridge were considered an adequate defence on the southern side
throughout the medieval period, though it is difficult to understand how the ends
were protected from outflanking before the Norman castles were built. A wall
making an enclosed circuit would certainly seem to be more secure, and the
Romans evidently thought so too, for in the fourth century the east and west ends
of the landward wall were joined by a new wall that ran along the river-front
north of the wharves, and approximately on the line of Upper and Lower Thames
Street. The existence of a riverside wall or walls has long been known, for it was
too substantial to escape notice in the 19th century sewer excavations beneath
Thames Street. What was then uncertain was whether the various glimpses
allowed from time to time by sewer trenches were of a continuous defensive wall
or of a series of embankment walls such as we have today. The balance seemed to
incline fairly decisively towards the latter view when Marsden found in 1961 that
the wall observed by Roach Smith at the foot of Lambeth Hill made a right-

52   Riverside wall, Upper Thames Street, showing pile foundations (A), remains of chalk raft
(B), eroded Roman riverside wall (C), dumping (D), and remains of fourteenth-century
Baynard's Castle (E), (view to E). *Museum of London*

angled turn to the north at that point, and appeared to be the lowest of a series of terrace walls which incorporated re-used stones and were built on foundations of chalk laid on oak piles, like the riverside wall described by Roach Smith. The relationship of the latter to the terraces behind it remains problematical, but work in 1974–6 has suggested that it was not a river embankment, but had its base at $4\frac{1}{4}$ft (1.3m) above OD, considered to be above the Roman river level.[15] If this view is correct, the wall must be defensive, and this implies that it was continuous, though there may possibly have been a gap of some kind for the mouth of the Walbrook if a culvert was inadequate for the flow of the water. There must also have been gates to allow access from the city to the waterfront, and the angle made by the wall at the bottom of Lambeth Hill may be the east side of one of these. Charles Hill has pointed out that an extension of the straight line of the road from the south gate of the Cripplegate fort would have come to this point.[16] It can only have done so if the Roman walls recorded in Knightrider Street had been demolished before the road was extended to the river. This is quite possible, since, as we shall see, there are indications that the riverside wall is of very late date.

Even with gates, however, the wall would have been a considerable inconvenience if goods in any quantity were to be transported from the wharves into the city, and it is significant that it was not built until after the decline of Londinium as a port, and also that it was never rebuilt in the Middle Ages, although its earlier existence was remembered. It was gradually destroyed by river action, which undermined its foundations as the tides of the Thames rose higher, and by the end of the Saxon period only traces of it remained. William Fitzstephen, who wrote a panegyric of London in the late twelfth century, may have seen these remnants, for he was fully aware, not only of the earlier existence of the riverside wall, but also of the process by which it had been destroyed. After describing the city wall as he knew it, with its seven gates and its external towers on the landward side, he tells us:

London was once similarly walled and towered on the south side, but that greatest of rivers, the Thames, abounding in fish, with the rise and fall of the tide flows on that side, and in the course of time has washed against those walls, loosened and overthrown them.[17]

The accuracy of Fitzstephen's account of the earlier existence of a riverside wall and of its destruction by the river has now been demonstrated. Excavations in the south-west corner of the walled city at Blackfriars, between the Mermaid Theatre and White Lion Hill (the flyover), in 1974–6, revealed portions of riverside wall of two different types of build. The longest stretch observed was in the eastern part of the site, and was some 130ft (40m) long. This was built on a foundation consisting of a chalk raft laid on oak piles (**52**). In this respect the wall here resembled that observed by Roach Smith further east under Lower Thames Street. Roach Smith's wall, however, had contained re-used sculptured stones immediately above the oak raft, and none were found here. Instead there were four courses of ragstone set in hard green mortar, with the facing stones in a rough herringbone pattern. Above this was the first tile course, which formed an internal off-set or ledge on the inner face of the wall, as in the landward wall. Then five more courses of ragstone were laid, followed by a second tile-course, this time double, and another internal off-set that was considerably wider. Five courses of ragstone above this was a third tile-course, also double, with another wide off-set on the inner face. The tiles in these courses were both flat building bricks of the kind used in the landward wall and flanged roofing-tiles (*tegulae*), which were set with their flanges keyed downwards into the mortar. The tile-courses do not appear to have run all through the wall, as in the landward wall, but as the outer face and much of the core of the wall had been eroded away, leaving a thickness of only 3–5ft (1–1.5m), it was not possible to be quite certain of this. The rubble concrete core of the wall consisted of ragstone mixed with lumps of chalk, flint, tile fragments and even pieces of *opus signinum* (concrete containing crushed tile). The north face of the wall consisted of lumps of ragstone arranged in a rough herringbone pattern, except between the second and third tile-courses, where there were courses of fairly neatly cut rectangular blocks, as in the facing of the landward wall. All the surviving inner face, however, was originally covered with a clay bank, to a height of more than 6½ft (2m) above the chalk raft, so none of it would have been seen. This presumably served the same purpose as the inner bank of the landward wall, giving additional strength to the lower part of the wall, but there are mortar spreads in the bank corresponding with the tile levels, so it was probably built up in stages as the work proceeded, and may also have provided a working platform for the builders. As with the landward wall, provision had to be made for the passage of spring waters, by means of a culvert through the base of the wall and a cutting in the bank behind. There was no evidence for an external ditch, which was quite unnecessary in view of the proximity of the river, so the materials for the bank must have been obtained elsewhere, perhaps from the river-bed. The position of the remnants of the riverside wall was evidently known in the later Middle Ages, and portions may have been still visible, as it was used as a foundation for the north wall of the fourteenth-century Baynard's Castle (**52**).

The pile foundations seem to have come to an end about 47 yards (43m) west of the modern flyover, and the construction of the wall further west, where it was studied in several places, was quite different. Here there was no chalk raft supported by piles, and the foundations were simply large ragstone blocks rammed into the clay. Charles Hill has argued convincingly that this difference was simply due to a change in the subsoil from loose gravels to firm clay as the line of the wall continued to the west.[18] The London Clay was sufficiently solid to serve itself as a foundation whereas the gravels required the raft and piles to spread the load. The western portions of the wall, however, were different in other respects also. They included tile courses on the inner face of the wall—here certainly only two tiles deep—but these did not form wide internal off-sets, as in the wall to the east. These wide off-sets Hill would also explain as due to the unstable subsoil, which made it necessary to reduce the weight of the wall, with

N

B12
B11A
B11
B14

B19
B18
B17
B16
B15

2 2
2

B20

B21

3

stream

3

riverside wall

Walbrook

2

R I V E R   T H A M E S

probable line of bridge

T

100   0   300 m
500   0   1000 ft

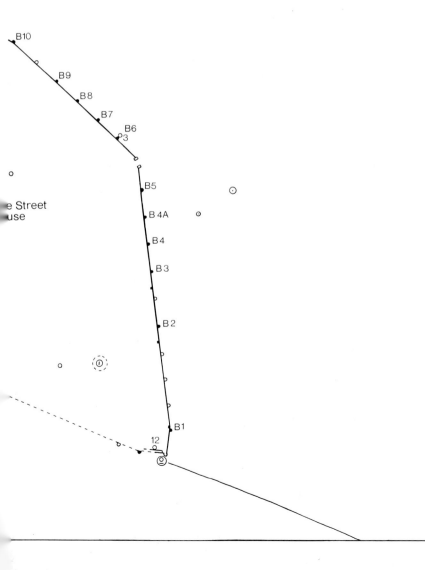

B10

B9

B8

B7

B6
3

B5

e Street
use

B 4A

B 4

B 3

B 2

B 1

12

Fig. 32 Map: features and finds of Londinium in the later fourth–early fifth century. *C. Unwin*

the internal bank compensating for the resulting loss of strength. No evidence for an internal bank was found in the western portion of the wall, though it could not be stated categorically that it had never had one; for this end of the wall seems to have been deliberately demolished by pulling or knocking the surviving inner portion to the north or landward side, and all Roman deposits against the north face of the wall must have been removed to make this possible. What was found in this area was the collapsed inner face of the wall lying on its side to the north of its foundations. The collapse could not have been the result of erosion by the river, which would have caused a collapse outwards into the water, as seems to have happened further to the east. The wall here must have survived as a dangerous fragment into the early Middle Ages, perhaps already partly undermined on its southern side, and it had to be demolished before any development could take place in its neighbourhood. The earliest recorded activity in this corner of the medieval city is in the twelfth century, and Thames Street overlying the fallen wall seems to have been first laid out as a road at this time.[19] Subsequently, probably in the late twelfth or early thirteenth century, a wharf was constructed here to the south of the Roman wall, apparently some time after the demolition had taken place.[20] The removal of a useless and dangerous ruin would have been an essential first step in this development.

The most interesting difference between the two stretches of wall at the western end of the riverfront, however, is that the collapsed portions in the extreme west contained large sculptured stones, including those from the monumental arch and the screen of deities, with two inscribed altars (see pp168–71, 176–81). These were re-used in a course along the inner face of the wall, with their upper surfaces forming a wide internal off-set of about 2ft 3in (700mm). This was evidently some distance above the surviving fragment of foundation, but its precise height can only be surmised. Hill has suggested a height of about $16\frac{1}{2}$ft (5m) above the foundations, but if the lowest tile course in the fallen fragment is equated with the single tile course in a fallen piece of the base of the wall found further west, and with the uppermost tile course of the wall to the east, both of which are on the same level, it would be about 3ft (1m) lower. It is in any case too narrow to have formed a parapet walk, and was simply a wide off-set, above which a narrower wall continued to the parapet base at an unknown height. Hill has pointed out that the width of the off-set seems to be equal to the sum of the widths of the three narrower offsets in the wall to the east, so that the upper narrower wall would have been of the same thickness in both stretches of wall. It is estimated from the width of the chalk raft that the thickness at the base of the wall was about 9ft (2.7m), reducing to $6\frac{1}{2}$ft (2m) in the upper portion above the offsets.

The most westerly fallen fragment, which was a piece of the base of the wall, lay under the former line of Upper Thames Street, just east of Castle Baynard Street, and only about 20 yards (18m) east of the Mermaid Theatre. Its position suggested that the riverside wall at this point was beginning to curve to the north to meet the landward wall west of St Andrew's Hill. Here the re-used sculptured blocks were in the foundations of the wall along its north side, and it was at the very base of the wall of that Roach Smith saw sculptured stone in the sewer excavations of 1841, in the stretch between Lambeth Hill and Queenhithe, where there was a raft of chalk and piles as in the more westerly portion examined in 1975–6.[21]

Between Queenhithe and Blackfriars, therefore, we have four variants: (1) with piles and chalk raft and with re-used sculptured stones in the base; (2) with piles and chalk raft and without re-used sculptured stones in the base or anywhere else in the surviving portions; (3) without piles and chalk raft and with sculptured stones forming an off-set higher in the wall; (4) without piles and chalk raft and with sculptured stones in the base. The presence or absence of the chalk raft and piles may be determined by local geological conditions, as Hill suggests; and the use of sculptured masonry from earlier buildings may be due simply to local availability. The rather patchy distribution of this material may indicate that it was derived from buildings in the immediate neighbourhood of the stretch of wall in which it was incorporated. It may be significant that the surviving fragments and the descriptions of the sculptured masonry from the wall east of Lambeth Hill and Trig Lane are all purely architectural ornaments. It is only the western end of the wall that has so far produced reliefs of deities and altars. Other variants, such as the placing of large slabs high or low in the wall, may be merely the result of different gangs using different methods. Certainly the riverside wall is much more diverse in structure than the remarkably homogeneous landward wall, but this does not necessarily mean that the different methods of construction were used at different times. A defensive wall was useless until it was completed, and it is improbable that this relatively short stretch of wall was built piecemeal over the years. It is much more likely that it was built on a single occasion when the urgency of the work made it necessary to recruit builders of diverse experience and traditions. There is a possible indication of a later rebuilding in the fallen portion that contained the sculptured stones from a higher level. The upper part, containing the stones, was separated from the lower by a fissure, and seemed to be of a different build, with hard white mortar and coarser facing-stones. It may, however, have been added in a later phase of construction by a different gang of workmen after only a brief time-lag. It was this portion that contained the pagan altars and religious sculptures, and it might be expected that these would have been early victims of a quest for building material in the Christian Londinium of the mid or late fourth century.

Our only real dating evidence for the western part of the riverside wall in Upper Thames Street, beyond the obvious fact that it is later than the inscription of 251–9 which was contained in it (p179), comes from the oak piles used in its foundations. These were subjected to a detailed study by Ruth Morgan, using a combination of tree-ring analysis and Carbon-14 dating from five samples. Tree-ring analysis by itself could not then give us an actual date for the Roman period in Britain, but was useful for relating the Carbon-14 date of the sample to the felling date of the tree. From this it was concluded that the foundation piles were cut between about 330 and 350 in radio-carbon terms,

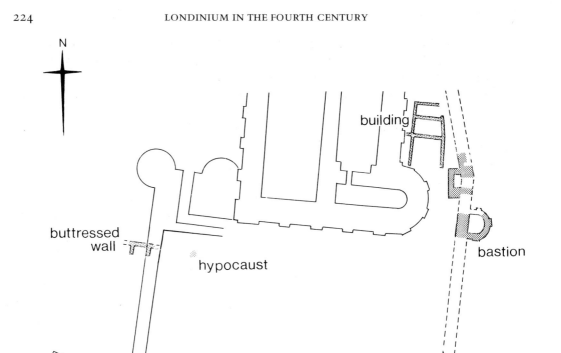

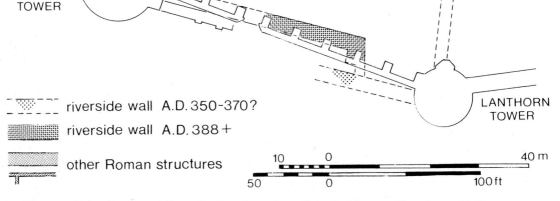

Fig. 33   Plan of earlier and later Roman riverside walls in the Tower of London, with Roman buildings of uncertain date to the north. *After G. Parnell*

though recalibration would push the date into the late fourth century.[22]

   The other area where new light has been thrown on the riverside wall is at the eastern end of the Roman walled city, in the Tower of London.[23] Here an excavation by Geoffrey Parnell in 1976–7 brought to light a most remarkable Roman wall just inside the Inner Curtain wall of the Tower, on which it converges slightly to the west (fig 33). The site is due south of the White Tower and east of the Wakefield Tower, and the wall has been preserved for display. It is quite different from any of the walls studied on the western side of the city. In this case the footings of the wall were slight; gravel had been laid to level the ground, and above this was a mixture of flint, ragstone and chalk puddled in clay, on which the wall itself had been built. The north and inner face consisted of extraordinarily neat courses, mostly of squared blocks of ragstone, mixed with Purbeck marble, sandstone, chalk, tufa and tile. The south and outer face, seen only in a limited area, consisted of ragstone with a double course of tiles 3ft 8in (1.1m) from the base, which had no plinth. The thickness of the wall was 10½ft (3.2m), its core consisting of layers of ragstone mixed with lumps of chalk, tile and *opus signinum*, alternating with bands of gravelly yellow mortar. Running through the core, parallel with the north face, was timber lacing, apparently at the level of the first offset, 5ft (1.5m) from the base. There were also traces of a 'brace-timber' across the wall, though corresponding lacing along the south face was not found. The wall did not continue in a straight line to the east, to meet the landward wall, but turned to the south at an angle of about 100°, evidently to

53   Later Roman riverside wall making angle at eastern end, Tower of London (view to SW), with Inner Curtain wall of Tower behind. *G. Parnell*

form a defensive promontory at its junction with the landward wall. The corner of the angle was built of several large stone blocks from an earlier building, re-used here to form a quoin, the angle of which seems to have been determined by their shape (53). Mortar had been smeared between the courses on both faces of the wall, and on the north side this pointing had remained extraordinarily fresh, as if it had only just been finished. It was completely unweathered, and must have been covered immediately with dumped soil. From this came a large quantity of late Roman pottery, and no fewer than thirty fourth-century coins, the latest of which was a small bronze coin of Valentinian II, dated 389–92. It is clear that the dump against the wall cannot have been made earlier than the last few years of the fourth century, and the condition of the mortar that it protected shows that the wall was then quite new.

Of the three historic occasions when the riverside wall might have been built—the visit of Constans in 343, the restoration of Britain's defences by General Theodosius in 369 and the final Roman expedition organised by Stilicho at the very end of the fourth century—the new evidence from the Tower of London now seemed to point unequivocally to the last. The beautifully built wall that was revealed for a length of 23 yards (21m) within the Inner Curtain, and the defensive projection it made at its junction with the landward wall can hardly be earlier than this time, and the engineering skill it shows has the stamp of the Roman army; it is most unlikely to have been built by any hypothetical sub-Roman defender of London in the fifth century. It also seemed to imply that the other Roman defences of the riverfront were probably of the same date, which could be reconciled with the Carbon-14 date of the foundation piles if sufficient allowance were made for recalibration. It then seemed likely that the riverside wall was the farewell gift of the Romans to Londinium.

Further investigations on the south side of the Inner Curtain in 1977–8, however, proved that this last assumption was quite wrong. They were undertaken to trace further the southward extension of the Roman wall and its eastward return, which was indicated by a scarping of the internal bank of the landward wall close to the Lanthorn Tower. Walling was found where it was expected, but this proved to be an *earlier* riverside wall, which had remained standing to the west of the junction of the two walls after the new wall had been built, so that a narrow corridor was formed between the two. This may have been used as a defended approach from the riverfront to a gateway in the new wall, and dumping at the eastern end of the corridor may have formed part of a ramp leading from the river to the gate. We do not know how far the older wall continued to the west after the new wall had been built, but a wall recorded in 1958 showed that it originally extended west of the Wakefield Tower, and there is little doubt that it was part of a continuous riverside wall. Its foundations were laid on a chalk raft supported by rows of wooden piles, exactly like the riverside wall built on the gravel subsoil in the western part of the city.[24]

This find, together with the discovery of another portion of timber-piled riverside wall at New Fresh Wharf, just east of London Bridge, provided more samples for dendrochronological examination and Carbon-14 dating.[25] From this investigation it appeared that the latest piles had been felled some twenty years later than had been indicated by the study of the Blackfriars material, giving a radio-carbon date of c. 350–70, with calibration bringing the date nearer to 400. It is most unlikely that the defence of the western part of the city was begun *before* that of the eastern part below the bridge, which was more directly under threat from possible attacks by river, so that logically the construction should have begun at the Tower end. A possible explanation of this relatively small discrepancy is that stock-piled timber felled some twenty years earlier had been used at Blackfriars. An immense quantity of timber would have been needed, and all possible sources for it would have been sought, including perhaps second-hand piles which could be re-used. A more serious problem is the need for calibration, which brings the date of the earlier riverside wall at the Tower uncomfortably close to that of the latter, which is well-dated archaeologically. It could be regarded as merely a strengthening of the earlier defences at their vulnerable junction with the landward wall, and as such could have been built in a second phase of the work quite soon afterwards. The differences in construction are so great, however, that a much longer time-lag seems necessary. Although the piles can be compared with one another and dated in terms of years within a floating chronology, this is at present anchored to the chronology of real time only by the flexible link of radio-carbon dating with its standard deviation of error, which cannot be eliminated altogether by the multiplication of samples. Jennifer Hillam and Ruth Morgan, who undertook this research, state that the radio-carbon date produced 'would not be inconsistent with the well-documented Theodosian reconstruction which followed the *barbarica conspiratio* of 367'.[26]

Of the three known occasions in the fourth century when the huge task of building the timber-piled riverside wall might possibly have been undertaken, the most likely is undoubtedly the second, when General Theodosius took measures for the further protection of Britain in 369. He had learnt the strategic value of Londinium from personal experience, and although the city had apparently held out against the recent marauders, in spite of its vulnerable riverfront, next time it might not, particularly if it were subjected to a naval attack via the Thames. If the first riverside wall, as represented by the widely distributed portions of wall built on chalk and piles, was built or commenced in 369, the inner wall at the Tower can reasonably be attributed to Stilicho's expedition some thirty years later, as the archaeological evidence suggests. Unless further evidence of a second wall is found elsewhere, it seems better to regard this as a local refortification for strengthening the defences in the south-eastern corner of the city, which may have become particularly important in late Roman times. Whether any of the variants of construction at the western end of the riverside wall can be attributed to this later period is quite uncertain; they have nothing in common with the second wall at the Tower, except the re-use of stone blocks from earlier buildings, and this practice is also associated with the portion under Upper Thames Street that had the chalk and pile foundation of the first riverside wall.

The Bastions

Another addition to London's defences that in all probability first appeared in the fourth century was the earliest series of bastions. These were fortified towers, semi-circular or horseshoe-shaped in plan, which were built on the outside of the city wall. Their purpose was to provide a field of fire covering the base of the wall and the approaches to it, and in Roman times an important weapon used for the purpose was the *ballista*, a spring-gun or catapult that could shoot iron-headed bolts with great force and fair accuracy. Bastions were a form of fortification that became popular in the late third century, and were a prominent feature of the forts of the Saxon Shore built at that period. They do not seem to have been added to the walls of Romano-British cities, however, until the fourth century was well advanced. This may well have been the result of a single decision, and coin evidence at Great Casterton has shown that there the bastions were built after 358.[27] The innovation can therefore probably be attributed to the reorganisation of defences under General Theodosius in 369. As we shall see, the scanty evidence we have from London tends to confirm this date for the building of the first bastions on the landward wall. The London bastions, however, are not all of the

Fig. 34   Plan of bastion 10, Camomile Street, as recorded in 1876, showing sculptured fragments from tombs in fill. *Drawing as published by J. E. Price in 1880*

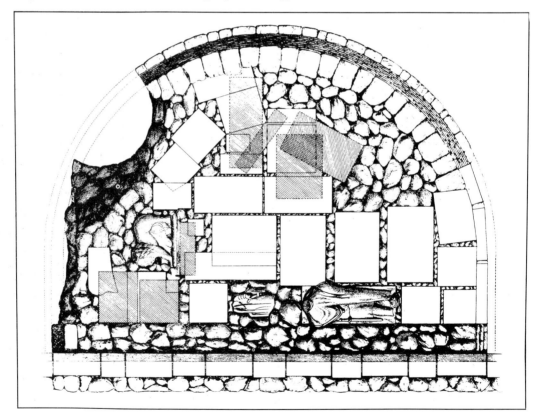

same date. They fall into two main groups: those west of the Walbrook, which, with one exception, are hollow from the base; and those east of it, which, with two exceptions, have their bases packed solid with re-used Roman monumental stones, including sculptures, much of it from the tombs and funerary monuments of the Roman cemeteries beyond the walls. There appears to be a gap between them in the long stretch of wall on the north side of the city, facing the headwaters of the Walbrook and Moorfields, and this was perhaps considered safe from attack because of the marshy nature of the terrain. Since three hitherto unknown or unrecognised bastions have been found in recent years, however, and a convincing case has been argued for the former existence of five more in the eastern group of bastions alone, it is clear that our knowledge of the series is far from complete (see fig 32, pp220–1).

The only well-dated bastion is 11A, one of the western hollow-based group, found by Professor Grimes in 1965, in the stretch of wall between Cripplegate and the corner bastion (12), which still stands at the north-west corner of the second-century fort. Only stumps of the walls and their foundations survived, but the latter cut through and clearly post-dated a deposit containing thirteenth century pottery. Moreover, details of structure were remarkably like those already observed in its neighbours. It had a gravel floor like that of bastion 14, and its foundations rose towards the back to rest on a ledge made in the fort wall, over a wedge-shaped deposit of occupation soil, exactly like the foundation of bastion 15.[28] There is good reason to suppose, therefore, that the group of bastions on the west side of the fort is medieval in date, and there is at least a strong suspicion that the whole western series of hollow-based bastions may be of the same date. It may also be noted that worked stones with 'traces of Norman mouldings and of foliage of the early-English period' are said to have been found in the foundations of bastion 16 west of Aldersgate Street.[29] Surviving arrow-slits in bastion 14 indicate that the hollow bastions of the Middle Ages were manned by archers.

The eastern series of bastions is very different, however. They contain so much material from monuments in the Roman cemeteries that it seems certain that these were still standing when the bastions were built. Moreover, at the base of the core of each bastion that has been fully recorded were large coping-stones, that must surely have come from the battlements of the late second century city defences. This has been questioned because they are unlike the coping-stones from city walls in north-western Europe and more like certain massive coping-stones from walls and monuments in some continental cemeteries. In London, however, these stones have only been found in close proximity to the wall and occur on its western side, north of Ludgate and south of Newgate, as well as on its northern and eastern sides, from the Camomile Street bastion near Bishopsgate to bastion 2 near Tower Hill. It is unlikely that walls sufficiently thick to carry coping-stones more than 2ft (0.6m) wide would have escaped notice in all three extramural cemeteries, where hardly any masonry foundations have been detected, and it is very much more probable that the stones came from the battlemented parapet of the city wall, which would of course have been removed behind each bastion when the latter was built. The dissimilarity of the coping-stones from the crenellations of Gaulish city walls (eg at Trier)[30] can be explained by a change of fashion if these were of substantially later date. Some of the coping-stones re-used in the bastions have lateral projections, as in fact do some from Trier, indicating that they came from a more complex structure than a simple parapet wall. Some of the bastions, also, notably bastion 9 in Bevis Marks, contained more coping-stones than could have been obtained from the portion of parapet wall destroyed when the bastion was built. The most likely explanation seems to be that the building of the bastions was accompanied by the modification of other structures in the city wall, possibly the internal turrets and almost certainly the gates, which would presumably have been rebuilt in the late Roman fashion with projections serving the same purpose as the bastions, and taking their part in the mutually-supporting cross-fire provided by the new system (fig 35). Aldgate certainly had bastion-like projections in the later Middle Ages, though these extended across the line of a ditch that was apparently not filled before the early thirteenth century, and therefore should have been built after that date.[31]

One other piece of evidence, unfortunately long lost, that might have supported a medieval date for the eastern group of bastions, is the reported discovery of the handle of a green-glazed pitcher at the foundation of bastion 14 in Camomile Street, 'beneath the lowest bed of stone and near to the centre of the structure'. At the time it was taken as evidence for a post-Roman date, although J. E. Price, who reported on the bastion in 1880, four years after its discovery, was already qualifying his conviction with the caveat that has since been the mainstay of those who would prefer to attribute a late Roman date to the eastern group of solid bastions at least. He pointed out that green-glazed pottery is by no means unknown in Roman times, though unfortunately his doubts did not impel him to include in his report a drawing of the sherd, which was perhaps already missing.[32] The weakness of the argument, of course, is that lead-glazed pottery in Roman Britain is not particularly common and is normally found in an early context, so that the odds against a piece being found beneath the foundations of a fourth-century bastion must be considerable.

Nevertheless the question remains open, and evidence strongly suggesting, but not completely proving, a late Roman date for bastion 6, just north of Aldgate, was found by Peter Marsden in 1971. The foundation had been dug through an earlier deposit containing fourth-century material, and was overlaid by a later and thicker layer of refuse containing pottery of the fourth century, with nothing recognisably later, together with coins of 364–75. The latter deposit had obviously accumulated after the bastion was built, and if it is no later than the pottery and coin evidence suggests, would fit very well the notion that the bastions were added to the wall as part of General Theodosius' programme of reconstruction in 369.[33] This bastion still stood more than 3ft (1m) high, and contained a number of large sculptured stone blocks, including the inevitable coping-stone (54). It is unfortunate that this bastion could not have been completely excavated when it was uncovered in subsequent work at Aldgate.

54 Surviving portion of bastion 6, north of Aldgate, containing coping-stone (C) in its fill (view to W). *Museum of London*

This would probably have produced conclusive dating evidence, perhaps with the added bonus of a sculpture or inscription from the core; but as the bastion was not under threat of immediate destruction no funds were available for the purpose, and it has again been covered.

The foundation of a hitherto unknown bastion between Nos 4 and 5, in the northern part of the site of 8–10 Crosswall, between Aldgate and the Tower, was found by John Maloney in 1979–80, and has been numbered 4A in the series.[34] It was squarish in plan, and composed of layers of ragstone, flints and lumps of *opus signinum* embedded in gravel and capped with rammed chalk. The foundation, which was 4ft 9in (1.45m) in depth, was stepped down in two stages into the

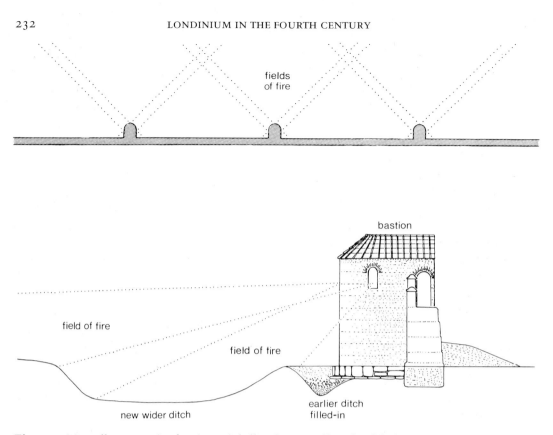

Fig. 35   Mutually supporting bastions. A *ballista* has a small angle of declivity, so that ground near the base of a bastion could only be covered by its neighbour. *C. Unwin*

bottom of the ditch. Only one small portion of the base of the bastion itself remained, and this contained a portion of the tombstone of a young girl, named Marciana, probably of the third century. Although the ditch had been filled before the foundation was cut into it, the builders were evidently well aware of its presence, and deepened the foundation at this point so that it did not rest on unstable ground. Again the evidence for a late Roman date is only circumstantial, but the bastion had been destroyed not later than the thirteenth century, and the outer face of its foundation had been cut away by a mediaeval ditch. The importance of this find is that it demonstrates that the eastern bastions were regularly spaced along the wall, at intervals of about 180ft (55m). A slightly wider gap occurs between bastion 5 and Aldgate and between bastion 10 and Bishopsgate, due, Maloney suggests, to the measurements being laid out from east to west—from the river wall to Aldgate, and from Aldgate to Bishopsgate— using a standard measurement that could not be divided equally into the distance required. On this hypothesis there are six missing bastions to be found between bastions 1 (Wardrobe Tower) and 11 (All Hallows London Wall), giving a total of 18 in the landward wall east of the Walbrook (fig 32). These would form a single unified defensive system, and ought therefore to be of one period.

Fitzstephen tells us that the riverside wall had towers like the landward wall, and in view of the vindication of his statements by the archaeologists, the old hypothesis that the Lanthorn, Bell, Wakefield and Middle Towers stand on the foundations of earlier bastions is inevitably revived.[35] Maloney points out that these towers, standing on the known line of the late Roman river-wall, are all between 170 and 185ft (51.8–56.4m) apart, and are therefore spaced at approximately the same distance as the eastern bastions of the landward wall. If the Wardrobe Tower was built on an earlier bastion, why not these?

Acceptance of this hypothesis has obvious implications for the dating of the whole eastern group. If some of these bastions stood on a wall that had been destroyed by the river before the Norman Conquest, they must be pre-medieval in date. Bastion 4A in the landward wall no longer existed in the thirteenth century when bastion 11A on the western side of the city was built, and it was constructed when the position of the original late second century ditch was still known. So also was bastion 11, on which the vestry of All Hallows, London Wall, was subsequently built. This likewise had a square foundation which extended over the original Roman ditch, where it was supported by a fill of chalk, flint and other stones. On either side of this was the silt of the ditch, which seems to have remained open here even after the building of the bastion, perhaps because in this marshy area it performed a useful function as a drain. Re-used Roman blocks and architectural fragments were found in the base of the bastion.[36] It is usually described as hollow, though it is not clear how much of the original bastion survived intact. In view of its subsequent re-use, it is possible that the core had been removed, and this may also be true of the other hollow bastion of the eastern group, re-used as the Wardrobe Tower of the Tower of London.

Normally the addition of bastions to a town's defences required the digging of a new and wider ditch, usually flat-bottomed, somewhat further away from the wall. This was not only a replacement for the old city-ditch but an integral part of the late Roman defensive system, since it slowed up the advance of any attackers and kept them longer under fire from the bastions. It may be represented by a sloping surface contemporary with bastion 6, but it has mostly been destroyed by the wide City Ditch dug in the thirteenth century. The filling of the original V-shaped ditch outside the Roman city wall inevitably accompanied the building of the bastions, and in the neighbourhood of bastion 6 this cannot have happened before the mid-fourth century, for a coin of Constans dated 341–6 was found with earlier material in its fill.[37]

Apart from the troublesome piece of missing evidence from the Camomile Street bastion, however, there is nothing to suggest that any of the eastern bastions are medieval, and there is a strong indication that bastion 6, at least, was already standing in the late fourth century. Moreover the presence of coping-stones in the fill of this bastion and of bastions 2, 3, 9 and 10 seems to show that the crenellated parapet of the late second century wall was still intact until they were built. Bastions were normally built in series to give each other covering fire, and the regularity of spacing leaves little doubt that this was the case here, and that the whole group was set up in a fairly short time. Variations of structure may mean no more than they do in the riverside wall, with which these eastern bastions may well be contemporary. This method of fortification is so characteristic of the late Roman period that it would be astonishing if it had been omitted in Londinium, particularly at a time when the much greater task of building a riverside wall was considered worthwhile.

What is puzzling, however, is that it does not seem to have been extended to the western half of the city, where there is no indication of a Roman date for any of the bastions, and there is clear evidence that four at least were not built before the thirteenth century. The eastern side of the city was certainly more vulnerable to the Saxon sea-raids that constituted the greatest danger to south-east Britain in the later Roman period. The north side of the city west of bastion 11 was protected by the marshes outside, and a considerable detour was necessary to reach the west side, since it must be assumed that the bridge at least was strongly defended, no doubt quite as effectively as it was against Viking attacks in the tenth and eleventh centuries. Nevertheless it must surely have been intended originally to complete the defensive circuit, but for some reason the task was abandoned when the more urgent part of the work had been done. It was not resumed until nearly 900 years later, when defences were needed against fellow-countrymen rather than foreign invaders. The irregularity of spacing on the western side, as contrasted with the eastern, also indicates that these bastions were built at a different time, although, as Maloney has pointed out, there were greater difficulties in achieving regular spacing owing to the position of the gates. Nevertheless the medieval defenders were obviously less concerned with this, for it was then that irregularities were allowed to appear in the eastern series also, where some bastions were evidently refurbished and used, while others, such as 4A, were demolished.

There is no evidence that the eastern half of the city was cut off and made into a separate citadel in late Roman times, for this would have required a new internal western defensive line along the east side of the Walbrook, of which there are no traces whatsoever. Nevertheless it had priority in defence, as is demonstrated also by the building of the second riverside wall, and it was to be the scene of the latest Roman activities in London.

It is possible that we may yet find evidence that the western group of bastions was at least begun in late Roman times. It might be expected that the series would have been commenced at the river and continued to the north, and in the stretch of wall just north of Ludgate Hill there is a possible hint of a former Roman bastion. Here Charles Hill found one of the great coping-stones that were so often re-used in the bases of the late Roman bastions on the eastern side of the city. It was no longer *in situ*, however, and may therefore simply have fallen from the parapet wall; but it was in this area also that the tombstone of the centurion Vivius Marcianus was found when St Martin's Church was rebuilt after the Great Fire, too near the city wall to have been in position on his tomb, and with damage that seems to have been caused by re-use. Had this been incorporated in the core of a bastion like the funerary monument of the soldier from Camomile Street?

Moreover the complex of successive ditches studied here by Hill included one that might just possibly be the hypothetical second Roman ditch.[38]

The one solid bastion on the western side of the city (bastion 17, west of King Edward Street) had little in common with those on the eastern side. Its foundation, which was not extended outside the base of its walls, was not stepped down into the Roman ditch, but simply ignored it and went straight down into the brick-earth beneath, 7ft (2.1m) below the plinth of the wall. No re-used carved or shaped stones were seen in its core, and the only obviously Roman material was a quantity of tile fragments worked into the masonry. There was a second and wider ditch observed to the west of the bastion, but it lacked the expected character of the late Roman ditch, being V-shaped. The situation here was complicated by the presence of a small stream which passed through the wall immediately west of the bastion, which it would have tended to weaken. This may account both for the unusually deep foundations of the bastion and for its solid base. There seems no good reason to suppose that it was of Roman date.[39]

It will be realised from this brief survey that we need to know a lot more about both the riverside wall and the bastions, and their history may be more complicated than it appears at present. There seems little doubt, however, that the inception of both can be attributed to the later fourth century, and there is a strong probability that they formed part of the restoration of British defences by General Theodosius, who was fully aware of the strategic value of Londinium from personal experience. It is possible that the subsequent failure to complete the circuit of bastions was due more to the lack of troops to man them adequately than to any decline in building ability or in the will to defend the city.

10

From Londinium
to London

Historical background

The expedition of Stilicho, to which the later riverside fortification at the Tower of London may probably be attributed, was the last serious attempt by central authority to retain Britain as part of the western Roman empire. Thereafter in the face of increasing barbarian threats it stood alone, protected only by its already depleted army. It was probably discontent with this situation, particularly in the army itself, that led to the rise of three short-lived usurpers. The first, appropriately, was himself a soldier; his name was Marcus, and he survived his election in 406 by only a few months. Surprisingly the next was a civilian named Gratian, a member of the urban aristocracy, whose brief elevation testifies that some political power was still wielded by the cities of Roman Britain. The great need, however, was for an effective military leader, and after four months Gratian was replaced by a soldier with the auspicious name of Constantine. A large-scale invasion of the Gallic provinces by barbarians from across the Rhine had taken place at the end of 406 and posed an obvious threat to Britain, though in fact the Germanic invaders moved into south-west Gaul and Spain. Constantine III gave first priority to the restoration of the Rhine frontier, and like Maximus before him crossed over to the Continent in 407, taking most of the surviving garrison of Britain with him. Although he survived for a few years and was even recognised as a legitimate emperor by Honorius, the Emperor of the West, any hope of his success in reuniting the empire was destroyed by the defection of part of his army, which joined forces with the barbarians in Spain. Meanwhile the troubles of Britain, including a barbarian onslaught of unknown origin, had led to revolt and the expulsion of Roman officials, according to the Greek historian Zosimus. This was probably not a revolt against the tottering Roman Empire as such, but rather against the unsatisfactory Constantine III who had left Britain in the lurch, and was quite possibly led by the same civilian notables who had supported his predecessor. The insurgents had apparently taken up arms and had been successful in freeing the cities from barbarian harassment. The initiative in Britain seems at this time to have been firmly in the hands of the local councils, and it was evidently these bodies who in 410 addressed a joint appeal for help to Honorius. With the Goths at the gates of Rome itself there was little the unfortunate emperor could do, except send the famous letter (Rescript of Honorius) renouncing responsibility for the defence of Britain. His instruction, significantly addressed, not to the *vicarius* or any military commander, but to the local councils, was merely that the *civitates* should look to their own defences—as they seem already to have done with some measure of success. The part played by Londinium is unknown, but its council was presumably one of the recipients of the letter. It is possible that the very late Roman refortification of the riverfront at the eastern corner of the city was undertaken as a result, rather than eleven years earlier by the orders of Stilicho.

If the emperor had now accepted the inevitability of abandoning Britain to its fate, the Church had not; and in religious matters at least Britain remained part of the Roman world for most of the first half of the fifth century. The Roman Church was still combating heresies with more vigour and success than the Empire had achieved in resisting the thrust of the barbarians. In Britain the heresy of Pelagianism was particularly strong; it was a doctrine of free will, taught by Pelagius, himself a Briton, although he had left his native land many years earlier. He was particularly opposed to the doctrine formulated by St Augustine of Hippo, who taught that salvation is entirely dependent on the grace of God, and cannot be achieved by the human will. This deterministic theology had been accepted as the orthodox belief of the Church, and Pelagianism was declared a heresy in 418, but continued to flourish in Britain. This was probably largely due to isolation from the main stream of Catholic thought, although it has also been suggested that the heresy may have had a political appeal for those who advocated strenuous independent action in self-defence, or for those who sought social reform.[1] To many, then as now, the Pelagian emphasis on the importance of good works must have seemed more relevant to the problems of the day than the Augustinian advocacy of submission to the Divine Will and to the discipline of the Church. Orthodoxy had its champions in Britain, however, and complaints about the Pelagianism of a British bishop named Agricola were sent to the Gaulish ecclesiastical authorities and to Pope Celestine. As a result, Germanus, bishop of Auxerre, was sent into Britain to rout the heretics in 429. He was subsequently canonised, and his biography, written later in the fifth century, gives us a unique glimpse of Britain nearly 20 years after the Rescript of Honorius. This is important for a study of Londinium, since there is no doubt that Germanus passed through the city, although it is not mentioned by name. He did however cross the Channel and subsequently visited the shrine of St Alban at Verulamium, so that his route was obviously along Watling Street. It is said that he preached 'at cross-roads and in the country' (*per trivia per rura*), the 'cross-roads' probably being street-intersections or squares in towns, so that some sort of town life was presumably still continuing, if such details are reliable. He met a man 'of tribunary power', whose blind daughter he miraculously cured, with the implication that there was still an administrative organisation of Roman style with magistrates, presumably belonging to one of the *civitates*. The Pelagians, whom he defeated in argument, are described as 'conspicuous by their wealth, splendidly dressed and surrounded by crowds of supporters' (*conspicui divitiis, veste fulgentes, circumdati assentatione multorum*).[2] We do not know where this meeting occurred, though it was evidently in a town of south-eastern Britain. It could equally well have been at Canterbury, London, Colchester or St Albans itself, the one place we know Germanus subsequently visited. The story demonstrates the survival of an educated Romano-British aristocracy, whose wealth must have been derived from the land, and who continued to enjoy considerable local support, presumably derived from traditional tribal loyalties. There is no reason, however, to suggest that this class had ever played a significant role in the later history of Londinium, which may have suffered a mortal blow when the Roman officials, its natural occupants, were overthrown in 408. It would be unwise to infer, therefore, on the analogy of such tribal capitals as Verulamium and Wroxeter, where occupation has been demonstrated archaeologically to continue well into the fifth century, that this was necessarily the case with Londinium. The strategic value of London as a centre of communications was diminished by the military isolation of Britain from the Continent, but it could still be important to anyone seeking to control a large part of the country that included the south-east. The need for co-operation in defence between the *civitates* had produced such a ruler in Vortigern, a shadowy war-lord who would probably have been regarded by the Romans as a minor usurper, but in the revival of native tradition took on the role of high king. It is even possible that he owed his position to hereditary rank rather than skill in war. This might explain the curious episode that occurred during the visit of Germanus. The bishop, who had formerly been a soldier, took over the command of the British force sent against a marauding band of Saxons and Picts, which he ambushed in a valley among high hills, possibly in north Wales, and routed to shouts of 'Alleluia', suffering no losses himself though many of the barbarians were drowned in a nearby river as they fled. If this battle really took place in north Wales, as later Welsh traditions suggest,[3] Vortigern was attempting to defend a large part of Britain, including tribal territories at least as far apart as those of the Cornovii and Cantiaci.

It was for his ultimately disastrous strategy in the latter region that he was remembered with obloquy by subsequent generations. His main problem seems to have been a shortage of manpower, and this induced him to follow a long-established Roman practice by inviting Hengist, a Saxon leader of Jutish origin, to settle with his people on Thanet, in return for the protection given by his warriors. The date of this event is as uncertain as all other dates in this period, but probably falls between 425–30. Archaeology has demonstrated that this was only one of several such settlements of Anglo-Saxon soldier-farmers in strategic places in the lower Thames area and on the southern approaches to London, at Mucking, Mitcham and Ham, and was certainly not the first of these. Hengist owes his fame and Vortigern the opprobrium of history less to the circumstances of the original alliance, which was normal late Roman practice, than to the fact that Hengist led a successful revolt of the Anglo-Saxon mercenaries many years later. The implications of the policy of Vortigern and his immediate predecessors are that the Thames was still an important route into Britain, and its protection was given high priority. This should also mean a continuation of the strategic role of London, and it might be expected that the strongly fortified Roman city would have served as a convenient headquarters for a ruler such as Vortigern. It can hardly have been his customary place of residence, however, and his tribal affinities probably normally kept him elsewhere, except when emergency demanded close and immediate co-operation between the *civitates*. The revolt of the latter which resulted in the expulsion of officials about 408–9 was in a sense the revolt of the tribal capitals against London, and, although no political vicissitudes could lessen the city's geographical advantages as a centre of communications, these must have been much less important in daily affairs than they had been under the late Roman Empire, in which administration, though devolved, was in theory at least closely knit under a central authority. The failure of that authority had removed a great part of the reason for London's existence. Even its purely military function as a strategic fortress demanded a standing garrison large enough at least to man its walls, and lack of manpower was obviously one of Vortigern's main problems.

Officials and soldiers in late Roman London

Before considering further the possibility that London survived as a centre of sub-Roman power into the fifth century, it is necessary to examine such evidence as we have for its general state in the later fourth and early fifth centuries. This is sparse enough, but certain deductions can be made from the few excavations that have produced information relevant to the period, from scattered finds, and from a single historical source.

The *Notitia Dignitatum* is a list of military and civilian posts of the empire, and is apparently a copy of an official document of the late fourth century, though it incorporates some material then out-of-date, and also seems to have been subjected to later revision up to about 420–5.[4] London (Augusta) is mentioned once as the place where the treasury was kept and the officer in charge of it was stationed—*Praepositus thesaurorum Augustensium*. From this it would appear that in theory, and probably also in practice, there was an imperial treasury in London as late as about 395—a good enough reason for the refortification of the riverside wall then, apart from any consideration of the strategic potential of the city.

The fact it was the eastern end of the wall that received special attention does not necessarily signify that the south-eastern corner of the city formed a special enclave at that date, like the later Tower of London, still less that it contained the treasury. Only the discovery of late fortifications cutting it off from the rest of the walled city would justify such a suggestion. Nevertheless the Tower is the only part of the Roman city that has as yet produced undoubted evidence of structural work at the very end of the fourth century. We have already seen (Chapter 9) that an inner riverside wall was built parallel with the first at this period, within what is now the Tower of London, and that this formed an obtuse angle to meet the outer wall some 15 yards (14m) west of the junction of the latter with the landward wall; the two riverside walls co-existed, with a narrow corridor between them that may have served in some way as a strongly defended approach from the river (fig 33). In 1979, a continuation of the inner wall was found by Geoffrey Parnell about 15 yards (14m) west of the first stretch. Its line had converged on that of the existing inner curtain wall of the Tower, so that here only a portion of the north side was visible. It was, however, possible to excavate the area to the north of it, which produced a valuable section. Further east the wall had been free-standing, but here it was built in a construction trench, within which was a line of timbers that appear to have been posts for scaffolding. From deposits through which the construction trench had been dug came no fewer than forty-eight coins, which amply confirmed the coin evidence found further east, dating the wall as not earlier than the last years of the fourth century (p226). The coin series found in 1979 ended with an issue of Theodosius I and another of Arcadius, both of the period 388–402. They demonstrate conclusively that the inner wall found here cannot have been commenced before 388. The deposits from which they came lay directly on a scatter of ragstone waste which could be interpreted as masons' debris from the building of the earlier riverside wall to the south. Overlying them, at a distance of 18ft (5.8m) north of the later wall, was a thin spread of sand and crushed chalk, possibly the remains of a floor or working surface contemporary with its building. Above this was a thin layer of dark silt, probably representing a phase when this surface was exposed to rains and hill-wash, and covering the silt was a well-constructed floor, made of gravel and yellow mortar surfaced with a finer mortar. Although the stratification was interrupted by medieval disturbances, there seems no doubt that this floor was laid *after* the wall was built in the 390s or later.

Geoffrey Parnell has suggested that there may indeed have been a late Roman stronghold in the south-east corner of the city, and that this could have determined the lay-out of the Norman Tower of London. The possible relationship of the Lanthorn, Wakefield and Bell Towers to late Roman bastions of the riverside wall has already been discussed (233). Parnell also draws attention to the fact that the ground floor chamber of the Bell Tower lies above a massive build-up, and that an excavation in the boiler-room of the Queen's House, just to the north of it, has shown that the curtain wall adjoining it was inserted through a mass of clay that was undoubtedly dumped to a height of $12\frac{1}{2}$ft (3.8m) above the natural level of the London Clay in that area. This might suggest that the late thirteen-century Inner Curtain wall on the east side was built on the line of a pre-existing north–south feature. More evidence is obviously required, particularly of the date of this feature, which could of course by Norman, as Parnell points out. The old traditions, mentioned sceptically by Stow, that the Tower is of Roman origin, might however yet be vindicated![5]

We have no certain evidence that the late Roman activity in the south-east corner of the city was of a military character, but two remarkable hoards from

55 Silver ingot stamped EX OF. FL. HONORINI ('from the workshop of Flavius Honorinus'), found with gold coins of Arcadius and Honorinus in Tower of London, 1777. Length 4in (10.1cm). Probably early fifth century. *British Museum*

that area might suggest the presence of soldiers or officials. During digging for foundations in the Tower of London in 1777, very near the site of the recent excavations, a small but valuable hoard was found consisting of two gold coins (*solidi*) of Arcadius, from the mints of Rome and Milan, and another of Honorius, from the mint of Milan, together with a silver ingot 4in (10cm) long and weighing 1lb troy (373gm). This was stamped EX OF FL HONORINI ('from the workshop of Flavius Honorinus') (**55**). Ingots were presented to soldiers on such occasions as an emperor's accession, quinquennial or even on his birthday. They were often accompanied by gold solidi, and the accession donative, at least from 361, is known to have been five gold solidi and one pound of silver.[6] The Tower hoard could therefore be the major portion of such a donative, perhaps for the accession of Honorius and Arcadius in 395. It can be argued against this interpretation that the coins are from more than one mint, and that the stamp on the ingot is not an official one. The name of a silversmith, however, occurs both on bars of silver from Yugoslavia and on plates from Bulgaria made for distribution to commemorate the tenth year of the reign of Licinius, so it would appear that individual maker's names did sometimes appear on objects made for an official donative. Ingots closely resembling the one from the Tower, but with the stamp CVRMISSI, have been found in Kent and also in the hoard of loot deposited at Coleraine, Northern Ireland, after 410. Kenneth Painter has suggested that it is an abbreviation for *curator missionum*, the official in charge of issues of donatives, and is inclined to attribute all such ingots to imperial donatives of the fourth century.[7]

The problem of these ingots and their date has recently been given greater relevance to a study of late Roman London by the discovery that another hoard of similar ingots was found in 1898, apparently in the same corner of the Roman city, less than 300 yards (275m) from the hoard of 1777. In 1978, the British Museum purchased a silver ingot of similar form to the one from the Tower, with the stamp in two lines EXXOF/VINCI, 'from the workshop of (?)Vincius'. This came from Capard House, Co. Laois, Eire, where it had been for at least the last 50 years, according to the vendor, and its original find-spot was unknown. Since then two other ingots have come to light, in the possession of two residents of Dublin, and these are said to have come from the grounds of Capard House, where other antiquities, including a fragment of a Mediterranean amphora, were recovered from a rubbish tip in the grounds. They are stamped respectively EXOFF/TVCIVS and EXOFFC/ATILICA, both in two lines (respectively from the workshops of Tucius and Atilica). The one stamped by Atilica, which weighs 337gm, has a paper label stuck on its back, on which is written in four lines, 'Silver Ingot/Roman c.350 AD/Found by Mr Hopkins/Tower Hill 1898'. The appearance of the label and the handwriting seems to be consistent with the date of discovery mentioned.[8] It is almost certain that all three ingots came from the same hoard, for they are sufficiently rare to make it virtually impossible for a collector to have assembled three from different sources. Two elements of doubt remain: first, of course, is the label genuine? Circumstances seem to be in its favour, for the man through whose hands both ingots passed, and who still retains the third ingot, was evidently unaware that the label gave it any additional interest. The other doubt arises from the fact that the hoard came to light in Ireland, where two other hoards containing these ingots have been found, accounting for 11 out of the 26 hitherto known from the British Isles, the remainder of which all came from southern England.[9] Can we be quite sure that the hoard came from Tower Hill, London, and not from some unknown 'Tower Hill' somewhere in Ireland? There is no reason to doubt the provenance of the 1777 Tower hoard, however, and this gives credibility to the purported later discovery of very similar stamped ingots in the same neighbourhood.

The precise dating of both hoards is obviously of great importance for the history of London, and the bold statement 'c.350AD' on the label of the Tower Hill ingot raises the question whether the 1898 hoard also may have been accompanied by coins. If so, they are likely to have been of gold, and gold coins are even more prone than silver ingots to vanish without record. The suppression of the supporters of Magnentius in 353 would have been a likely occasion for the abandonment of a hoard. A mid-fourth-century date for the Tower Hill ingots, however, would rule out any possible historical connection between the two hoards, such as might be expected, in view of their unusual character, similarity and close proximity. The 1777 hoard cannot have been deposited before about 395, and most solidi of Honorius and Arcadius found in Britain were minted in the early fifth century. It could of course have incorporated an earlier silver ingot, however, and the ingots from both hoards are so similar in form and style as to make it likely that they were produced at least in the same quarter-century. Is it possible to make any deductions on a typological basis from the useful corpus of stamped ingots assembled by Kenneth Painter for his discussion of the ingot from Kent?[10] The ingot from the Tower of London is of the kind he describes as double-axe shaped. The corners are rounded, and the breadth at the expanded ends is more than half the overall length. These are characteristics it shares with all three ingots of the 'Tower Hill' hoard, as well as with ingots from Canterbury, Richborough and Reculver. The same type also occurs in the two hoards of pirate loot from Ireland, with stamps that are also found in Kent. The continental ingots with stamps that indubitably identify them as imperial largesse are mostly of quite different types,—round, square, oblong and irregularly octagonal, with angular corners[11]; these date from 305 and 350. The only one with an imperial stamp that closely approaches the British form is one from Dierstorf near Hanover, and this bears busts of late style, believed to be those of Theodosius III, Valentinian III and Galla Placidia. It could have been issued as a donative on the accession of Valentinian III as emperor of the west in 425. This ingot has one straight end—a variant found also in Kent—but otherwise closely resembles the London and other British examples, while another ingot from the same hoard has both ends incurved and very rounded corners, exactly like those from the Tower, Tower Hill and Richborough.[12] This ingot and a third from the Dierstorf hoard, which has straight ends, both have official stamps of the Trier mint, which produced coins as late as 428, so that they are not necessarily any earlier. The use of the abbreviation PVS for *pusulatum* ('pure silver') on one of them, would suggest a date between 367 and 428 when this abbreviation was used on coins. The broad double-axe shaped ingot, which often has distinctly incurved ends, seems therefore to be definitely late, as far as our information goes; it is quite different in proportions from the double-axe shaped silver bars from Eni Eri, Bulgaria, that were found in association with dishes made for a donative of Licinius, and evidently date from the early fourth century.[13] These have a width less than a third of their length, straight ends, and corners that are only slightly rounded. If they represent the ancestral form of the British ingots, as is possible, a considerable period must have elapsed to account for the change.

Typologically, therefore, these ingots are likely to be of the later fourth or early fifth centuries, as might also be expected from their presence in fifth century Irish hoards; and this date is confirmed by the coins found with the one from the Tower. Their relative abundance in southern Britain is in marked contrast with their apparent scarcity on the Continent where, apart from the three from Dierstorf, Painter was able to find only one fragment from Belgium that is approximately of this form. The total number of this type from Britain, including those from the Irish hoards, now amounts to thirteen, all of which have only the stamp in two lines of the workshop from which they came, or in two cases no stamp at all. Two stamps occur both in Irish hoards and in Kent, and the circumstances strongly suggest that the ingots were produced in south-eastern Britain. John Kent is of the opinion that the silver was obtained by coin-clipping,

0   5 cm

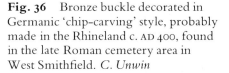

Fig. 36 Bronze buckle decorated in
Germanic 'chip-carving' style, probably
made in the Rhineland c. AD 400, found
in the late Roman cemetery area in
West Smithfield. *C. Unwin*

which also seems to be confined to Britain.[14] He argues that this treatment of
silver *siliquae*, which removed the emperor's name and titles, could only have
taken place after imperial authority had been removed, and that the ingots are
therefore likely to have been produced after 410. The issuing authority would
then presumably have been either the independent *civitates*, who used this means
to pay for their defence, or a ruler such as Vortigern, who was also concerned with
the defence of the south-eastern area where the ingots seem to originate. Such a
late date would account for the various barbarisms in the inscriptions, such as
incorrect endings and letters that are doubled or reversed. On this hypothesis it
would be necessary to abandon the interpretation of cvrmissi as the title of a
Roman official, and revert to the original explanation that it was simply the rather
barbaric name of a silversmith, in no way different from the other craftsmen
whose names appear on the stamps.

Whichever theory is correct, there seems little doubt that these ingots are not
earlier than the late fourth or early fifth century, or that they were used in one way
or another to buy the services and loyalty of troops. These would no doubt have
been the barbarian mercenaries who had become the mainstay of the Roman
army. Direct evidence for the presence in Londinium of late Roman soldiers is

provided by two military buckles, one with a 'dolphin' ornament from Lothbury, where it had probably been lost in the Walbrook stream, and the other a highly ornate example found in the cemetery beyond the city wall in West Smithfield, north of Newgate (fig 36). Such equipment was issued by the Roman army in the late fourth and early fifth centuries, and is unlikely to have reached Britain from official sources after about 407, though the possibility of later copying in a British workshop must be borne in mind. Late Roman belt-fittings have been found in graves outside other Romano-British towns, notably at Dorchester-on-Thames and Winchester, and the status of the soldiers who wore them has been the subject of much debate. Until recently they were generally considered to be *laeti*, irregular troops who were allowed to settle with their families to form a defensive militia, but it now seems as likely that they were detachments of the regular army, and there is even a possibility that such belt fittings were sometimes part of a civilian uniform.[15] Since these objects are not closely datable, and date at this period of transition is an important criterion for interpretation, great caution is obviously necessary. The significance of the highly decorative Smithfield buckle, presumably worn by a person of some rank, may be quite different from that of the relatively plain dolphin buckle, which is a type with a wide distribution that includes not only the whole length of the Danube-Rhine frontier, but also North Africa as well.[16] A set of belt-plates and buckle even more elaborately decorated than the Smithfield buckle was found in a grave at Mucking overlooking the Thames estuary—a strategic site where Saxon occupation seems to have begun very early in the fifth century, if not in the late fourth, according to Myres' dating of the Saxon pottery found there.[17] In this case at least, the 'late Roman' equipment was presumably worn by a mercenary officer who was also a person of importance in the Saxon community that used the pottery; moreover, it is difficult to believe that an ornament of such barbaric splendour was any kind of official issue from a military workshop. The circumstances here point to a settlement of federate Saxons with a military role, officered by their tribal leaders, who wore the uniform of the Roman army but embellished it by commissioning equipment of this kind to their own taste, no doubt from craftsmen in Britain. Vera Evison has suggested that this and other less elaborate buckles from Mitcham, Orpington and elsewhere in south-eastern Britain were products of the same insular school of metalwork, which was derived from the late Roman workshops of northern Gaul, probably through the migration of craftsmen.[18] The Mucking buckle can be attributed to the early fifth century, but it remains uncertain whether the last Roman rulers or their successors were responsible for the introduction of Saxon soldiers into the Thames estuary. The Smithfield buckle is likewise elaborately ornamented by the same technique of faceting, known as chip-carving, but is more closely akin to buckles found in Germany, and may be an import from the Rhineland.[19] In that case it is probably of somewhat earlier date—late fourth to early fifth century, and before rather than after 407. At this time it is as likely to have been part of the uniform of an official in government service as of an army officer, regular or otherwise.

The western half of the city in late Roman times

It would be wrong to give the impression that Londinium had contracted in the late fourth century to the area of a citadel at the south-eastern corner of the walled Roman city, on the analogy of some Gaulish towns. Nevertheless, some contraction, favouring the eastern half of the city, does seem to have taken place, although it did not result in a shortening of the defensive line when the riverside wall was built, probably late in the third quarter of the century. This would have made it necessary to build a new western landward wall east of the Walbrook, but the amount of building would have been little more than was required for the riverside wall west of the Walbrook, and a much smaller defensive force would have been adequate for the shorter line of wall. The fact that this was not done can probably be attributed less to vested interests west of the Walbrook than to the strength of the existing western defences, which dominated the Fleet valley, itself a good natural line of defence with which the marshes of the Walbrook could not be compared. It is just possible also that some use continued to be made of the Cripplegate fort, though its ditches within the city walls had long been filled in.

Records of finds of coins of the later fourth century, after 364, are not particularly numerous for the City of London, but from the Museum of London catalogue and a few published sources[20] it has been possible to trace twenty sites where they have been found. Three of these were just outside the city wall on the east side; of the remainder within the walls, eleven were on the east side of the Walbrook and six on the west—a substantial, but not overwhelming, preponderance of sites in the eastern half of the city (map, fig 32). It may be significant, however, that in three of the four cases west of the Walbrook where there is a record of stratification, the coins came from 'black soil' in Friday Street, 'black occupation (soil)' in Aldermanbury, and drainage gullies filled with dark earth north of Guildhall,[21] suggesting they were lost during the activity that produced the dark earth, characteristic of large areas in the western part of the city in late Roman and Saxon times (see pp140–4). There is only one record of the association of late Roman coins with a substantial building west of the Walbrook. In 1841 a hypocaust was found with pillars of tiles supporting a mosaic floor, with pattern of rosettes on a white ground, at a depth of 18ft (5.5m) in the north-east corner of St Paul's Churchyard, and a coin series terminating in Valens (364–78) was found 'beneath the ruins'.[22] It is not clear whether the coins lay beneath the floor of the hypocaust itself, thus dating the construction to the later fourth century, or, as is more probable, under the fragments of mosaic and fallen hypocaust pilae above this floor, circumstances which would suggest its demolition in this period. In the latter case, a close parallel can be cited from the eastern half of the city, in Lime Street, where coins of Valens and Gratian, dated 364–75 and 367–75, were found in the filling of the hypocaust that probably resulted from the destruction of the building, for which there was evidence of a late third-century construction (p199). There was evidence of burning but also of some robbing of the ragstone walls.[23] The walls of the building in St Paul's Churchyard are not mentioned, and this might indicate that they had been robbed for the stone of which most buildings of this class and period were constructed in London. There is a distinct possibility that both these substantial residences were demolished in the years following the troubles of 367 to provide building material for the riverside wall. The St Paul's Churchyard building is the only one in the west of the city for which we have some evidence of existence in the second half of the fourth century. It must have been reasonably extensive, and in all probability included other portions of building observed in Paternoster Row, where a mosaic at a higher level (12½ft—3.8m—deep), 'with a design of birds and beasts in compartments within a border of guilloche and rosettes' is said to have extended for 40ft (12m).[24] The co-existence of any building in this area with the late Roman 'dark earth' deposits to the north on the GPO site would obviously be of great interest if it could be proved, but the idea of a city 'villa' engaged in intramural agriculture must be considered with caution until the nature of the 'dark earth' can be determined with more certainty. For the present it seems more reasonable to regard large domestic buildings of some luxury in fourth century London as the residences of officials. Peter Salway has suggested that a great part of the late Roman city could have been occupied by an imperial palace with its grounds, as was the case with Arles and Trier, where the fourth-century palace quarter lay in a part of the town clear of the earlier public buildings.[25] The idea of the 'dark earth' representing parks and gardens is an attractive one, but for the present we lack the new palace west of the Walbrook to go with them. Certainly the one residence that is evidently late Roman has no such pretensions, and is separated from the neighbouring 'dark earth' deposits of the GPO site by the main highway to Newgate and the west. The possibility that a major late Roman building complex once existed somewhere in the western half of the city, perhaps like the earlier palace on the terraces above the river, cannot however be ruled out in our present state of ignorance. A new palace quarter would only have been created in the presence of an emperor, or one claiming that title, such as Clodius Albinus, Geta or Carausius, and if it ever existed the splendour must have departed long before the later fourth century. It is hard to believe that the western half of the city at that time would have merited its inclusion within the new defences if there had been no overriding topographical consideration.

The late Roman house in Lower Thames Street

It may be significant that the one Roman building we know where occupation certainly continued into the early fifth century is on the eastern side of the city close to the river. Before the Coal Exchange in Lower Thames Street was swept away in the interests of development, privileged visitors were allowed to descend by a spiral iron stairway into its basement, where a Roman hypocaust, with a considerable part of its upper floor still surviving, had been preserved when the Coal Exchange was built. Plans made during the construction of the Coal Exchange in 1848 and of warehouses to the east of it in 1859 showed that the hypocaust room was part of a considerable Roman building complex. The removal of the Coal Exchange, though much to be regretted, had one advantage

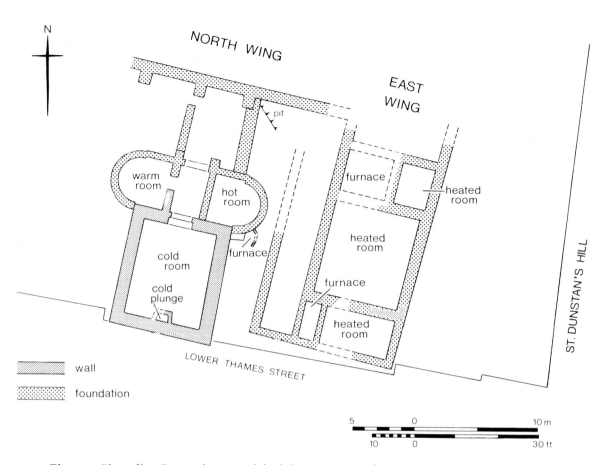

Fig. 37 Plan of late Roman house with bath-house, on site of Coal Exchange, Billingsgate, Lower Thames Street (p248). *After P. R. V. Marsden*

for the historian of London; it gave a valuable opportunity for investigation of the important Roman remains that still survived beneath it.

The hypocaust was part of the warm room of a bath-house, centrally placed in a courtyard between three wings of a building that were linked by a corridor (fig. 37). The south side of the courtyard was presumably open to the river, and like other buildings on the riverside it was constructed on terraces, with the north wing built between retaining walls. The bath-house was evidently a private one belonging to the building, as was customary in later Roman times, and although a close dating for the construction has not been obtained, it is not earlier than the Antonine period, and it seems likely that this was one of the large and substantially built establishments that appeared in London in the third century. Peter Marsden, who excavated it, has suggested that the relatively large size of the bath-house and its central position may indicate that the building was not a private residence but an inn or hostel.[26] Its function was evidently sufficiently basic to ensure its continued use in much the same form for a long period of time, and the great interest of the building lies in the fact that it was still occupied at the very end of the Roman period, and we have some indication of its subsequent fate. The east wing of the building, the only one of which we have any detailed knowledge, had under-floor heating by hot-air channels from a stokehole at its southern end. Scattered over the floor of the furnace-room and the adjacent corridor was a hoard of more than 270 small bronze coins, mostly very corroded and illegible. Nearly all those that could be identified were of the last imperial issues that reached Britain in bulk, dating between 388 and 402. A coin of Honorius was not earlier than 394, and two of Arcadius from the mint of Aquileia were not earlier than 395. The hoard was therefore being accumulated to the very end of the

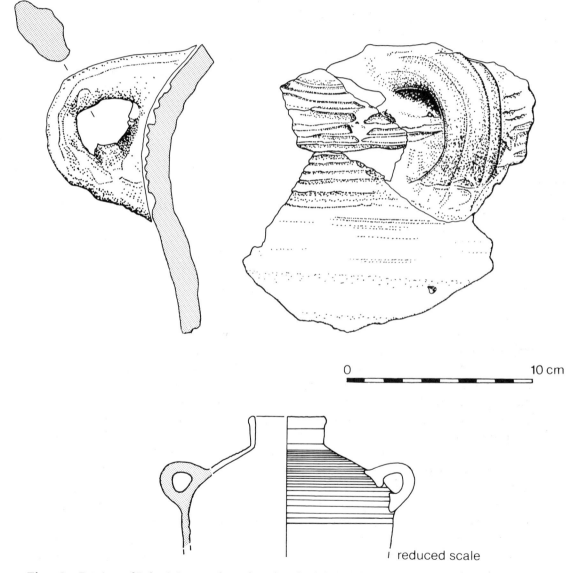

0   10 cm

reduced scale

Fig. 38   Portion of Palestinian amphora found under ashes in furnace compartment at south end of east wing of late Roman house, Billingsgate, Lower Thames Street (see fig. 37). *C. Unwin, after P. R. V. Marsden*

fourth century, and had evidently been kept somewhere in the house nearby. The circumstances in which it was scattered on the floor of the furnace-room can only be guessed, but this happened before the collapse of the roof, the debris of which overlay the coins. The abandonment of the hoard has no sinister implications, since coins would have ceased to be used in Britain as a means of exchange within a few decades of the date when these were issued. Tiny coins with a negligible metal content must then have become valueless, not even worth the trouble of picking up if by mischance they were scattered on the floor.

One other find of great interest was made at the north end of the same furnace-room, where the ash from the last fire used for heating the east wing still lay. Under it was a coin of Theodora (337–41), not necessarily indicating a date for the ash earlier than the scattered coin hoard, since it has been pointed out that 'most hoards of copper coins deposited around 400 contain up to two per cent of coins struck between 330 and 348, still in recognizable condition'.[27] It is possible, therefore, that it also came from the scattered hoard, and that the date of the ash is 400+. Under the ash also were fragments of an amphora, of a type that came from the eastern Mediterranean, probably from Gaza (fig 38). Since the type first appears in Athens in the middle of the fifth century, it was at first thought that the amphora gave an impressively late date to the wood-ash. It is now known, however, that in Palestine it occurs as early as the fourth century, so that the date of its appearance in Greece is merely that of a trade pattern. Its significance in London is precisely the same, and until it occurs there in a closely dated context such as we are unlikely to find for the fourth and fifth centuries, its value for dating will be limited. Other examples of east Mediterranean amphorae, not all from the same source, have certainly been found in London, for example in a great dump of late Roman material overlying the ruined offices or staff quarters in the south-eastern part of the Cannon Street palace, a wing that seems to have continued in use to a late date and had finally been occupied when in a dilapidated condition by 'squatters' who had built a rough hearth there.[28] There are also fragments from Late Saxon silting at New Fresh Wharf, where they are evidently residual.[29] Another came to light as an unstratified workman's find from the site of St Dionis Backchurch in Lime Street. A possible example comes from the late robbing of a Roman flint wall in St Thomas Street, an event that could not be dated more precisely than 'between c 400 and 1000'.[30] None of these helps to date the London imports. All that can be said is that they do not conflict with the date at the end of the fourth or more probably early in the fifth century that is suggested by the coin evidence from Lower Thames Street. A further clue can be found in the nature of the trade to which these fragments testify. In the south-west of Britain fragments of amphorae from the eastern Mediterranean and Black Sea have been found on a number of Dark Age sites, sometimes with imported table-ware that can be paralleled by finds from Athens dated between about 460 and 600. It has been argued that this Atlantic trade with the Byzantine empire was impossible in the middle decades of the fifth century because of the activities of Vandal pirates based on the coast of north Africa.[31] This is not altogether convincing, since piracy cannot exist without trade, and later generations of merchants were prepared to risk the passage of the straits of Gibraltar in spite of the danger from Barbary pirates. Nevertheless it can be accepted that Mediterranean imports were arriving at south-western sites in the later fifth century. As we shall see, a date as late as this is impossible for the Lower Thames Street amphora, but it is hard to see any reason for the development of trade in Mediterranean products between Britain and the Empire of the East while they were readily available from much nearer sources. The amphorae would have contained wine or olive oil, both of which could have been obtained more easily and presumably much more cheaply from Gaul, Spain, Italy or even North Africa before the general disruption of the Empire of the West by barbarian invasion early in the fifth century. This was a process extending over a number of years, but the crucial event for British supplies could have been the Vandal invasion of Spain in 409. The eastern traders probably stepped into the breach remarkably quickly, for the Church had an interest in the distribution of wine and oil, both of which were necessary for sacramental purposes, and it had contacts and influence throughout the Roman world. It is difficult to believe, however, that it would have been worth anyone's while to have brought wine from the eastern shores of the Mediterranean to London earlier than about 410. Since trade is a two-way process, it must also be asked what goods were to be found in Britain at this period, for which wine could be exchanged to provide a profitable cargo for the long return journey. It is unlikely that the traditional British exports of earlier times were being produced in quantities greater than were required for very local consumption, or that there was a sudden enthusiasm in the east for British cloaks or hunting-dogs. The return cargo is more likely to have been provided by the troubled nature of the times. Barbarian raiders and invaders did not have everything their own way, and if captured would have been sold into slavery. It is possible that London's brief revival as a trading centre was based on this traffic. It would have been a convenient entrepôt to which captives taken on the Rhine frontier or in Gaul could be sent for safe-keeping and eventual sale.

Although there is a strong argument for the continued use of the Lower Thames Street house into the fifth century, and probably at least into its second decade, there is an equally valid reason for believing that it did not survive until the middle of the century. The sequence of events is clear, even if their date can be fixed only within a quarter-century or so. There was no violent destruction, merely the quiet abandonment of the building to the destructive forces of time and weather. The stokehole fire was lit no more, and the inhabitants, who had been living in some degree of Romanised comfort, enjoying the benefits of central heating and drinking imported wine, had all departed. Some of the pleasures of civilised life had probably been abandoned earlier, for the bath-house does not seem to have been used for its proper purpose for some time, perhaps because fuel was short or the last occupants had lost the habit of bathing in the elaborate Roman way. It remained in use, however, perhaps as a store, at least until the end of the fourth century, for coins of the House of Theodosius, including one

56 The end of Roman London; collapsed roof tiles of east wing of late Roman house, Billingsgate, Lower Thames Street (see p253). *Museum of London*

probably of Arcadius, were found on the pink mortar floor of the frigidarium. The abandoned building suffered the natural decay that might be expected. First the windows were broken, and the fragments of their glass lay immediately on the floor-surface, overlaid by silt which accumulated as the rains poured in and hill-wash spread from the open doors. Finally the winds lifted the roof-tiles and brought them crashing to the floor, so that the building stood as a roofless shell (**56**). This happened to both house and bath-house, the voussoir tiles of which lay broken on the floor of the frigidarium. After the collapse of this roof the building received visitors, who were presumably scavenging for anything worth retrieval from the ruin. They included a woman, who lost her bronze disc brooch, of a very distinctive early Saxon type, among the roof-tiles overlying the frigidarium floor (**57**r). This *ought* to give us a *terminus ante quem* for the collapse of the bath-house roof and consequently for the abandonment of the building, but unfortunately there is disagreement among scholars concerning its precise date. It is identical with a brooch found in a grave of the early Saxon settlement at Mitcham, which also contained a glass cone-beaker considered to be of the second half of the fith century (**57**l). Unfortunately another, of slightly different design but obviously of similar date, was associated in another Mitcham grave with a pottery pedestal bowl that Dr Myres considers to be not later than about 400. M. G. Welch has traced altogether eight similar brooches from various sites in south-eastern England, and concludes that they were manufactured in the same workshop, probably in Surrey, in the first half of the fifth century, and were

57 Bronze disc brooch from fifth-century Saxon grave at Mitcham (l); and (r) identical brooch, much corroded, from collapsed bath-house roof of late Roman house, Billingsgate, Lower Thames Street (p253). *Museum of London*

deposited in graves around the middle of that century.[32] Dr Myres would prefer a
date nearer 400 on the evidence of the association of the pottery bowl with one of
the brooches,[33] while Dr T. M. Dickinson believes that the pottery dating should
be reconsidered, and that the grave containing the brooch and bowl cannot be as
early as c400, but need not be as late as c450.[34] It is generally agreed that these
brooches of tinned bronze are unlikely to have been passed on from one
generation to the next, and were probably worn only within twenty-five years or
so of their manufacture. The early date postulated by Myres must be ruled out in
the light of the coin evidence from Lower Thames Street, since a considerable
time must be allowed for the collapse of the bath-house roof after the
abandonment of the building. The vaulted roof of voussoir tiles should in fact
have survived much longer than the roof of the east wing. The date of the Saxon
visit to the ruined building must therefore have been within a decade or so of 450.
The period within which it was abandoned by its last occupants is consequently
circumscribed. If we allow ten years before the collapse of the voussoir roof,
which should be an under-estimate, the date of abandonment must fall between
400 and c440, or between c410 and c440 if the argument is accepted that the East
Mediterranean trade developed only after the collapse of the Western Empire. A
date between about 420 and 430 seems likely on the present evidence.

One other event of purposeful human activity occurred before centuries of
oblivion descended on this site. At some time after the collapse of its roof, the
ragstone walls of the east wing of the house were demolished to ground level, and
the stone was removed, evidently for building purposes elsewhere. It is unlikely
that Saxons were responsible for this at any date earlier than the seventh century,
for they had no tradition of building in stone, and were apparently unable to build
masonry walls until the craft was reintroduced, together with other features of
Mediterranean civilisation, by the Roman Church, following the Augustinian
mission at the end of the sixth century. The stone and tiles from this Roman house
may have gone towards the building of a church such as All Hallows-by-the-
Tower, where a wall and arch of the late seventh or eighth century still survives
(**60**). There remains the possibility of stone-robbing in the fifth century. It might
just possibly have taken place before the loss of the Saxon brooch, but the
evidence for natural decay and silting within the building before the fall of the
roof indicates it can hardly have occurred before 430, and a date in the second half
of the fifth century would be more likely. Inevitably for this period one's
thoughts turn first to fortifications. According to the traditional history of the
Anglo Saxon Chronicle, when the great revolt of Saxon settlers was led by
Hengist in the middle of the fifth century, the Britons were defeated in Kent at
Crecganford (probably Crayford), in 457 by the Chronicle's dating, and fled in
great fear to London. This might have occasioned repairs to the city defences, for
which material had to be sought within the walls. It is clear that the Saxon
intruders in Lower Thames Street were not hostile raiders, since they were
accompanied by women. They may have formed part of the standing garrison;
or, since it is by no means impossible that the earlier Surrey settlers had remained

true to their alliance, these also could have been refugees from Hengist. There are also the possibilities that a sub-Roman Briton had a Saxon wife—after all, Vortigern himself is said to have set the example—or that a brooch made in a Saxon workshop was worn by a member of another ethnic group. All the brooch really tells us is that there were people about in Londinium when it was in a ruinous condition in the middle of the fifth century; they may well have included those with some memory of Roman building methods.

After the walls were demolished, there is no indication of further occupation or activity on the site for centuries. Layers of dark silt and hill-wash accumulated over what remained of the east wing of the house, and these contained only late Roman pottery, no different from the fragments found in the refuse of the rather squalid final phase of occupation in the building itself. Both groups included sherds of soft, coarse hand-made ware in Roman style that was evidently a local product of the early fifth century. It was also found in the late dump on the palace site in Cannon Street, from which came the East Mediterranean amphora sherd. Peter Marsden records it also from St Dunstan's Hill, immediately east of the Coal Exchange site, and from the late layers against bastion 6, north of Aldgate. Outside the City it has been found at Old Ford in a clay-lined pit which contained coins of the reign of Honorius, and at Hammersmith in an uncertainly dated fourth-century context.[35] There is nothing Anglo-Saxon about it, and it is obviously a local attempt to supply the need for kitchen-ware when products of the large-scale factories were no longer available in very late Roman or sub-Roman times.

The material from the silt layers in Lower Thames Street is therefore residual, and gives no indication of their date, which seems to extend over hundreds of years, during which there was no occupation or evidence of activity on this site. Then a rammed gravel surface was laid down, probably as a road beside the river, and pottery found in its make-up shows that this was no earlier than the twelfth century.[36]

The problem of 'the Gap'

It would be rash to make generalisations from a single site, but most archaeologists who have worked in the City would consider the Coal Exchange site untypical only in one respect—that it presents clear evidence of occupation well into the fifth century; in this it is at present unique. In the surprising gap in occupation, real or apparent, it is however quite typical. Those without personal experience of work in the City or north Southwark have been inclined to attribute failure to produce evidence of continued occupation as due to lack of interest in the post-Roman period—'a tendency to concentrate upon the study of Roman London without an equal regard for the archaeology of the subsequent periods'.[37] This is certainly now untrue of the Anglo-Saxon period, on which great efforts have been made, so far with little result. The problem of 'the gap', which has always intrigued London archaeologists, has received great attention from highly skilled investigators, and evidence for rectangular timber-framed huts with sunken boarded floors, of the Saxon 'Grubenhaus' type, has been found on a number of sites in the western half of the city, where late Roman occupation is lacking or represented only by 'dark earth'. Yet these on pottery dating are consistently of the *later* Saxon period—on the *Financial Times* site in Cannon Street a little earlier than the Norman Conquest;[38] at Watling Court, Cannon Street, late Saxon (c 850–1100); at Milk Street one set into the edge of a north–south Roman gravelled roadway is 'provisionally of ninth-century date', and in the western part of the same site traces of timber buildings of the tenth or eleventh century directly overlay the dark earth. Only at Bread Street is there a Saxon hut that might be of somewhat earlier date, in the Middle Saxon period (c 650–850).[39] An embankment on the riverside at New Fresh Wharf, consisting of timber-laced rubble backed by the remains of the Roman waterfront, which had been partly dismantled, was surfaced with planks, some from a clinker-built boat, laid on birch piles. A Carbon 14 date taken from the latter was 760 ± 100 years—also in the Middle Saxon period.[40] The embankment formed a sloping hard on which boats could be beached in front of the riverside wall. The area where this was possible was limited at its western end by a series of vertical pointed stakes, subsequently inserted into the embankment, presumably for defensive purposes, since the site is only just downstream of the probable position of the bridge. The attractive suggestion has been made that this formed part of the defences against the Vikings under Alfred, and it is evident both from archaeology and historical records that there was recovery in London and the beginning of its reorganisation as an Anglo-Saxon town in the Middle Saxon period, although archaeology would suggest that this was on a very small scale. An intensive search for Anglo-Saxon pottery in recent excavations has produced a small quantity of the Middle Saxon Ipswich ware and a much more substantial amount of later Saxon pottery, including red-painted imported wares from the Rhineland, testifying to the revival of London's trade across the North Sea.

It is the period c 450–600 in London's history that is shrouded in almost complete darkness, hardly relieved by any gleam of light from historical records or from archaeology. There are a few finds from the City in the old museum collections that have been attributed to this period—a cruciform brooch found in Tower Street; a wheel-turned pot of Merovingian type with bands of stamped decoration found in Gresham Street, and believed to be an import from north France of the second half of the sixth century; a somewhat similar wheel-turned pot with bands of stamped decoration, believed to be an import from Germany of the late sixth or early seventh century, and without provenance, although it is assumed to be from the City as it was in the old Guildhall Museum collection; and a glass stemmed-beaker minus its base, an import from the Rhineland attributed to the fifth–early sixth century, and found in Lime Street.[41] From outside the City, there is also a glass palm-cup of the sixth–early seventh century found at St Martin's-in-the-Fields.[42] This is about the sum-total of our archaeological evidence for a human presence in London between about 450 and (say) 625. I do not include the hoard of pewter ingots stamped with Christian inscriptions and the name SYAGRIUS, from the Thames at Battersea, as I do not now believe that the stamp refers to the Roman ruler of north Gaul who was overthrown in 486. The name normally appearing on ingots is of the officer or craftsman responsible for their production—in this case almost certainly in a British work-shop under Roman rule. Marsden has pointed out that the name Syagrius is known in the fourth century, and there is no reason to suppose that the hoard is post-410.

The near completeness of the pots and glasses suggests rather strongly that they came from pagan graves, of which two at least would have been within the city walls. Moreover, the exotic character of these goods might suggest the presence of foreign traders, perhaps already beginning to take advantage again of London's good communications. If they were few in number and transitory, they could have kept a trickle of life running through the city without necessarily leaving much record of their presence in the form of structures or occupation debris. The possible presence of a few graves of transient visitors, however, spread over a long period of time, does not conflict with the view of most archaeologists who have worked in the City, that for at least 150 years London was derelict and virtually abandoned. Moreover, we have yet to find an object of this period in any archaeological context, and we know that collectable antiquities of every kind have been brought to London in subsequent ages. There is a warning of the great need for caution from the case of the complete prehistoric beaker, acquired by Guildhall Museum with the information that it had been found in a Tudor well in the City!

Some historians have been reluctant to believe that London with its strong fortifications could possibly have been abandoned in times of danger, arguing that if it was a refuge in 457, it must have continued to be so in the troubled period that followed. Refugees, however, have to make a living for themselves sooner or later, and a London without trade, industry or government service can only have supported the tiny population that could live on the produce of the river, the fields within and for a short distance beyond its walls, and the neighbouring forests. Its circuit of nearly $4\frac{1}{2}$ miles (7km) of defences with gatehouses and bastions would have needed a standing garrison of at least 1,000 men to maintain a minimal 24-hour watch, an impossible number of mouths to be fed from a local subsistence economy. In the absence of an organised state that could spread the burden more widely by some form of taxation such as corn levies, London can only have been provided with an adequate garrison for a brief emergency, if at all. Under these circumstances life in the walled city could be more dangerous than in the open countryside, where there was a better chance of escape from a surprise attack. At best a Dark Age army, without organised supplies and living off the land, must have been very small in comparison with a Roman or modern force, and its hope of success lay in its mobility and skilful use of terrain. To such a war-band a walled city that it was unable to defend adequately could easily become a death-trap. The possibility remains that a small citadel that could easily be defended in the south-eastern corner of the city might have continued to be useful—if it existed.

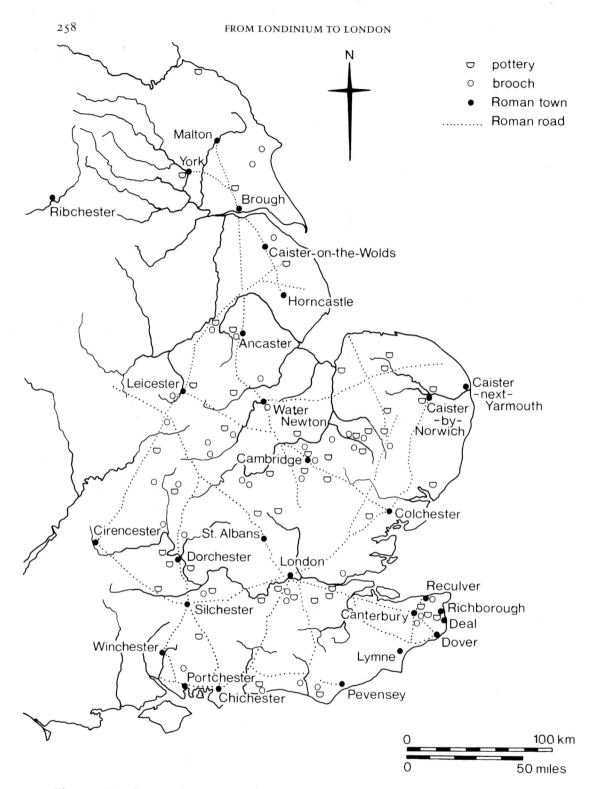

Fig. 39 Distribution of Saxon pottery and brooches of c. AD 475–500, showing 'empty' area north of the Thames. *After J. N. L. Myres*

It has been argued that London was still a centre of British resistance and a strategic stronghold in the later fifth century, forming part of a sub-Roman territory that also included Colchester and Verulamium.[43] This area north of the Thames lacks pagan Saxon burials, and partly for that reason is also devoid of the Saxon brooches and pottery that are characteristic of this period (map, fig. 39). Unfortunately we have no datable British or sub-Roman artifacts of the later fifth century to be set against them to provide evidence of a resisting population at this date in the relevant area. John Morris has pointed out that there is a concentration north-east of London of Ambros- place-names, which he suggests are derived from Ambrosius, the successful sub-Roman leader of the period, and could be sites of his garrisons.[44] Archaeologically, however, the army of Ambrosius remains as yet a phantom.

The hinterland of London in the fifth and sixth centuries

We know very little about the occupation of the London area in the fifth century, or even at the end of the fourth. Coin hoards that were abandoned in the early fifth century have been found in Rotherhithe and west of the Brockley Hill settlement.[45] As with the hoard in Lower Thames Street, the reason for their abandonment may well have been the disuse of coinage in the second or third decade of the fifth century, rather than the troubles of the times.

On coin evidence from Lefevre Road, the site at Old Ford continued in occupation at least to the end of the fourth century, and a structure with an associated clay-floored cellar seems to have been still in use after 383 (**58**). The cellar was back-filled after 395 on coin evidence and almost certainly in the fifth century, for its fill contained the base of a glass vessel attributed to that date and also sherds of the hand-made gritty local pottery of the kind found in Lower Thames Street.[46] In Bishop's Park, Fulham, however, this same ware appeared in a level antedating a gravel surface that on other considerations should be fourth century, so that in itself it cannot be taken as an indication of a fifth century date.[47] The so-called Romano-Saxon ware, a late Roman pottery with decoration of bosses and depressions similar to that of some Saxon pottery, has been found both in London and Essex, but is probably merely another Romano-British ware of the fourth century;[48] it throws no light on fifth-century occupation.

There was Anglo-Saxon occupation in the earlier fifth century south of the Thames at Mitcham, Ham, Orpington and Northfleet, and north of it at Hanwell in west Middlesex and at Mucking in Essex. These probably began as federate settlements by the consent of Romano-British authorities in the London area, intended to occupy, farm and defend depopulated areas of strategic importance on the approaches to London. They did, however, continue to be occupied in the later fifth and sixth centuries, and we do not know whether they still played a part in the defence of the London area. If they co-existed with continued successful British resistance in this region, it must be assumed that they were at least not hostile to it.[49]

Another important feature of the countryside near London must now be

58 Late Roman tile structure at Old Ford that was still in use in the late fourth century, and was associated with a cellar probably back-filled in the fifth century. *J. Earp*

considered, for there is little doubt that it is to be attributed to the pagan Saxon period, although its precise date and political significance remain obscure. Mortimer Wheeler many years ago suggested a Dark Age date for linear earthworks consisting of bank and ditch that run intermittently for many miles, mostly through wooded claylands (clay-with-flints), on the Chilterns to the south of the Icknield Way, and crossing it to the Thames further west in the neighbourhood of Nuffield.[50] They are traditionally known as Grim's Ditches, a name very suggestive of a pagan Saxon origin, since Grim or Grime is another name for Woden, equated with the Devil in later Christian times. Wheeler pointed out that their position near the brow of the Chiltern ridge delimited the valley lands on the remoter side of the hills of the London Basin. They are obviously not intended to protect an enclave based on London, but rather to contain it and prevent encroachments on the territory to the north-west, since the ditches are on the London side of the embankments. They must be envisaged not as a battle-line, but as a frontier defence, designed as a cleared strip that could easily be patrolled to prevent infiltration through the woods. They imply a stable frontier under potential threat from the south-east, and if they are of this period give considerable support to the idea of an independent power under sub-Roman or British leadership in Essex and the London area. According to Gildas, the British victory at Mons Badonicus, probably about 500, was followed by a period of peace, in which the British were evidently the dominant military power. This seems a likely historical context for the Chiltern dykes.

There is, however, another similar earthwork much nearer London. This is also called Grim's Ditch, and can be traced intermittently from Cuckoo Hill, Pinner, to Harrow Weald Common, and after a considerable gap seems to end in Pear Wood, Brockley Hill, immediately west of Watling Street. Like the Chiltern dykes, this also has its ditch on the south-eastern side towards London. More recently there was a tendency to regard these earthworks as pre-Roman, like the similar Belgic dykes in the neighbourhood of St Albans. Excavation in Pear Wood in 1973, however, proved conclusively that Grim's Ditch there could not be earlier than the fourth century, a date when there was no conceivable reason for constructing a defensive line facing Londinium.[51] It could of course be later, and it now seems likely that Wheeler was right after all in his attribution of the linear earthworks called Grime's Dyke or Grim's Ditch to the fifth or sixth

Fig. 40 Grim's Ditches in the Chilterns and Middlesex. *After R. E. M. Wheeler and S. A. Castle*

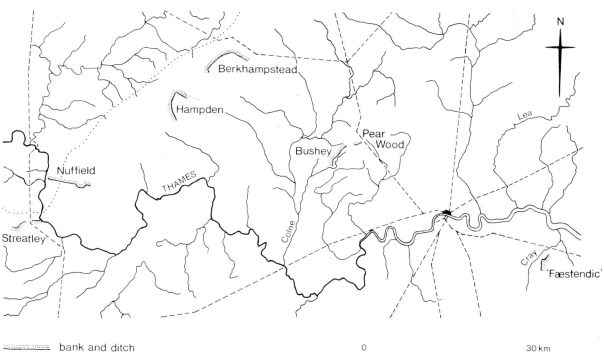

century. If they represented political frontiers, however, two different periods must be represented, with the Middlesex earthwork earlier or later than that of the Chilterns. On the assumption that it was earlier, it has been suggested that the Middlesex earthwork was a political boundary between the territories of two sub-Roman communities centred respectively on Verulamium and Londinium.[52] It can be accepted that Verulamium and its region may have constituted a separate power in the mid-fifth century, but why should it have been so concerned to prevent, or at any rate control, the movement of people from Londinium, its natural ally against the dangers of the time? For the Pear Wood earthwork must surely imply that there was at least a check-point on Watling Street, the route from Kent and the Continent. It is possible that a defensive measure of this kind might have been taken after the British defeat at Crecganford, and the subsequent flight of refugees to London. John Wacher has suggested that plague was a major cause of the abandonment of Romano-British cities in the fifth century, and referred specifically to the plague of about 443, mentioned by Hydatius.[53] Malcolm Todd, however, has questioned its relevance to Roman Britain,[54] and in fifth-century Londinium there was certainly no gross aggregation of population, such as Wacher considers would have been a necessary condition for an epidemic, except possibly very briefly after Crecganford. Plague would have been as good a reason as any for seeking to control the movement of population, since the infiltration of a few plague-stricken families would have been infinitely more dangerous than that of a few hundred raiders. It is doubtful whether this would have been realised in time for major works like the Grim's Ditches to be carried out, however, and it is more probable that the Middlesex earthworks, like those of the Chilterns, were simply intended to define a frontier and stake a claim.

The similarity of the two series, in fact, suggests rather strongly that they were following the same tradition, and it seems more likely that the Middlesex dykes are the later, and represent an encroachment from the north-west on the former British territory. By this time—presumably well into the sixth century—it is better to abandon these ethnic simplifications and recognise that we are dealing with a mixed community that was now as much English as British. In the days of its strength the political enclave containing London must have maintained some control over the south bank of the Thames in its narrower portion and, as Wheeler pointed out, there is an earthwork on the east side of the valley of the Cray, south of Bexley, consisting of bank and ditch, remarkably like the Grim's Ditches north of the Thames, and like them it faces towards London. This has been identified with the 'Faestendic' that is mentioned in a charter of 814.[55] If it marks the Kentish boundary of the territory, as Wheeler suggested, this contained not only the early Saxon communities north of the Thames at Hanwell and Mucking, but also in all probability those south of it at Mitcham and Orpington as well.

The historical and topographical evidence from the hinterland of London does not therefore suggest abandonment during the later fifth and early sixth centuries, but the presence of a population under a vigorous if declining political leadership that was able to maintain its position, at least for a time, although we are quite unable to recognise its presence in archaeological terms. How far is this true of Londinium itself? Here full weight must be given to the negative evidence from many sites that have been closely studied by archaeologists. If there are hardly any artifacts that we can recognise of the period, there ought at least to be structural evidence of the surfaces on which the occupants lived and the supports of the roofs that sheltered them, to say nothing of the bones of the meat they ate, all of which might be accompanied only by abraded sherds of earlier Roman pottery, but which should appear in the stratigraphical sequence between the recognisable Roman features and those of the later Saxon period. Their absence on sites where the stratigraphy for this phase seems complete should indicate an absence of occupation there. Yet there are relatively few such sites, and our total archaeological cover is only of a tiny proportion of the area of the walled city. Moreover, allowance must be made for erosion of structures and occupation levels, perhaps by the very process that created the dark earth (p143). Commonsense would suggest that the city was at no period completely devoid of occupants, but that it no longer had any relevance to the needs of the age. A small citadel may still have served from time to time as the temporary base of a mobile war-band, but if it stood on the site later occupied by the Tower of London most traces of it may have been obliterated by later mediaeval building. Little more can have remained of London's once vital strategic role in an era of small armies that could not hope to man its walls. The city was still a convenient meeting-place, but in the absence of trade and organised government meetings were seldom necessary. People no doubt still came and went, since the Roman roads compelled them to pass through London, but they had few reasons to stay, and gradually the old street-plan was being lost as new short cuts were made through the more easily traversable ruins from one gate to another. The really massive ruins, such as those of the forum, remained and would serve as a quarry for builders of a later age, but part at least of the basilica may already have been demolished. The extent to which farming was going on within the city walls must be left an open question until the problem of the true significance of the 'dark earth' can be solved. If it had already commenced in later Roman times there is no reason at all why it should not have continued, if there was a population to be fed.

The return of the Romans

Britain had never been cut off entirely from what remained of Roman civilisation. Appeals to secular authority for military aid—to Honorius in the first instance in 410, and subsequently in 446 to Aëtius commander-in-chief in the west—were perforce ignored, since on both occasions there were more pressing tasks for Roman armies on the Continent itself. The Roman Church, however, endeavoured to intervene against the spiritual dangers of heresy through the agency of Germanus, the indefatigable bishop of Auxerre, who visited Britain for that purpose in 429 and again as an old man in about 448, when he was accompanied by Severus, bishop of Trier. The need for a second visit may indicate that Pelagianism was still firmly rooted in Britain, but also implies the presence of an organised Christian community that was concerned about theological doctrine in the middle of the fifth century. There is no doubt, as the history of Patrick shows, that Christianity survived in the west of Britain in a not totally disorganised fashion until it was subsumed by the new monasticism, itself of Mediterranean origin, about the end of the fifth century.[56] Both Jocelyn Toynbee and Charles Thomas have insisted on the complete Romanity of the so-called Celtic Church,[57] which provides a thread of continuity between Roman Britain and the later history of the west and north. The positive evidence of surviving Romano-British place-names[58] and the negative evidence of pagan Saxon avoidance strongly suggest that there was continuity of a British population north of the Thames, among whom Christianity must have survived. Yet the history of the Augustinian mission indicates that there was no organised Church in this area at the end of the sixth century, and the bishopric of London had to be recreated in 604, when St Paul's was built by the newly converted King of Kent in the western wastes of Londinium. If any British occupants remained in the derelict city to give their name to the Walbrook[59] and to perpetuate the memory of a Christian church on Cornhill, they then had no religious leader with a rival claim on the bishopric. This one historic incident clearly illuminates the obliteration of Londinium as a centre of urban civilisation, and its lack of continuity as a city in any real sense.

59 Gold thrymsa minted in London, with name LONDUNIU on reverse, about 640, from the Crondall hoard. Enlarged, actual diameter 12mm. *Original in Ashmolean Museum*

To a Roman Pontiff Londinium was the obvious place for a bishopric, and Pope Gregory I had intended it to be the prime see of southern Britain. The historical accident that the kingdom of Kent had a Christian queen determined instead that this should be established at Canterbury, but in Rome it was inconceivable that London should not also become a centre of ecclesiastical authority. The founding of the bishopric in 604 was undoubtedly the first step towards the city's recovery, since it led in due course to the re-establishment of the administrative element that was as necessary to London as the revival of trade. Yet it is indicative of the total collapse of the urban tradition in Britain that the new bishopric failed to strike roots in London for many years. The unmanned city walls could not protect Mellitus, the first bishop, when Essex relapsed into paganism, and he was driven out in 616. His eventual successor, Cedd, preferred to establish himself in the ruins of the old Saxon Shore fort at Bradwell-on-Sea, Essex, but it was probably during his bishopric that London's first Saxon mint was founded. This produced gold coins, copied from the Merovingian *tremisses* and called 'thrymsas', about the middle of the seventh century, with the name LONDUNIV or LONDIOIIO upon them (**59**). Thrymsas were also produced at Canterbury, and as the obverse bust is usually accompanied by a cross or staff, it is generally assumed that they were minted under ecclesiastical authority.[60] The London thrymsas should therefore imply that in spite of the rural preference of its bishop, a product of the northern Church, some sort of ecclesiastical administration had already been set up in the city.

When Cedd died about 664–5, the bishopric of London and Essex was an established office that was worth purchasing by the unemployed refugee, Wini, who had been expelled from the bishopric of Winchester. The cynical vendor was the king of Mercia, who had established his overlordship over Essex, now divided into two kingdoms, one Christian, which evidently included London, and the other pagan.[61] Neither Cedd nor Wini seems to have spent much time in London, but Wini's successor, Erkenwald, who became bishop about 675, may have devoted more attention to his local diocesan duties, since in later tradition he was remembered, not only as the founder of Barking and Chertsey Abbeys, but also as 'the Light of London'. It was a time when England was still divided into independent kingdoms, often warring, of which first one and then another became dominant. London became the centre of Church administration of one minor kingdom, but was closely linked with others, particularly with the dominant power, and this must have made a substantial contribution to the city's recovery. It was paradoxically an advantage that Essex never itself became dominant, but was subjected in some measure to whatever kingdom achieved that position; so that St Paul's was built by a king of Kent, the bishopric was sold by a king of Mercia, and a king of Wessex called Erkenwald 'my bishop'. The comings and goings of ecclesiastics between the various dioceses of Britain, and between Britain, Gaul and Rome, ensured that London's convenience as a centre of communications was again appreciated. The opening up of travel routes for religious purposes, particularly with Rome itself, also led to the development of

pilgrimages in the late seventh century, as Bede relates, by many English people, 'both noble and simple, layfolk and clergy, men and women alike', and the insular isolation, which had been disastrous for London, had ended.[62]

At least one major religious house now found it necessary to maintain a permanent establishment in London. Barking Abbey built a church near Tower Hill, still called All Hallows Barking, and its surviving Saxon arch, revealed by bomb damage in 1940–1, is the one upstanding and visible example of Saxon architecture in London (**60**). Built of ragstone and Roman tiles from the ruins of Londinium after the Roman style, it is a reminder that the Church also brought back the Roman art of building in stone. There is no means of dating the arch more closely than to the earlier Anglo-Saxon period, but the similar use of Roman tiles for arches in Cedd's church at Bradwell-on-Sea suggests that it was probably not built later than the bishopric of Erkenwald, the founder of Barking Abbey, or his immediate successors—ie in the late seventh or early eighth century.

The revival of trade, and particularly of overseas trade, was necessary for the full recovery of London, and the opening up of travel routes together with the reintroduction of coinage favoured its development. Bede, writing in the early eighth century, described London as a trading centre for many nations who visited it by land and sea. Tony Dyson has drawn attention to an even earlier reference to the port of London in the charter of Frithuwald, attributed to 672–4. This refers to a grant of land to Chertsey Abbey, apparently in Southwark, 'by the port of London, where ships come to land, on the same river on the southern side by the public way'.[63] A centre of commerce that seemed impressive to Bede might still have operated on a tiny scale by Roman or medieval standards, but it cannot be doubted that London's commercial revival had already begun. Bede in fact also refers to a specific instance of this commerce, which demonstrates that the old trading connection across the North Sea had already been re-established. The story is of a Northumbrian prisoner-of-war, captured by a Mercian ealdorman after a battle in 679, and subsequently sold as a slave to a Frisian in London.[64]

It is significant that Frisia was converted late in the seventh century by English priests, who obtained holy relics from Rome for the dedication of churches there.[65] The re-emergence of London as a trading centre long before the political unification of England clearly owes a great deal to the re-establishment of its overseas links, for which the Church may have been largely responsible. A network of communications was as important to the Roman Church as it had been to the Roman Empire, and in this London's geographical advantages, both natural and man-made, predetermined its role. It was, however, a case of resurrection or rebirth rather than survival, since for 200 years London had had no function as a city. *Londinium* died early in the fifth century but was never forgotten; its walls and ruined buildings stood as monuments to its past greatness,

60 Saxon arch built with Roman tiles and ragstone in the Church of All Hallows-by-the-Tower, probably late seventh–early eighth century. *Museum of London*

but travellers who came and went had no reason to linger. *Lundonia*, with a notable change of gender and vowels, was born in the seventh century, with the Church of Rome as its midwife. It was at first a puny infant, but the vigour derived from natural advantages and the heritage from its imperial forbear eventually asserted itself. As with Londinium in the beginning, its strength lay in commerce, but its links with a supra-national organisation, at a time when no national authority had yet emerged, may have helped to develop the independence of spirit that was characteristic of London in its dealings with later English kings.

Glossary

Ammianus Marcellinus Fourth-century historian who wrote a continuation of the history of Tacitus, dealing with the years 96–378, of which only the last part survives, covering the period 353–78.

Antonine period The reigns of Antoninus Pius, his adopted son Marcus Aurelius, and the latter's son Commodus, 138–92.

Antoninianus Coin of base silver characterised by radiate crown of emperor, introduced by Caracalla about 214, probably as equivalent to two denarii, though only one-and-a-half times the weight of a denarius. Much debased later in the third century, when it was often copied by forgers.

Civitas A unit of local government with magistrates and council, usually developed from a native tribe, which was encouraged to build an urban centre (civitas capital).

Colonia A settlement of Roman citizens, often to provide for veteran soldiers, and usually in a strategic centre, as at Colchester, Lincoln and York. Also conferred as a title of the highest degree of civic dignity on capital cities.

Claudian period The reign of Tiberius Claudius, 41–54.

Denarius Silver coin of earlier Empire, equivalent to four brass sestertii or sixteen copper asses.

Dux Britanniarum Fourth-century general in command of the defences of northern Britain.

Equestrian rank The second order (*ordo*) of nobility in the Roman world, the 'Knights', to which certain military and civilian offices were reserved (eg that of procurator).

Flavian period The reigns of T. Flavius Vespasianus and his sons Titus and Domitian, 69–96.

Gildas A sixth-century monk who wrote an account of events in Britain, including those of the fifth century. The latter are mainly based on oral tradition, but Gildas is our best source for British history of the period.

Hadrianic period The reign of P. Aelius Hadrianus, 117–138.

Heptarchy The seven kingdoms into which Anglo-Saxon England was divided before 900. These were Kent, Essex, Sussex, Wessex, Mercia, East Anglia and Northumbria.

Mansio A public lodging-place for officials travelling on public service, located in every important centre and at intervals of about 25 miles along the main roads.

Maximian Ruler of the west as Augustus in 286–305 in partnership with Diocletian, ruler of the east (see *Tetrarchy*). Abdicated in 305, but resumed rule in 306. Abdicated again in 308, and committed suicide after failure of revolt against Constantine in 310.

Neronian period The reign of Nero, 54–68.

Oppidum A fortified settlement, often serving as political and trading centre of a tribal community.

Peregrinus The citizen of any state other than Rome. All provincial peoples with any form of local autonomy but without Roman citizenship were *peregrini*.

Quinarius A half-denarius in the early Empire, but also applied by numismatists to the smaller coins issued by Allectus, with the value-mark Q, whose equivalent value is unknown.

Saxon Shore This term—*Litus Saxonicum*—was used in late Roman times for the eastern and southern shores of Britain between the Wash and the Solent, presumably because this part of the coast was subject to Saxon harassment. With its nine forts it was under the command of the Count of the Saxon Shore in the late fourth century. The term was also applied to part of the Gaulish coast opposite.

Senatorial rank The first order (*ordo*) of nobility in the Roman world, to which the principal offices of state were reserved, including, in the earlier Empire, governorships of most provinces and the command of legions. Later its share in provincial government was much reduced.

Severan period The reigns of L. Septimius Severus and his son Caracalla, 193–217.

Tetrarchy System of shared rule by four emperors, established by Diocletian in 293. There were two seniors (*Augusti*), ruling the east and west respectively, each assisted by a junior (*Caesar*) who would, it was intended, in due course succeed him.

Trajanic period The reign of M. Ulpius Traianus, 98–117.

Abbreviations and Selected Bibliography

ALCOCK, L. 1971, *Arthur's Britain*, London

Ant. Journ., *Antiquaries Journal*, journal of Society of Antiquaries of London

Arch., *Archaeologia*, publication of Society of Antiquaries of London

Arch. Cant., *Archaeologia Cantiana*, annual journal of Kent Archaeological Society

Arch. Journ., *The Archaeological Journal*, journal of the Royal Archaeological Institute

B.A.R., *British Archaeological Reports*, Oxford

BIDDLE, M., HUDSON, D. M. and HEIGHWAY, C. M., 1973, *The Future of London's Past*, Worcester

B.M., British Museum

Britannia, annual journal of Society for the Promotion of Roman Studies, containing summaries of finds of the year in Roman Britain, including London, since 1970

BROWN, A. E. and SHELDON, H. L., 1974, 'Highgate Wood: the Pottery and its Production', *Lond. Arch.*, II, No 9, Winter 1974, 222–31

BURGESS, C. and NEEDHAM S., 1980, 'The Later Bronze Age in the Thames Valley', in Barrett J. and Bradley, R. (eds), *Settlement and Society in the British Later Bronze Age*, *B.A.R.* 83, 437–69

CANHAM, R. A., 1978, *2000 Years of Brentford*, H.M.S.O., London

CASEY, J., 1978, 'Constantine the Great in Britain — evidence of the coinage of the London Mint, AD 312–314', *Coll. Lond.*, 181–93

CASTLE, S. A., 1972, 'Excavations at Brockley Hill, Middlesex, Sulloniacae, 1970', *Trans. L.M.A.S.*, XXIII, pt 2, 148–59

CASTLE, S. A., 1975, 'Excavations in Pear Wood, Brockley Hill, Middlesex, 1948–73', *Trans. L.M.A.S.*, XXVI, 267–77

CHAPMAN, H. and JOHNSON, T., 1973, 'Excavations at Aldgate and Bush Lane House in the City of London, 1972', *Trans. L.M.A.S.*, XXIV, 1–73

CLARK, J., 1980, *Saxon and Norman London*, M.O.L. publication, London

C.O.L.A.T., City of London Archaeological Trust

Coll. Lond., *Collectanea Londiniensia*, Special Paper No 2, London and Middlesex Archaeological Society, 1978

COTTRILL, F., 1936, 'A Bastion of the Town Wall of London, and the Sepulchral Monument of the Procurator, Julius Classicianus', *Ant. Journ.*, XVI, 1–7

D.U.A., Department of Urban Archaeology, Museum of London

D.U.A. Archive, archival reports of excavations in the City of London by the Department of Urban Archaeology of the Museum of London, held in the Museum.

DUNNING, G. C., 1945, 'Two Fires of Roman London', *Ant. Journ.*, XXV, 48 77

DYSON, T., 1980, 'London and Southwark in the seventh century and later', *Trans. L.M.A.S.*, XXXI, 83ff

FRERE, S., 1974, *Britannia, a history of Roman Britain*, London, 2nd ed

GRIMES, W. F., 1968, *The Excavation of Roman and Mediaeval London*, London

HAMMERSON, M., 1978, 'Excavations under Southwark Cathedral', *Lond. Arch.*, III, No 8, Autumn 1978, 206–12

HASSALL, M., 1973, 'Roman Soldiers in Roman London', in Strong, D. (ed), *Archaeological Theory and Practice*, London, 231–7

HAVERFIELD, F., 1911, 'Roman London', *J.R.S.*, I, 141–72

HILL, C., MILLETT, M. and BLAGG T., 1980, *The Roman Riverside Wall and Monumental Arch in London, Excavations at Baynard's Castle, Upper Thames Street, London, 1974–76*, L.M.A.S. Special Paper No 3

HOBLEY, B. and SCHOFIELD, J., 1977, 'Excavations in the City of London, First Interim Report, 1974–5', *Ant. Journ.*, LVII, 31–46

J.B.A.A., Journal of the British Archaeological Association

JOHNSON, T., 1975, 'A Roman Signal Tower at Shadwell, E1', Interim Note, *Trans. L.M.A.S.*, XXVI, 278–80

JONES, D., et al., 1980, *Excavations on the site of Billingsgate Buildings, Lower Thames Street*, L.M.A.S. Special Paper No 4

J.R.S., *Journal of Roman Studies*, annual journal of Society for the Promotion of Roman Studies, containing summaries of finds of the year in

Roman Britain, including London, prior to 1970

KENT, J., 1978, 'The London Area in the Late Iron Age: an interpretation of the earliest coins', *Coll. Lond.*, 53–8

KENYON, K. M., 1959, *Excavations in Southwark*, S.A.S. Research Paper No 5

LAMBERT, F., 1915, 'Recent Roman Discoveries in London', *Arch.*, LXVI, 225–74

LAMBERT, F., 1921, 'Some Recent Excavations in London', *Arch.*, LXXI, 55–112

L.M.A.S., London and Middlesex Archaeological Society

L.M.A.S. Special Paper No 1, *The Archaeology of the London Area: Current knowledge and problems*, 1976

L.M.A.S. Special Paper No 2, *Collectanea Londiniensia, Studies in London archaeology and history presented to Ralph Merrifield*, Bird, J., Chapman, H. and Clark, J. (eds), 1978

L.M. Cat., London Museum Catalogue.

Lond. Arch., *The London Archaeologist*, quarterly journal, valuable for up-to-date news of London archaeology

LONGLEY, D. and NEEDHAM, S., 1980, 'Runnymede Bridge, Egham', in Barrett, J. and Bradley, R. (eds), *Settlement and Society in the British Later Bronze Age*, B.A.R. 83, 397–436

MCISAAC, W., SCHWAB, I. and SHELDON, H., 1979, 'Excavations at Old Ford, 1972–1975', *Trans. L.M.A.S.*, XXX, 39–93

MALONEY, J., 1979, 'Excavations at Duke's Place: the Roman Defences', *Lond. Arch.*, III, No 11, Summer 1979, 292–7

MALONEY, J., 1980 (1), 'The Roman Defences of London', *Current Archaeology*, No 73, Vol 7 No 2, August 1980, 55–60

MALONEY, J., 1980 (2), 'The Discovery of Bastion 4A in the City of London and its Implications', *Trans. L.M.A.S.*, XXXI, 68–76

MARGARY, I. D., 1948, *Roman Ways in the Weald*, London

MARGARY, I. D., 1967, *Roman Roads in Britain*, London

MARSDEN, P., 1965 (1), 'The County Hall Ship', *Trans. L.M.A.S.*, XXI, pt 2, 109–117

MARSDEN, P., 1965 (2), 'A Boat of the Roman Period Discovered on the Site of New Guy's House, Bermondsey, 1958', *Trans. L.M.A.S.*, XXI, pt 2, 118–31

MARSDEN, P., 1967, *A Ship of the Roman Period from Blackfriars, in the City of London*, Guildhall Museum publication

MARSDEN, P., 1969, 'The Roman Pottery Industry of London', *Trans. L.M.A.S.*, XXII, pt 2, 39–44

MARSDEN, P., 1975, 'The Excavation of a Roman Palace Site in London, 1961–1972', *Trans. L.M.A.S.*, XXVI, 1–102

MARSDEN, P., 1976, 'Two Roman Public Baths in London', *Trans. L.M.A.S.*, XXVII, 2–70

MARSDEN, P., 1978 (1), 'The Discovery of the Civic Centre of Roman London', *Coll. Lond.*, 89–103

MARSDEN, P., 1978 (2), 'The Excavations of a Roman Palace Site in London: Additional Details', *Trans. L.M.A.S.*, XXIX, 99–103

MARSDEN, P., 1980, *Roman London*, London

MERRIFIELD, R., 1955, 'The Lime Street Hoard of Barbarous Radiates', *N.C.*, 6th Ser., XV, 113–34

MERRIFIELD, R., 1962, 'Coins from the Bed of the Walbrook and their Significance', *Ant. Journ.*, XLII, 38–52

MERRIFIELD, R., 1965, *The Roman City of London*, London

MERRIFIELD, R., 1969, *Roman London*, London

MERRIFIELD, R., 1975, *The Archaeology of London*, London

MERRIFIELD, R., 1977, 'Art and Religion in Roman London, an inquest on the sculptures of Londinium', in Munby, J. and Henig, M. (eds), *Roman Life and Art in Britain*, B.A.R. 41, 375–97

MILLER, L., 1982, 'Miles Lane: the early Roman Waterfront', *Lond. Arch.*, IV, No 6, Spring 1982, 143–7

M.O.L., Museum of London

MORRIS, J., 1973, *The Age of Arthur*, London

MYRES, J. N. L., 1969, *Anglo-Saxon Pottery and the Settlement of England*, Oxford

N.C., *Numismatic Chronicle*, journal of the Royal Numismatic Society

NORMAN, P., 1904, 'Roman and later Remains found during Excavations on the Site of Newgate Prison, 1903–1904', *Arch.*, LIX, 125–42

NORMAN, P. and READER, F. W., 1906, 'Recent Discoveries in Connexion with Roman London', *Arch.*, LX, 169–250

NORMAN, P. and READER, F. W., 1912, 'Further Discoveries relating to Roman London, 1906–12', *Arch.*, LXIII, 257–344

PAINTER, K. S., 1972, 'A Late Roman Silver Ingot from Kent', *Ant. Journ.*, LII, 84–92

PAINTER, K. S., 1981, 'A Roman Silver Ingot', *B.M. Occasional Paper*, No 35, Dept of Greek and Roman Antiquities, Acquisitions 1976

PARNELL, G., 1977, 'Excavations at the Tower of London, 1976–7', *Lond. Arch.*, III, No 4, Autumn 1977, 97–9

PARNELL, G., 1978, 'An earlier Roman Riverside Wall at the Tower of London', *Lond. Arch.*, III, No 7, Summer 1978, 171–6

PARNELL, G., 1981, 'Tower of London: Inmost Ward Excavations 1979', *Lond. Arch.*, IV, No 3, Summer 1981, 69–73

PHILP, B. J., 1977, 'The Forum of Roman London: Excavations of 1968–9', *Britannia*, VIII, 1–64

P.P.S., *Proceedings of the Prehistoric Society*

PRICE, J. E., 1870, *A Description of the Roman Tessellated Pavement found in Bucklersbury: with observations on analogous discoveries*, London

PRICE, J. E., 1880, *On a Bastion of London Wall, or Excavations in Camomile Street, Bishopsgate*, London

Proc. Soc. Ant., Proceedings of the Society of Antiquaries of London

R.C.H.M., 1928, Royal Commission on Historical Monuments (England): *An Inventory of the Historical Monuments in London*, III Roman London, 1928

R.C.L., R. MERRIFIELD, *The Roman City of London*, 1965. Bold numeral is Gazetteer and Map reference

R.I.B., COLLINGWOOD, R. G. and WRIGHT, R. P., *The Roman Inscriptions of Britain*, I, Oxford, 1965

R.I.C., MATTINGLY, H, et al (eds), *Roman Imperial Coinage*.

RILEY, W. E. and GOMME, L., 1912, *A Ship of the Roman period discovered on the Site of the new County Hall*.

ROACH SMITH, C., 1859, *Illustrations of Roman London*, printed by subscription

RODWELL, W., 1975, 'Milestones, Civic territories and the Antonine Itinerary', *Britannia*, VI, 93

ROSKAMS, S., 1978, 'The Milk Street Excavation', *Lond. Arch.*, III, No 8, Autumn 1978, 199–204; No 9, Winter 1978, 227ff

ROSKAMS, S., 1980, 'G.P.O. Newgate Street, 1975–9: the Roman levels', *Lond. Arch.*, III, No 15, Summer 1980, 403–7

ROSKAMS, S. and WATSON, L., 1981, 'The Hadrianic Fire of London—a reassessment of the evidence', *Lond. Arch.*, IV, No 3, Summer 1981, 62–5

SALWAY, P., 1981, *Roman Britain, The Oxford History of England* vol IA, Oxford

S.A.S., Surrey Archaeological Society

SCHOFIELD, J. and DYSON, T., 1980, *Archaeology of the City of London*, C.O.L.A.T., London

SHELDON, H., 1972, 'Excavations at Parnell Road and Appian Road, Old Ford, E3', *Trans. L.M.A.S.*, XXIII, pt 2, 101–47

SHELDON, H., 1974, 'Excavations at Toppings and Sun Wharves, Southwark, 1970–1972', *Trans. L.M.A.S.*, XXV, 1–115

SHELDON, H., 1981, 'London and South-east Britain', in King, A. and Henig, M. (eds), *The Roman West in the Third Century*, B.A.R. International Series 109, 363–82

SHELDON, H. and SCHAAF, L., 1978, 'A survey of Roman sites in Greater London', *Coll. Lond.*, 59–88

S.L.A.E.C., Southwark and Lambeth Archaeological Excavation Committee

Southwark Excavations, 1972–74, S.L.A.E.C. Report, Joint Publication No 1 of L.M.A.S. and S.A.S., 1978

TATTON-BROWN, T., 1974, 'Excavations at the Custom House Site, City of London, 1973', *Trans. L.M.A.S.*, XXV, 117–219

THOMAS, C., 1981, *Christianity in Roman Britain to A.D. 500*, London

TOYNBEE, J. M. C., 1963, *A silver casket and strainer from the Walbrook Mithraeum in the City of London*, Leiden

TOYNBEE, J. M. C., 1964, *Art in Britain under the Romans*, Oxford

Trans. L.M.A.S., Transactions of London and Middlesex Archaeological Society

TURNER, E. G. and SKUTSCH, O., 1960, 'A Roman Writing-Tablet from London', *J.R.S.*, L, 108–11

V.C.H., 1909, *Victoria County History of London*, I, London

WACHER, J., 1975, *The Towns of Roman Britain*, London

WEBSTER, G., 1978, *Boudica*, London

WELCH, M. G., 1975, 'Mitcham Grave 205 and the Chronology of Applied Brooches with Floriate Cross Decoration', *Ant. Journ.*, LV, 86–93

WHEELER, R. E. M., 1930, *London in Roman Times*, L. M. Cat., No 3

WHEELER, R. E. M., 1935, *London and the Saxons*, L. M. Cat., No 6

WHIPP, D., 1980, 'Excavations at Tower Hill, 1978', *Trans. L.M.A.S.*, XXXI, 47–67

Notes and References

1 London before the Conquest (pages 1–22)

1 J. D. Cowan, 'The Earliest Bronze Swords in Britain and their Origins on the Continent of Europe', *P.P.S.*, XVII (1951), 195–213

2 J. D. Cowan, 'The Hallstatt Sword of Bronze: on the Continent and in Britain', *P.P.S.*, XXXIII (1967), 377–454

3 Longley and Needham, 1980, 397–436; also *Current Archaeology*, No 68 (1979), 262–7

4 M. O'Connell and S. Needham, 'A Late Bronze Age hoard from a settlement at Potters Sports Field, Egham, Surrey', *Lond. Arch.*, III (Winter 1977), 123–30

5 Burgess and Needham, 1980, 437–69

6 C. Burgess, 'The Bronze Age', in C. Renfrew (ed), *British Prehistory*, 1974, 196f, 311, n 205

7 E. M. Jope, 'Daggers of the Early Iron Age in Britain', *P.P.S.*, XXVII (1961), 329–30

8 R. Canham, 'The Iron Age', in L.M.A.S. Special Paper No 1, 1976, 48

9 P. J. Drury, 'Non-classical and Religious Buildings in Iron Age and Roman Britain', in W. Rodwell (ed), *Temples, Churches and Religion in Roman Britain*, B.A.R. 77, 1980, 52–4

10 J. V. S. Megaw, *Art of the European Iron Age*, 1970, 139

11 W. F. Grimes, 'Some Smaller Settlements: a Symposium', in S. S. Frere (ed), *Problems of the Iron Age in Southern Britain*, 1959, 25–6

12 E. Ekwall, *The Concise Oxford Dictionary of British Place-Names*, 1960, 63

13 Kent, 1978, 53ff

14 D. F. Allen, 'Iron Currency Bars in Britain', *P.P.S.*, XXXIII (1967), 312ff

15 C. Julius Caesar, *De Bello Gallico*, v

16 *Ibid*, ii,3

17 Rosalind Dunnett, *The Trinovantes*, 1975, 9–12

18 D. W. Harding, *The Iron Age in Lowland Britain*, 1974, 223–6

19 Kent, 1978, 56

20 R. S. Rattray, *Ashanti*, 1923, 199–202

21 M. Sharpe, *Middlesex in British, Roman and Saxon Times*, 1919, 35–9

22 Canham, 1978, 32–3, 148

23 *Southwark Excavations 1972–74*, II, 508–9

24 D. W. Harding, *loc cit*, 225

25 C. Julius Caesar, *loc cit*, v, 22, 14

26 R. E. M. and T. V. Wheeler, *Verulamium: a Belgic and two Roman Cities*, 1936, 16ff

27 B. Cunliffe, *Iron Age Communities in Britain*, 1974, 80–3

28 C. Julius Caesar, *loc cit*, v

29 The identification of the Catuvellauni as the tribe of Tasciovanus and his successors rests only on Cassius Dio's statement that the Bodunni were tributaries of the Catuvellauni. Kent suggests that the Catuvellauni may have been a subsidiary kingdom of the Trinovantes ruled by Caratacus in his father's lifetime

30 D. F. Allen, 'The Belgic Dynasties of Britain and their Coins', *Arch.*, XC (1954), 1–46

31 The names of Tincommius and Dubnovellaunus occur in a list of suppliant kings who came to Augustus, given by the *Monumentum Ancyranum* (*Res Gestae Divi Augusti*, vi, 32), AD 14

32 T. D. Pryce and F. Oswald, *Arch.*, LXXVIII, 74ff

33 G. Marsh, 'Nineteenth and Twentieth Century Antiquities Dealers and Arretine Ware from London', *Trans. L.M.A.S.*, XXX (1979), 125–9

34 K. Jackson, *Language and History in Early Britain*, 1953, 308 footnote

35 M. Gelling, *Signposts to the Past*, 1978, 37

36 *Southwark Excavations 1972–74*, I, 56–7, 102–3, fig 33, 1

37 J. Clark, 'Trinovantum—the evolution of a legend', *Journal of Medieval History*, VII (1981), 138ff

2   The Claudian Invasion and the Beginning of Londinium (pages 23–40)

1   Cassius Dio, lx, 19–22

2   C. Julius Caesar, *De Bello Gallico*, iv

3   G. Suetonius Tranquillus, *De Vita Caesarum—Divus Claudius*, 17; *Bulletino della Commissione Archeologica Comunale di Roma*, LXX (1942), 71. The inscription from the arch commemorating the conquest of Britain, constructed AD 51–2 in the ancient Via Lata (Via del Corso), is now in the courtyard of the Palazzo dei Conservatori

4   *Southwark Excavations 1972–74*, II, 501ff

5   R. Merrifield and H. Sheldon, 'Roman London Bridge:– A View from Both Banks', *Lond. Arch.*, II, No 8 (1974), 183–91

6   Margary, 1967, 55–6

7   Southwark Excavations 1972–74, I, 22–4, 239–43

8   *Ibid*, I, 22, 59–61, 181–2

9   *Ibid*, II, 588–93

10   The Grades are those of Sutherland—C. H. V. Sutherland, 'Romano-British imitations of bronze coins of Claudius I', American Numismatic Society, *Numismatic Notes and Monographs*, No 65, New York, 1935

11   Philp, 1977, 7–16

12   Grimes, 1968, 183–4, fig 42

13   Chapman and Johnson, 1973, 3–6

14   R.C.H.M., 1928, map opposite p 154

15   A. H. Graham, 'The Geology of North Southwark and its Topographical Development in the Post-Pleistocene Period', *Southwark Excavations 1972–74*, II, 501–17. See also *ibid*, I, 16, fig 2

16   Marsden, 1978 (1), 91

3   The First Londinium, its Death and Rebirth (pages 41–60)

1   Haverfield, 1911, 149–50

2   Merrifield, 1969, 28ff

3   Tacitus, *Annals*, XIV, 33

4   C. T. Lewis and C. Short, *Latin Dictionary*, Oxford, 1900, defines *negotiator* as:
'I one who does business by wholesale, wholesale dealer, a banker, a factor; IIA a trader, tradesman (post-Augustan); IIB a factor, agent entrusted with the management of a business.'
The earlier restrictive use of the term is discussed by W. Smith, W. Waite and G. E. Marindin, *A Dictionary of Greek and Roman Antiquities*, 3rd ed, London, 1891, II, 226, citing Ernesti, *Opuscula Philologica—De Negotiatoribus*

5   Philp, 1977, 9

6   Philp's Period II, Period I being the primary activity on the site before any structures were built. Layers of carbon in this phase may represent the burning of brushwood to clear the ground.

7   J. P. Bushe-Foxe, *Excavations of the Roman Fort at Richborough, Kent*, IV, 1949, 28, fig 10

8   Chapman and Johnson, 1973, 58–64

9   Excavation notes by A. Boddington on 160–162 Fenchurch Street, 1976 (D.U.A. Archive)

10   S. Frere, *Verulamium Excavations*, I, 1972, 14–22, fig 8

11   Verbal comment by B. Philp in January, 1980

12   Marsden, 1978 (1), 92

13   *R.C.L.*, fig 24, Z and Z1, **240**, **243**

14   Dunning, 1945, 51; revised in *R.C.L.*, 90

15   MS notebook by Q. Waddington, M.O.L. archive. I am indebted to Peter Marsden for drawing my attention to this

16   R.C.H.M., 1928, 155. The Mark Lane burial is probably not earlier than late first century, and suggests that the city boundary had not been extended at that date

17   Chapman and Johnson, 1973, 6–7, 13

18   Roskams, 1980, 403ff

19   For a full discussion of these events, see Webster, 1978, 93ff

20   G. C. Boon, *Silchester: The Roman Town of Calleva*, 1974, 46

21   K. V. Carroll, 'The Date of Boudicca's Revolt', *Britannia*, X (1979), 197ff

22   Webster, 1978, 111

23   Tacitus, *Annals*, XIV, 33

24   Geoffrey of Monmouth, *Historia Regum Britanniae*, V, 4

25   Norman and Reader, 1906, 176

26   Anne Ross, *Pagan Celtic Britain*, 1967, 104ff

27   But see G. Marsh and B. West, 'Skullduggery in Roman London', *Trans. L.M.A.S.*, XXXII (1981), 86–102, where the ritual significance of the Walbrook skulls is accepted but their Boudican context doubted

28   Roach Smith, 1859, 28

29   R. G. Collingwood, 'Inscriptions of Roman London', in R.C.H.M., 1928, 171

4 The Transformation of Londinium, AD70–125 (pages 61–89)

1 Haverfield, 1911, 169f
2 I am much indebted to Mark Hassall for a helpful discussion of legal and constitutional problems, but he must be absolved of all responsibility for the views advanced here
3 P. Marsden, *Trans. L.M.A.S.*, XXI, pt 3 (1967), 213
4 A section about 36ft (10.9m) west of the west wall of the basilica showed no metalling (*Trans. L.M.A.S.* XXII, pt 2 (1969), 18), and the line of the buttressed wall was off-set about 16ft (4.9m) west of this wall
5 MS notes by F. Cottrill; *R.C.L.*, **236**
6 Philp, 1977, 49, Nos 81–88
7 *R.C.L.*, **229**
8 Philp, 1977, No 51
9 MS notes by F. Cottrill, and *J.R.S.*, XXIII (1933), 205. *R.C.L.*, **225**, **232**
10 *J.R.S.*, XXI (1931), 236–8
11 Philp, 1977, Samian Nos 103–16; coarse pottery Nos 81–90
12 MS notes by A. H. Oswald, cited in *R.C.L.*, **239**. See also Philp, 1977
13 *R.I.B.*, **9**
14 Marsden, 1975, 1–100
15 *Ibid*, 54–9
16 *Ibid*, Feature 73, 57–8
17 *R.I.B.*, **8**. Unfortunately only the last three letters of the title of *iuridicus* are present in the fragment, and other interpretations are possible
18 W. Maitland, *The History and Survey of London*, 1756, I, 17. Marsden, 1975, 3, 99, fig 44a
19 C. Wren, *Parentalia*, 1750, 265f
20 *R.I.B.*, **19**
21 *Ant. Journ.*, XLIII (1963), 123–8
22 Grimes, 1968, 15–40
23 *R.I.B.*, **5**
24 *R.I.B.*, **21**. The formula H.S.E. (*hic sita est*)— 'she lies here'—suggests a date before the end of the first century
25 *R.C.L.*, 142–3, **86**, **182**, **233**, **312**, **348**
26 Marsden, 1976, 3–30
27 J. Carcopino, *Daily Life in Ancient Rome*, 1956, 257
28 Marsden, 1976, 30–40
29 Marsden, 1975, 70–1
30 *R.C.L.*, **86**, **104**

5 Londinium in its Heyday (pages 90–114)

1 Miller, 1982, 143–7
2 Tatton-Brown, 1974, 122. For interim reports of the New Fresh Wharf excavations, see Hobley and Schofield, 1977, 34, and Schofield and Dyson, 1980, 18–19. I am indebted to Gustav Milne for information in advance of publication about the quay found on the Peninsular House site
3 I am much indebted to Chris Green of the D.U.A. for this and other information on pottery imports prior to its publication
4 Wheeler, 1930, 54–5
5 The second alternative is Professor Richmond's original translation (*Ant. Journ.*, XXXIII (1953), 207), the first a suggested amendment by Professor A. W. Van Buren, quoted by K. Painter (*B.M. Quarterly*, XXI (1967), 102–3)
6 Turner and Skutsch, 1960, 108–11
7 Margary, 1967, routes **14** and **150**, 59–64
8 *Trans. L.M.A.S.*, XXV (1974), 93–4; *Southwark Excavations 1972–74*, 31, 159, 391–2
9 Wheeler, 1930, 32, pl VII
10 For information on the G.P.O. site I am much indebted to Stephen Roskams, who by skilful excavation traced eight phases of activity from pre-Boudican to Antonine times, and has fully written up his findings in a D.U.A. archival report
11 P. R. V. Marsden, 'Archaeological finds in Southwark and Bermondsey, 1961', *Trans. L.M.A.S.*, XXI, pt 1 (1963), 81
12 L. Ercker, *Treatise on Ores and Assaying*, 1580, trans. A. G. Sisco and C. S. Smith, Chicago, 1951
13 J. J. Hatt, *Celts and Gallo-Romans*, London, 1970, 275
14 See R. Higgins, 'Jewellery' in D. Brown and D. Strong (eds), *Roman Crafts*, London, 1976, 55, 59
15 *J.B.A.A.*, XXXIV (1878), 254
16 Grimes, 1968, 97
17 MS of John Conyers (B.M. Sloane MSS, 958, fol 105). *R.C.H.M.*, 1928, 140. The site is incorrectly shown on the R.C.H.M. map as being at the *NW* corner of the Cathedral, a mistake repeated by Merrifield, *R.C.L.*, 1965
18 Strype's edition of Stow's *Survey of London*, 1755, II, Appendix I, 23
19 P. V. Webster, 'More British Samian Ware by the Aldgate-Pulborough potter', *Britannia*. VI (1975), 163ff

20 Marsden, 1969, 41–4
21 Norman and Reader, 1912, 285–6
22 G. Marsh and P. Tyers, 'Roman pottery from the City of London', *Trans. L.M.A.S.*, XXVII (1976), 228ff
23 Dunning, 1945, 52ff
24 *R.C.L.*, 91, fig 10
25 Information kindly supplied by G. Marsh in advance of publication

26 The dating is at present provisional as detailed study of the pottery has not been completed
27 Roskams and Watson, 1981
28 Guildhall Museum, *Discoveries on Walbrook 1949–50*, n.d., pl IV. *R.C.L.*, **265**
29 *R.C.L.*, 89ff
30 Roskams, 1980
31 C. Roach Smith, *N.C.*, IV (1841–2), 147–68, 186–94

6   The Hinterland of Londinium (pages 115–139)

1 *Southwark Excavations 1972–74*, I, figs 5, 6, 7
2 Merrifield, 1969, 63–7
3 Margary, 1948, 48–50
4 *Trans. L.M.A.S.*, XX pt 4 (1962), 170–3
5 *Southwark Excavations 1972–74*, I, 21, fig 4; II, 423
6 Margary, 1967, 59ff, 62ff
7 *Britannia*, VI (1975), 268–9: X (1979), 317; Canham, 1978, 150
8 A charter of Ethelred II recording the boundaries of lands belonging to Westminster Abbey. See *Trans. L.M.A.S.*, N.S. IX (1953), 101–4
9 Grimes, 1968, 182–3
10 R.C.H.M., 1928, 165
11 J. Stow, *Survey of London*, Kingsford ed, II 43
12 Margary, 1967, 57–8
13 *R.C.L.*, **319, 325**
14 As shown on Horwood's Map of 1799
15 R.C.H.M., 1928, 145
16 *R.C.L.*, **362**
17 *Trans. L.M.A.S.*, XXIII, pt 1 (1971), 42ff; pt 2 (1972) 101ff
18 *Proc. Soc. Ant.*, XXIII (1909–11), 236–7
19 *The Essex Naturalist* XXXI, 3 (1964), 208–12
20 *Trans. L.M.A.S.*, 1st ser., III (1868), 563
21 Merrifield, 1969, 56
22 *Trans. L.M.A.S.*, 1st ser., III (1868), 191ff
23 Sheldon and Schaaf, 1978, 65
24 *Ibid*, Gazetteer No 65
25 *Ibid*, Gazetteer No 30
26 A. L. F. Rivet and C. Smith, *The Place Names of Roman Britain*, 1979, 347. Translations of the names are also taken from this work
27 Rodwell, 1975, 93
28 *Ibid*, 90–4. The temptation to call the town zone the *territorium* has been resisted, since elsewhere in the empire this term was applied to much larger areas (but see Rodwell, *ibid*, 99)
29 The dubious Iter XX has been omitted in view of the uncertainty of the site of Durolitum. If it really was at Chigwell, the distance given in the Itinerary (15 miles) is

greater than the actual distance (12–12½ miles).
30 Sheldon, 1972, 127–9
31 *Ibid*, 129, citing K. J. Bonser, *The Drovers*, 1970, 218
32 R.C.H.M., 1928, 148
33 *R.I.B.*, **16**
34 R.C.H.M., 1928, 147
35 Grimes, 1968, 182–3
36 Margaret Gelling, 'The Boundaries of the Westminster Charters', *Trans. L.M.A.S*, N.S. XI (1953), 101–3
37 Grimes, 1968, 184
38 R.C.H.M., 1928, 165–6. Two pots of black-burnished ware containing burnt bones would normally be attributed to the fourth century, when cremation was rare
39 The more romantic view that there was continuity of a traditional cult from a shrine at a martyr's tomb in a Roman cemetery to the sanctuary of an English church is hardly tenable because of the wide time gap between them—at least 600 years
40 Grimes, 1968, 186–7
41 P. S. Mills, 'A Roman Well on Welbeck Street, W1', *Trans. L.M.A.S.*, XXXI (1980), 77
42 *Southwark Excavations 1972–74*, 32
43 Cato and Varro, cited by H. Sheldon, *ibid*
44 *Southwark Excavations 1972–74*, report by H. Willcox, 411–13
45 For references, see Sheldon and Schaaf, 1978, Gazetteer Nos 50, 52, 58, 60, 61, 74, 75
46 *V.C.H. Essex*, III, 198; *Arch.*, I (1779), 72
47 *Essex Journal*, XII No 3 (1977), 51–61
48 Sheldon and Schaaf, 1978, Gazetteer Nos 1, 4
49 Brown and Sheldon, 1974, 222–31
50 I. N. Hume, 'Romano-British Potteries on the Upchurch Marshes', *Arch. Cant.*, LXVIII (1954), 72–90
51 A. H. Graham, in *Southwark Excavations 1972–74*, 1978, II, 513. The wattle 'floor' at about O.D. in Brentford (*Antiquity*, III (1929), 20–32) is re-interpreted as a collapsed bank revetment, for which a Southwark

parallel is cited

52 D. Defoe, *Tour Through Britain* (1724), I, 234; discussed Merrifield, 1977, 396

53 H. Sheldon and B. Yule, 'Excavations in Greenwich Park, 1978–9', *Lond. Arch.*, III, Autumn 1979, 311–17

7   Londinium in the Antonine and Severan Periods (pages 140–171)

1 Grimes, 1968, 121–2

2 *Southwark Excavations 1972–74*, site reports

3 Marsden, 1965 (2), 118–31

4 Schofield and Dyson, 1980, 13

5 *Ibid*, 13–14; *Britannia*, X (1979), 313, 317

6 Kenyon, 1959, 14; *Southwark Excavations 1972–74*, I, 40

7 H. Sheldon, 'A Decline in the London Settlement, A.D. 150–250', *Lond. Arch.*, II, Summer 1975, 278–84

8 Information kindly given in advance of publication by Dominic Perring, who directed the excavations at Watling Court and Well Court on behalf of the D.U.A.

9 John Morris, 'London's Decline, A.D. 150–250', *Lond. Arch.*, II, No 13, Winter 1975, 343–4

10 For a fuller account of the military history of Britain in this period, see Frere, 1974, 176–90

11 *Ibid*, 211

12 Merrifield, 1962, 38–52

13 John Morris's suggestion that the stream was boarded over or otherwise covered and that occupation continued (*Lond. Arch.*, II, No 13, Winter 1975, 343–4), as was the case in the 16th century, is incompatible with W. F. Grimes's section (Grimes, 1968, fig 23b, 93–7) which showed the Walbrook continuing as an open stream, flowing at ever higher levels, throughout the Roman period and later, eventually as a mere runnel through silt without well-defined or stable banks

14 *Southwark Excavations 1972–74*, 36

15 Sheldon, 1981

16 *Ibid*

17 Marsden, 1976, 51

18 (a) Tatton-Brown, 1974, 125
   (b) Schofield and Dyson, 1980, 19. I am informed by John Schofield that a later (1981) reassessment of the dendrochronological evidence gives a date early in the third century for the construction of the new waterfront

19 Hobley and Schofield, 1977, 34–5. Also Schofield and Dyson, 1980, 18–19

20 *Arch*, LIX, pt 1 (1904), 130ff; LXIII (1912), 294f

21 P. R. V. Marsden, 'Archaeological Finds in the City of London 1966–8', *Trans. L.M.A.S.*, XXII, pt 2 (1969), 22

22 There is no question of its being an earlier earth rampart cut by a later wall, as has sometimes been suggested. It has been clearly demonstrated more than once by archaeological sections that the bank was thrown up against the inner face of the wall, probably soon after its construction.

23 Maloney, 1980 (1)

24 Grimes, 1968, 50–1

25 *Trans. L.M.A.S.*, XXII, pt 3 (1970), 516

26 Marsden, 1967, 47–9

27 The estimate is for the new wall only, excluding the fort walls which were incorporated. These were not provided with a plinth and presumably already had their own battlements of a different kind.

28 Frere, 1974, 284–6

29 Hill, Millett and Blagg, 1980, pt 4(b), 180, 182

30 Roach Smith, 1859, 19

31 Marsden, 1975, 73–8

8   Londinium in the Third Century (pages 172–204)

1 Roach Smith, 1859, 150ff

2 John Evans, *N.C.* (1882), 57–60; (1883), 278–81

3 R. Merrifield, *N.C.* (1956), 247–54

4 Toynbee, 1964, 55

5 *R.I.B.*, **19**

6 Frere, 1974, 207

7 *R.I.B.*, **11**

8 *R.I.B.*, **17**

9 *R.I.B.*, **327, 334**

10 Hill, Millett and Blagg, 1980, 195–8

11 *Ibid*, 204–6; Merrifield, 1977, 383–6

12 Jones et al., 1980, 72–6

13 *R.C.L.*, **264**

14 *R.C.L.*, **151**; D. Dawe and A. Oswald, *11 Ironmonger Lane*, 1952, 112–14

15 Toynbee, 1964, 98

16 *Ibid*, 90

17 Ibid, 77

18 *Ibid*, 86

19 *Ibid*, 94

20 *Ibid*, 167–8

21 Toynbee, 1963, 8

22 Toynbee, 1964, 170. It seems more likely that

this is an imported sculpture than that a
Danubian sculptor was working in Britain on
imported marble, as Professor Toynbee
suggests

23 *Southwark Excavations 1972–74*, II, 319
24 *Ibid*, 39–40
25 Hammerson, 1978, 206–12
26 J. M. C. Toynbee, *The Art of the Romans*,
    1965, 97–8, 102–5
27 *Southwark Excavations 1972–74*, I, 42
28 Nothing like the Southwark ash-chest or the
    hunter-god can be found in the vast corpus of
    Gallo-Roman sculptures compiled by E.
    Espérandieu, *Recueil Général des Bas Reliefs,*
Statues et Bustes de la Gaule Romaine, Paris,
1907 et seq
29 Johnson, 1975, 278–80
30 I am indebted to Chris Green of the D.U.A.
    for this information
31 J. Casey, 'Tradition and Innovation in the
    Coinage of Carausius and Allectus' in J.
    Munby and M. Henig (eds), *Roman Life and
    Art in Britain*, B.A.R. 41 (ii), 1977, 219
32 *Trans. L.M.A.S.*, XXVI (1975), 78
33 Merrifield, 1955, 113–34
34 *R.C.L.*, pl 12; **17**; 193–4
35 Riley and Gomme, 1912; Wheeler, 1930,
    151–4; Marsden, 1965 (1), 109–17

9   **Londinium in the Fourth Century** (pages 205–235)

1   J. C. Mann, *Antiquity*, XXXV (1961), 316–20
2   The alternative suggestion that the most
    important province in Britain, with London
    as its capital, was named after Galerius
    Maximianus, the *eastern* Caesar, seems highly
    improbable
3   Frere, 1974, 241, citing Bury, *Cambridge
    Historical Journal*, I (1923), 1–9 and E. Birley,
    Acta et Dissertationes Archaeologicae, III (1963),
    83–8
4   R. A. G. Carson and J. P. C. Kent, 'Constant-
    inian Hoards and other Studies in the later
    Roman Bronze Coinage', *N.C.*, 6th ser, XVI
    (1956), 88–9
5   *R.I.B.*, **4**
6   Casey, 1978, 181–93
7   *R.I.C.*, VI, 121
8   Zosimus, *The Decline of Rome*, II, 15
9   Eusebius, *De Vita Constantini*, I, xxv
10 Ammianus Marcellinus (J. C. Rolfe ed),
    XXVIII, iii, 8. Unfortunately the surviving
    account is only a reference back by
    Ammianus to events described in a lost earlier
    book
11 *Ibid*, XX, i, 3
12 *Ibid*, XXVII, viii, 7. '. . . ad Lundinium, vetus
    oppidum, quod Augustam posteritas appellavit.'
13 *Ibid*, XXVIII, iii, 1. '. . . ab Augusta, quam
    veteres appellavere Lundinium.'
14 S. Johnson, *Later Roman Britain* (1980), 98
15 Hill, Millett and Blagg, 1980, 66
16 *Ibid*, 68
17 Translated from William Fitzstephen, *Des-
    criptio Nobilissimae Civitatis Londoniate*
    (c 1175): '*Similiterque ab Austro Londonia
    murata et turrita fuit; sed fluvius maximus
    piscosus Thamensis, mari influo refluoque, qui
    illac allabitur, moenia illa tractu temporis alluit,
    labefactavit, dejecit.*'
18 Hill, Millet and Blagg, 1980, 61
19 *Ibid*, 16–17
20 *Ibid*, 46
21 Roach Smith, 1859, 18–19
22 Hill, Millett and Blagg, 1980, 88–93.
    Recalibration is the process of adjusting radio-
    carbon dates to calendar dates, by correcting
    the error found in checking radio-carbon
    dates against known tree-ring dates given by
    the long-lived Californian Stone Pine
23 Parnell, 1977
24 Parnell, 1978
25 Jennifer Hillam and Ruth Morgan, 'The
    Dating of the Roman Riverside Wall at three
    sites in London'. *Lond. Arch. III*, No 11
    (Summer 1979), 283–7
26 *Ibid*, 287
27 Frere, 1974, 291
28 Grimes, 1968, 71–6
29 G. E. Fox, 'Notes on a Recent Discovery of
    Part of the Roman Wall of London', *Arch.*,
    LII pt 2 (1890), 610
30 A. Grenier, *Manuel d'Archéologie Gallo-
    Romaine*, V, pt 1 (1931), 520–1. The date of
    the city wall at Trier seems to fall between the
    reigns of Commodus and Postumus, and
    could therefore be up to 50 years later than the
    wall at London. (E. M. Wightman, *Roman
    Trier and the Treveri* (1970), 92–8)
31 *Trans. L.M.A.S.*, XXII, pt 2 (1969), 24
32 Price, 1880, 26–7
33 Marsden, 1980, 172
34 Maloney, 1980 (2)
35 Cf G. Home, *Roman London* (1948), 144–5
36 Norman and Reader, 1912, 271–4
37 Maloney, 1979, 295. Marsden, 1980, 172
38 The find is so far unpublished and a full
    assessment of the dating evidence from the
    ditches is not yet available
39 Norman and Reader, 1912, 276–9

10 **From Londinium to London** (pages 236–268)

1 For a convenient summary of the various views on Pelagianism in Britain, see Thomas, 1981, 53–60

2 Constantius, *Vita Germani*, 14

3 Morris, 1973, 63–4

4 See Frere, 1974, 260ff, where there is a critical discussion of the British section and its date

5 Parnell, 1981

6 Painter, 1981

7 Painter, 1972

8 Painter, 1981

9 To those listed in Painter, 1972, an ingot from Reculver must now be added, bringing the total for Kent to eight. T. Tatton-Brown, 'A New Late Roman Silver Ingot from near Reculver, *Kent Archaeological Review*, Winter 1980, 40–1

10 Painter, 1972

11 *Ibid*, pls XXX–XXXI

12 *Ibid*, pl XXIX, c, e

13 *Ibid*, pl XXIX, a, b

14 Dr J. P. C. Kent in conversation with the author. He pointed out that although late Roman *siliquae* are commonly found clipped in Britain, none of the clippings have ever been found, as they normally are for other periods when coin-clipping was common— e.g. in the 17th century

15 For a summary of recent doubts, with other references, see T. M. Dickinson, 'British Antiquity—Post-Roman and Pagan Anglo-Saxon', *Arch. Journ.*, CXXXIV (1977), 407–8

16 C. J. Simpson, 'Belt-buckles and Strap-ends of the Later Roman Empire', *Britannia*, VII, (1976), 205–6

17 Myres, 1969, 78

18 V. J. Evison, 'Quoit Brooch Style Buckles', *Ant. Journ.*, XLVIII (1968), 240–1

19 D. M. Wilson, *The Anglo-Saxons*, 1960, 134, Pls 30, 32

20 R.C.H.M., 1928, 189–90. Wheeler, 1930, 203

21 Museum of London Card Catalogue and Marsden, 1980, 167

22 R.C.H.M., 1928, 141

23 *R.C.L.*, 55, fig 6

24 *R.C.L.*, **18–20**. Roach Smith, 1859, 57–8 Britain, (1956), 153

25 Dr Peter Salway, in correspondence with the author

26 Marsden, 1980, 152–5

27 R. Reece, 'A Short Survey of the Roman Coins Found on Fourteen Sites in Britain', *Britannia*, III (1972), 276

28 Marsden, 1975, 78–9, fig 40, nos 243–4

29 Schofield and Dyson, 1980, 31 (fig)

30 *Southwark Excavations 1972–74*, II, 311, fig 148, no 945

31 Alcock, 1971, 208

32 M. G. Welch, Mitcham Grave 205 and the Chronology of Applied Brooches with Floriate Cross Decoration', *Ant. Journ.*, LV (1975), 86–93

33 *Ibid*, 93–5

34 Tania M. Dickinson, *Arch. Journ.*, CXXXIV (1977), 408, n 18

35 Marsden, 1980, 184–5 (fig), 214 (n 30)

36 *Ibid*, 186

37 Biddle, Hudson and Heighway, 1973, 16

38 Grimes, 1968, 155–9

39 Schofield and Dyson, 1980, 38

40 *Ibid*, 35–6

41 John Clark, *Saxon and Norman London*, 1980, 5 (pl). Information concerning the pots and their date is based on a recent assessment by Prof V. Evison. The Lime Street glass is of Harden class B i I ('Glass vessels in Britain, A.D. 400–1000', D. B. Harden (ed), *Dark Age Britain*, (1956), 153

42 Harden class X a n D. B. Harden, (ed), *loc. cit.*, 138, fig 25, 142

43 Morris, 1973, 108f

44 *Ibid*, 100–101

45 Sheldon and Schaaf, 1978, Gazetteer nos 2, 39

46 H. Sheldon, 'Excavations at Lefevre Road, Old Ford, E3, September 1969–June 1970', *Trans. L.M.A.S.*, XXIII pt I (1971), 52ff

47 P. Arthur and K. Whitehouse, 'Excavations at Fulham Palace Moat, 1972–1973', *Trans. L.M.A.S.*, XXIX (1978), 64

48 J. Gillam, 'Romano-Saxon Pottery; an Alternative Interpretation, P. J. Casey (ed), *The End of Roman Britain*, B.A.R. 71, 1979, 103ff

49 Continuity of occupation of the fifth-century Saxon sites in the London area after the great British victory at Mons Badonicus at the end of the century is in marked contrast with those in Sussex, where there seems to have been a break in continuity at this time. (Myres, 1969, 111–12)

50 Wheeler, 1935, 62ff

51 Castle, 1975

52 *Ibid*, 275–6

53 Wacher, 1975, 414ff

54 M. Todd, 'Famosa Pestis and fifth-century Britain', *Britannia*, VIII (1977), 319ff

55 Wheeler, 1935, 71–2, where W. de G. Birch, *Cartularium Saxonicum* I, no 346 is cited

56 Thomas, 1981, Ch 15

57 *Ibid*, 355

58 *Ibid*, map 45, 256

59 Meaning 'the stream of the Britons' from OE *Wealas*. E. Ekwall, *Street-Names of the City of London*, 1965, 193–4

60 G. C. Brooke, *English Coins*, 3rd ed, 1950, 4

61 Sebbi, the Christian king of Essex, was to die as a monk in London some thirty years later, and was buried at St Paul's in a stone sarcophagus that miraculously fitted his body after at first being too short; there is little doubt that it came from an earlier Roman burial. Bede, *History of the English Church and People*, iv, Ch 11

62 Bede, *op cit*, v, Ch 7

63 Dyson, 1980

64 Bede, *op cit*, iv, Ch 22

65 *Ibid*, v, Ch 11

Index

Figures in bold type e.g. **17** refer to Plate numbers